Sept 2, 2005

Dear Nigel

Thank you for your extraordinary insights. I love knowing you!

May every joy be showered upon you and your family,

With love,

John Cord

THE CHRISTIAN RIGHT

. . . OR *WRONG?*

"Your ability to first dissect Scripture with explanations and correlations, and then analyze arguments of notable religious figures is excellent."

—Ryan U., Palm Springs, CA

"Every page you write strengthens what I have always known about love and goodness and my resolve to live that way. God could have only selected a very, very special soul as a conduit to share this message. You have no idea how much you have revived my Spirit."

—Karen S., Coon Rapids, MN

"I must admit that from my study of religion and specifically the Bible, I never drew the logical conclusion or reached the simplicity of understanding that you seem to have."

—Steve D., Bagdad, KY

"I heard you on Orlando's 740 AM this evening on my way to the Central Florida Down Syndrome Association meeting. The important thing is that I think I finally heard someone able to put into the English language what has been gnawing me about organized religion since I was eight years old. That's a long time. I'm over 50."

—Patricia W., Orlando, FL

"You are awesome! Would you be offended if I called you a Christian with brains? I'd like to characterize your philosophy as 'Religion without Dogma.' You have got major kahunas. I'm blown away."

—Roland M., Milwaukie, OR

"I am currently doing a report on you in my school for a literary paper. Your book has meant a lot to me. I have had many friends and my mom read it, and they thought your book was great. At first they were against it, but then they sat down and read it. They realized that the book made a lot of sense. Your book has influenced me, my peers, and my mom. Thanks for writing this book."

—Ryan C., Aiken, SC

"Wow!!! I am so blessed by what you say, because I do believe with all of my heart that God has been teaching me this for the last few years and has brought me out of religion which is a shortstop to God. I have finally been able to pull all the way out of 'organized religion.' Sometimes we're in the 'system' so long that the SYSTEM is what we know, and we don't know God at all."

—Ruth H., Dallas, TX

"Thank you so much. I am reading it every night! I love it, love it, love it!"

—David D., Palm Springs, CA

"Your work is excellent. I am impressed with your writing ... content, style, research, and approach ... and I LOVE the different fonts that makes your book so easy to read."

—Kevin J., Pleasanton, CA

Comments welcome: johncord@aol.com

THE CHRISTIAN RIGHT

...OR WRONG?

EXPOSING THE CORRUPT TEACHINGS OF CORPORATE CHRISTIANITY AND ITS LEADING MEDIA EVANGELISTS

John Cord

BLUE DOLPHIN PUBLISHING

Previously published as *Big Ol' Christian Lies: False Teachings from the Pulpit* and *Betrayal of God: Christianity's Corporate Sabotage of Jesus and His Spirit,* 2002, EternalLight Publishing.

Published by Blue Dolphin Publishing, Inc.
P.O. Box 8, Nevada City, CA 95959
Orders: 1-800-643-0765
Web: www.bluedolphinpublishing.com

ISBN: 1-57733-142-7 softcover
ISBN: 1-57733-179-6 hardcover

Library of Congress Cataloging-in-Publication Data

Cord, John, 1958-
The Christian right— or wrong? : exposing the corrupt teachings of corporate Christianity and its leading media evangelists / John Cord.
p. cm.
Originally published: Big ol' Christian lies. Santa Barbara, Calif. : EternalLight Pub., 2002.
Includes bibliographical references and indexes.
ISBN 1-57733-142-7 (pbk. : alk. paper)
1. Christianity. 2. Evangelists—United States—Quotations. I. Title.

BR124.C648 2004
273'.9—dc22

2004006150

Printed in the United States of America

10 9 8 7 6 5 4 3 2

The enormity of deception, enslavement, suffering,
and bloodshed thrust upon humanity
by the saboteurs of the Spirit of God
is without measure.

May this work enlighten you to
His Message of the Spirit,
and move you to follow
it with greater faith.

TABLE OF CONTENTS

www.TheChristianRightOrWrong.com

INTRODUCTION

The world is full of religionists who use their sacred Scriptures to suit their own agendas. Had Bin Laden not sanctified violence as a means to further his "holy" cause, he would be just another selfish leader using spiritual texts for fear-mongering and separatism.

The global religions of Judaism, Christianity, and Islam are directly linked to the God of Abraham. All three are entrusted with God's Message of the Spirit, which instructs believers to overcome evil with Good, yet all three have, *past and present*, shown themselves remarkably separatist. They feed and breed idolatry (man-made rituals, fears, and superstitions), and continue to force suffering and death upon those of differing beliefs. Though each thinks itself the "way" to Salvation, all have grown into false religions, betraying God's Spirit.

Religious businesses that use Scriptures to secure power and control over the souls and pocketbooks of the masses for self-serving reasons were created by humans, not God.

Jesus rejected Israel's scholars and Temple priests because they had made an idolatrous business of God's Word to enrich, empower, and exalt themselves. His Message of the Spirit of the Law over the Letter of the Law attracted masses of Jews away from the Temple, a serious threat to the status of the scholars, priests, and their temple trade. Unable to defeat His Message, they went after the Messenger, seeing to it that He was captured, which led to His death.

God does not instruct the building of corporate temples for idolatrous worship, but the building of the Temple Within, *a Temple of Spirit built upon Selfless Love and Good Works.* He instructs you to overcome your evil with Good, and reveals these forces to be *relative to your heart and motivations.* He instructs you not to judge others as hellbound for their sins, because as you judge others for their sins, so shall you, *in the end,* be judged likewise for yours ("he that is without sin among you, let him first cast a stone," John 8:7).

Corporate religions are "mindsets" that, *to thrive*, must unite individual minds to their exclusive cause. Indoctrination usually begins in childhood, when enslaving the human mind to idolatrous worship is met with least resistance. The enemy of idolatrous religion is the Spirit Within, which breaks the yoke of idolatry and leads to Salvation.

Romans 8:11 (authored by Apostle Paul)

11. **But if the Spirit of him that raised up Jesus from the dead dwell in you, he that raised up Christ from the dead shall also quicken your mortal bodies by his Spirit that dwelleth in you.** [But if the Spirit of God that resurrected Christ dwells Within you, the Good Spirit shall quicken you unto Salvation.]

It is human selfishness grinding the gears of religions that serve-up separatism, intolerance, murders, and wars. Can we ever know the depths of misery that "Holy and Righteous" corporate religionists have wrought upon humanity in the name of God? What do you think September 11th was about? It was born of the same selfishness that birthed the Crusades, the Inquisition, the Ku Klux Klan, and every separatist, holier-than-thou zealot in history.

A bear cannot catch fish if it cannot see past the pond's rippling surface. The creature's success requires a shift of perception. *Realizing the Bible's Message of the Spirit requires a shift of perception.* We must look beyond the Bible's literal, "surface" messages of interwoven contrasts and contradictions to capture its underlying Message of the Spirit (we must see past the "ripples" to capture God's "food" for our souls).

Jesus reminds us that knowing the Spirit requires eyes that "see" and ears that "hear," which is not about opening our visual and auditory organs, but about opening our minds.

One famous scene shows Jesus and His Apostles upon the stormy Sea of Galilee. Jesus, asleep in the pitching boat, is awakened by them, as they fear for their lives, being of "little faith." Jesus shows His power of God, *the Spirit Within Him*, when He commands, "Peace, be still," calming the winds and waters (Mark 4:36-41; Luke 8:22-25). He is revealing that faith is the power to overcome evil (fear; chaos; ignorance) with Good (trust; peace; wisdom). Faith is the Spirit Within, the power to command peace and wisdom over fearful troubles and emotions.

Calming the stormy sea by bringing peace to its surface illustrates that you have the power to overcome your mind's troubles ("stormy seas") by lifting the Spirit Within to the forefront of your consciousness... *a shift of perception.*

The Bible is like a "stormy sea" when interpreted by fearful, unenlightened minds that lawyer its Scriptures to death. They bicker over the Letter of the Law and suppress its Message of the Spirit, giving rise to so many various and turbulent, contradictory interpretations of the Bible.

Judaism, Christianity, and Islam, *all born of the Bible,* use Scriptures to justify their corporate systems of idolatry, denying the Bible's "still, small voice" that is its quiet, constant undercurrent of the Good Spirit.

We are repeatedly instructed to overcome the "world" with the Spirit, and so too must we overcome the worldly, visible, literal, contradictory, "surface" messages of the Bible with its One Message of the Spirit. *We are to overcome the Letter of the Law with the Spirit of the Law.*

Corporate Christianity is split into hundreds of sects, because it denies Oneness and embraces separatism. God's Message of the Spirit is diminished, *even fully ignored* by religionists lacking eyes to *see* and ears to *hear.* If you choose to be spoon-fed the Bible from the minds of corporate religionists, beware to discern the "wheat" from the "chaff."

Eyes that *see* and ears that *hear* are needed in order to separate the Bible's fruitful "wheat" from its unfruitful "chaff" [the "wheat" is the Truth that supersedes all else (the Bible's Message of the Spirit; the Spirit of the Law); the "chaff" are lesser truths (inconsequential truths; the Letter of the Law)]. Lesser truths, when EXALTED over the Spirit, become lies. Preachers who serve-up *chaff* feed their audience Spiritless instruction. If *chaff* is to be served up, it must be kept in its proper perspective. Better to serve up only the *wheat.*

The "wheat and the chaff" is like Jesus' allegory in which a house built upon rock will survive, unlike a house built upon sand (Matthew 7:26-27). The "house" is your soul. Is your soul of the strong foundation of the Spirit of the Law (built upon the "rock"; fed upon the "wheat") or of the weak foundation of the Letter of the Law (built upon the "sand"; fed upon the "chaff")?

The Bible is like a desert of sand (Letter of the Law) threaded with a singular, direct path of rock (Spirit of the Law). The rock path is The Way to Salvation. Preachers who elevate the Letter of the Law over the Spirit of the Law are, *metaphorically speaking,* throwing a cloud of sand above the rock path, obscuring The Way for many of their followers.

■ ■ ◆ ■ ■

#14 - Hagee, John (February, 2000)

Are you sincere, are you real, or are you a cosmetic Christian? God is turning up the heat and He's exposing the hidden sin, the phony, the pompous, and the religious stuffed-shirts who have a form of godliness but deny the power thereof. God's exposing that in America.

If God is exposing Christian hypocrisy in America, then one of the ways He's doing it is through this book. You decide.

My authority to challenge corporate-Christian mindsets is the Bible's Message of the Spirit, which they unmistakably deny. I am an independent scholar who, *having never been indoctrinated in corporate religion*, is not beholding to Catholicism, Protestantism or any of man's church systems. I have been moved since early childhood to help others, and hope this work serves towards the fulfillment of that goal.

■ ■ ◆ ■ ■

#14 - Hagee, John (October 24, 1999)

Some people say, "Well, I really don't know if the Bible is true, it's so full of errors." How many of you have heard people make that asinine statement?

No, not an asinine statement considering: 1) the English-language Bible arrived through many language translations; 2) there are Biblical passages that, *when interpreted literally*, contradict other Biblical passages; and 3) the Four Gospels were written anywhere from 50 to 150 years after Jesus' death. Add to that the evident separatism that split Christianity into hundreds of sects, each built upon varying interpretations of Scriptures. *Is it any wonder why people question the validity of the Bible?*

(1 minute, 7 seconds later)

There is no error in Scripture. Perceived error is the fruit of stupidity. I wanna let that thought sit in just a little bit. Perceived error is the fruit of stupidity, and you can have a Ph.D. and be stupid.

There are depths of the Bible that have not yet surfaced into human consciousness. It is only natural for human minds to question perceived inconsistencies when working to unravel and decode the Bible's *complex, interwoven, historical, literal, spiritual, multi-dimensional, interconnected stories.*

What may appear to us as error is more likely our human lack of understanding. Let us agree that the Bible is without error, that all of its messages are truths. Are its truths to be weighed equally, none being greater or lesser? *God forbid*. Preachers who weigh all Scriptures equally, not discerning the greater from the lesser, commit a monumental injustice that breeds confusion and spiritual weakness.

■ ■ ◆ ■ ■

This work serves to educate and enlighten—through fair and thoughtful criticisms of public messages delivered by Christian leaders, messages that, collectively, reach hundreds of millions worldwide every week.

If you are reading these words, I am delighted you have come this far. I write matter-of-factly, with no intention of offending. If your mind reads this work and your anger is stirred towards me, then seek not to blame me. I do not have the power to make you angry or offended *or anything for that matter*. This work is a no-nonsense exposé of corporate religions, written not to insult, but to Enlighten.

I researched over 700 hours of Christian leaders who appeared on television ministries, talk shows, and news programs. I did not target any particular ministry or sect. In five years, I had transcribed over 600 pages of false teachings from over 70 preachers. These "traditional" lies about God and Christ are timeless, *passed on from generation to generation*, and, per Jesus, shall be taught to the very end. This book presents a robust sampling of the selfishness at the heart of corporate Christianity.

Of the many preachers studied, this book presents 40, most of whom are American televangelists. The fact that some preachers are cited more than others was not by design. All quoted materials are dated as to when they aired on television, spanning from mid-1998 through mid-2003 (an interesting block of years that presents a "before and after" snapshot of Christian teachings through the much-prophesied-about entrance into the new millennium).

This book is an updated, reworked version of *Big Ol' Christian Lies: False Teachings from the Pulpit*, which did not name the names of the excerpted preachers, as I wanted to direct the focus upon only their false messages. In time, I learned that naming names was essential to the credibility of the work, *having been accused of inventing the unnamed preachers*. Even so, it wasn't until I heard the Christless excuses spewed by Jerry Falwell and Pat Robertson regarding the atrocities of September 11th that I knew, absolutely, that names were to be named to add credibility to the work and to hold these leaders accountable for their false teachings.

Understand that any one message given by any one preacher within this book is not a full representation of that preacher's body of work. Undoubtedly, they believe they are teaching the "right thing," not aware that they are caught in a corporate web of idolatrous worship. Many of them have yet to think beyond their programmed "mindsets." You might ask: "So what?" *So plenty... because they are leaders who enrich, empower, and exalt their corporate religions by teaching hundreds of millions to embrace separatism and idolatry over the Oneness Message of the Spirit.*

■ ■ ◆ ■ ■

Please note that the parenthetical segments in this book are decreased in size (parenthetical segments are decreased in size, like this), so as not to be too distracting from the main body of text. I hope this is a help, not a hindrance.

Please also note that, throughout this work, words associated with God (Good) are capitalized, whereas words associated with anti-God (evil) are uncapitalized (some examples: God vs. satan; Heaven vs. hell; Selfless Love vs.

selfishness). I did this deliberately, not to confuse, but to keep separate, *consistently*, that which is associated with God from that which is not.

You will find Biblical verses *along with references to Biblical verses* throughout this book. If you come across a reference to a Biblical verse and want to read it, go to the Index of Biblical Verses to locate that verse (most of the Biblical verses referenced are presented elsewhere in the book; all scriptures are taken from the King James Version of the Bible).

All the quoted material in this work was transcribed verbatim. With extreme care, no quote was taken out of the context of any speech, interview, or sermon.

Due to the serious and potentially-controversial nature of this work, and to prevent being accused of having taken preachings out of context for critical review, it was necessary, *in some cases*, that I not chop-up a segment of preaching into shorter segments, but keep it intact, thereby more-fully showing the context in which the preaching was delivered.

I make no comments about how any preacher's message was delivered, though having witnessed hundreds of hours of all-over-the-place emotions and way-over-the-top theatrics, I find it hard to believe that preachers who scream, demand, patronize, mock, and judge, *doing so with tireless affectations*, are serving up God's word truthfully, sincerely, faithfully, and with humility.

Should you come to *see* and *hear* the Spirit more acutely after reading this book, the credit belongs to you and God, as Enlightenment comes via the Spirit Within, and is ultimately yours to accept or reject. Everything has its season, including your spiritual awareness, and everyone is at a different level of spiritual evolution, including myself and the preachers excerpted in this book.

I am well aware that my soul is at stake should I misinform you in any way. With all my heart, I present this work for your consideration, to *influence* you to realize and embrace the Enlightenments of the Spirit.

ENLIGHTENMENTS

This preparatory chapter defines, *methodically, and as simply as possible,* the main characters and issues of one of the most intense, complex books in existence: the Bible.

GOD

God is an Invisible Spirit (John 4:24; Colossians 1:15), and is only Good, having no evil whatsoever (Matthew 19:17; Mark 10:18). God is the Source, *or Selfless Giver* of all that is Good (the Source of Life, Love, Truth, Peace, and all other Goodness).

God is Three-in-One (First John 5:7): Father, Son, and Spirit, which is the Body (Father), Mind (Son), and Soul (Spirit) of Goodness. Oneness with Selfless Love and Good Works is Oneness with God in body (Father), mind (Son), and soul (Spirit).

THE SPIRIT

The Life-force of the Universe is the Spirit, the Soul of God, present in everything that has movement. Where there is no Spirit, there is no life (James 2:26). It was the Spirit that "moved" the ethereal matter of the Spiritual Universe (Genesis 1:2), after which our Physical Universe was created (Genesis 1:9).

The basic structural units of the Universe are atoms. This invisible, particulate matter is the "dust" of our Universe. When the human body dies, its atoms live on, disassembling one from another into different states of existence. The human body, built from "dust," shall return to "dust" (Genesis 3:19).

THE FATHER

The entirety of the Spirit of the Universe is the "body" of the Spirit: the Father; the Body of God.

THE SON

The Son, Jesus Christ, is the Head of the Body (Ephesians 1:22-23), the <u>Mind</u> of the Father (the God Conscience, or Good Conscience). He is also the Word of God (First John 5:7; Revelation 19:13). The Bible, *the word of God*, is a Message of Good Conscience. No one can be of God but through His Mind (no one can come to the Father but through the Son). The Mind of God is The Way of Christ that is built upon His Spirit of Selfless Love and Good Works.

Success in the Spirit comes to those who align their minds with His Mind. Crown yourself with His Mind, and you shall have the Crown of Life (Salvation; Revelation 2:10).

ANTI-GOD

As God is the Selfless Giver of all that is Good, anti-God is the selfish taker of all that is Good. The nature of anti-God is: selfish love (lust; selfishness; taker of the Spirit); death (taker of Life); deception (taker of Truth); evil (taker of Goodness); and darkness (taker of Light). Like God, the three-in-one anti-God has body (anti-Father; satan), mind (anti-Son, or anti-Christ), and soul (anti-Spirit).

A soul living and growing in anti-God uses its life *that God provided* not to magnify Good, but to magnify self. (Note: Through your free will, everything you do is <u>literally</u> "selfish," because you are the one doing it. But <u>spiritually</u>, selfishness is determined *according to your heart and motivations*, which cannot be hidden from God.)

Lucifer means "Light-bearer" (Light-collector), or taker of the Selfless Spirit. Light-bearers are souls who use life *for their own magnification*. They want, want, want everything to be *their* way for *their* comfort, rejecting, *even damning* those who disagree. They see themselves "Righteous and Holy," and seek to blame others for their problems. They play "victim," but are victimizers. They are "wolves in sheep's clothing," appearing to be Selfless and Good ("sheep"), but all the while motivated by selfishness ("wolves"; predatory takers of the Selfless Spirit).

Our souls were known by God before the Universe was created (Ephesians 1:4), at which time we were Pure. It was on the sixth day of the Creation that the human body was created to house the Pure soul (shown as Adam; Genesis 1:27, 2:7). The sixth day (6) signifies separation, as this is when the Pure soul became its own entity, separated from God in its individual personhood, *but not yet separated from its Oneness with God's Spirit*. Separation from God's Spirit followed of our own free will, by following in the likeness of Adam's sin (Romans 5:14). Consequently, *naturally*, our Pure souls "fell" from the *Realm of Life Eternal* (Heaven; Eden) into the *Realm of Life and Death*.

Those who build anti-Spirit (selfishness) over Spirit (Selfless Goodness) build separation (6) in body (Father), mind (Son), and soul (Spirit). Corruption in body, mind, and soul is separation from Father, Son, and Spirit, signified by 6 6 6, known as the "mark of the beast" (Revelation 13:16-17, 16:2, 19:20).

We are to overcome that which separates God in body, mind, and soul, as it is through Oneness with His Good Spirit that we are purified and prepared for Eternal Oneness.

MORE ABOUT THE SPIRIT

We tend to envision life as belonging to higher forms of creation, not belonging to such things as rocks. But the power spinning the atoms within a rock is Spirit alive. The Spirit is the power fueling the movement of every atomic and subatomic particle. All matter in our Universe owes its existence to the Spirit, the Power of Creation and Life.

Imagine the atoms in a stone, let's say a diamond. In simplest terms, a physical thing exists due to the positive and negative electromagnetic forces within its atomic structure. *Spiritually speaking,* the power that binds a diamond's atoms, making it a mineral of exceptional hardness, is the Spirit, as without the Spirit there is no electromagnetism, no possible opportunity for atoms to assemble and disassemble to even create diamonds. Without the Spirit there is no movement, *no existence.* The Creative Power that binds is Spirit (the force of Oneness, of Assembly; God is the Assembler of the Universe). The destructive force that separates is anti-Spirit (the force of separation, of disassembly; anti-God is the disassembler of the Universe).

Scientifically speaking, the atomic structure in the diamond is of balanced, highly-stable positive and negative electromagnetic charges. *Spiritually speaking,* the diamond owes its remarkable stability and invulnerablilty to the magnitude of Spirit alive in its crystalline structure. The seemingly "eternal" nature of the diamond is that of an atomic structure of far-greater strength in Spirit than anti-Spirit (the more an entity's Spirit, the less its anti-Spirit, as in the case of a diamond's "eternal" invulnerability over other, more-corruptible minerals).

Naturally, a diamond is not alive like you are, but it is very much a living thing in the sense that its building-blocks are arrayed and bonded by the Spirit, allowing its atomic components to exist as they do. What makes a diamond more stable than a piece of chalk is that the Spirit of the diamond is stronger. Chalk, being of weaker physical atomic bonds, *of lesser Spirit-strength,* is more vulnerable to corruption, to disassembling.

Both diamonds and chalk have value to us for their unique properties. Both are physical constructs of Spirit (Assembling-forces) and anti-Spirit (disassembling-forces) in different degrees. The "diamond Spirit" of greater physical stability is created through intense fire and pressure. The "chalk Spirit" of greater physical instability is created through the sedimentation and compaction of the calcite minerals in tiny sea shells.

Spiritually speaking, "fire" symbolizes the Spirit (Acts 2:3-4; Hebrews 12:29). Souls who remain true to the Spirit ("fire") while suffering trials and tribulations ("pressure") grow in the Spirit, *diamond-like*. Theirs is the "rock" foundation Jesus spoke of, upon which their souls shall grow further crystallized (Christ-allized) as they continue to remain true to the Spirit.

Those who build anti-Spirit chip away at their "rock" Spirit Within, eroding it into a "sand" foundation. They are like porous souls, *their soul's Light increasingly filled with holes of darkness the more they deny the Spirit.* Such souls are Spirit-takers ("Light-collectors"), their selfish souls built upon the chalk-like strength of Spiritual idleness, receiving and using (sedimentation and compaction) the Spirit for themselves, not prone to giving freely of their Spirit unto others *unless it serves their selfish desires* (Matthew 25:24-30).

Souls who tread The Way shall be "crystallized in the Spirit," *diamond-like*. Those who do not shall be "ground into powder," *like chalk*. As given in Matthew 21:42-44, those who fall upon His Cornerstone (those who embrace His "rock" Spirit) shall be saved, but those upon whom the Cornerstone falls (those who deny His Spirit) shall be ground into powder.

Like dross removed from silver tried in the fire (Psalms 66:10; Proverbs 25:4-5; Isaiah 1:25), the impurities ("dross") are removed from the entity ("silver") via the Spirit ("fire").

MORE ABOUT JESUS

Jesus told His Apostles that because they have known Him, they have known and seen His Father (John 14:7). Here, He reveals His Individual Personhood and His Oneness with His Father.

If Jesus' name had been "Mud," would He not still be the "Word made flesh" (John 1:14), the Mind and Spirit of God alive in the flesh? *Would He not still be the Mind and Spirit of Selfless Love and Good Works alive in your flesh?*

Jesus no longer walks on Earth, yet still lives on Earth. He lives within those who tread His Way of Selfless Goodness. His flesh was crucified, but His Spirit lives on (Acts 1:5-8, 2:17, 10:45). *He lives in you*. His Kingdom is Within you (Luke 17:21). He is the Spirit Within (the Christ Within; John 14:16-21). Building His Church is not about building buildings, but about building His Good Mind Within, making of your being a temple (church) of His Spirit.

Those who do not deny the Spirit, *no matter who they are, Christian or not, even if they speak against Jesus*, shall know Salvation (Matthew 12:31-33). It is not a matter of *talking the talk*, saying, "I believe in Jesus as Savior," but *walking the walk*, treading His Way of Selfless Love.

Selfless Love is giving of your Goodness joyfully, for want of nothing from the world, that others might see your Good example and follow. Selfless Love is non-judgmental. *Naturally*, we judge by way of our senses, emotions, intellect, and experiences. Judging is about observation, discrimination, and decision, and is essential to maneuvering through life. But non-judgmental love is different. It means not to curse others, *not to accuse and judge others as being lesser in God, worthy of damnation, or hellbound.* Be careful not to damn others for their sins, for as you judge, so shall you be judged.

Jesus said, *And when ye come into an house, salute it* (Matthew 10:12). Here, the subject is not just about houses, but people. Though "house" can refer to a home or environment, one's "house" is also one's "temple" (the human "house" or "temple" is of body, mind, and soul; God is the Spirit Within your temple; "Know ye not that ye are the temple of God," First Corinthians 3:16). Jesus is telling us that when you have dealings with another person ("when ye come into an house"), be respectful ("salute").

And if the house be worthy, let your peace come upon it: but if it be not worthy, let your peace return to you (Matthew 10:13). And if that person magnifies the Spirit, then continue sharing your Spirit, justifying your Holy Communion (your Good Fellowship). But if that person denies your Good Spirit, give no more of it ("let your peace return to you").

And whosoever shall not receive you, nor hear your words, when ye depart out of that house or city, shake off the dust of your feet (Matthew 10:14). Should anyone not receive or "hear" your Spirit, leave that person alone. Move on, departing in peace, taking none of his/her *dirt* (selfishness) with you.

We are not to damn others just because they are not at a higher level of knowledge and wisdom in the Spirit. Yet, when it is evident that your Good Spirit will not be accepted by another person, give no more of your Spirit (cast not "your pearls before swine," Matthew 7:6). Preserve your Spirit and peacefully move on. You cannot *make* someone respect the Spirit.

We all have "darkness within," or unreconciled sins within our souls. The more sin (selfishness) you sow, the more suffering your soul shall eventually reap. All sufferings are lessons that, *of your free will*, can either be compounded or overcome. No matter the suffering that comes before you, *whether seemingly "deserved" or not*, your soul is responsible for dealing with that darkness simply because it is happening to you. How do you deal with the darkness and suffering that becomes a part of your soul's life on Earth?

Human selfishness is the source of the suffering that humanity heaps upon itself. When faced with suffering, do you battle it with anti-Spirit (hatred, blaming, vengeance, jealousy, murder, etc.), building even more darkness within your soul? Only by overcoming suffering with the Light (love, forgiveness, peace, etc.) do you build the Spirit Within. Every measure of darkness that is overcome by the Light is a measure of darkness redeemed, purifying your soul in that same measure (as you sow to the Spirit in a particular measure, so shall you reap of the Spirit in the same measure, per the Parable of the Talents; Chapter 3).

Our sufferings are not without cause (Proverbs 26.2), but come so that we may know Salvation (Second Corinthians 1:6).

THE WAY, THE TRUTH, AND THE LIFE

In John 14:6, Jesus said, "I am the way, the truth, and the life: no man cometh unto the Father but by me." This verse, *taken out of the context of the Message of the Spirit*, is used to propagate the idolatrous worship of Jesus. Other verses taken out of context to support the idolatrous worship of Jesus include John 3:16 ("whosoever believes in Jesus should not perish, but have eternal life") and Matthew 10:32-33 ("whosoever shall confess Jesus before men, him shall Jesus confess before His Father in Heaven").

Truest "belief" in Christ is not ultimately by words or actions, but by Spirit. Ritual baptisms, *like baptism by circumcision, baptism by water, and baptism by confession*, account for nothing if there is not the *Baptism Within*, the "one baptism" of living in the Spirit (Galatians 5:6; Ephesians 4:5).

Matthew 7:20-21 (spoken by Jesus; likely authored by Apostle Matthew)

20. **Wherefore by their fruits ye shall know them.** [We are known to God by our works of Spirit or anti-Spirit.]
21. **Not every one that saith unto me, Lord, Lord, shall enter into the kingdom of heaven; but he that doeth the will of my Father which is in heaven.** [Not everyone who verbally confesses Jesus shall enter Heaven, but only those who do God's Will (confession in Jesus is not a verbal act, but is internal, justified only by conducting God's Spirit of Selfless Love and Good Works).]

First Corinthians 4:20 (authored by Apostle Paul)

20. **For the kingdom of God is not in word, but in power** [Salvation is not by speaking of one's belief in Jesus, but by conducting His Power (His Spirit is the Way, the Truth, and the Life of Selfless Goodness).]

"Outward" faith in Jesus through man-made, ritualistic, idolatrous worship separates humanity into two groups: those who have confessed Jesus as Savior (the Christians); and those who have not (the non-Christians). But Jesus divides humanity into those who exemplify His Spirit (the Spiritful) and those who do not (the Spiritless), *no matter their religion, politics, race, etc.*

Christianity's idolatry of Jesus, *at its extreme,* divides humanity into Christian and non-Christian, where all Christians go to Heaven, *no matter how evil*, and all non-Christians go to hell, *no matter how Good.* Such "sanctified" separatism gave life to such religious terrorism as: the Inquisition; the Crusades; extremist cults (the Ku Klux Klan, the Army of God, the Aryan Nation, Christian Identity, etc.); and the persecution of "heretics" (including the brutalization, enslavement, and murdering of Africans, Aztecs, Incas, American Indians, Australian Aborigines, Muslims, Jews, and other non-Christians).

The outward, idolatrous worship of Jesus over the inner worship of His Spirit is the source of corporate Christianity's us-versus-them exclusivity, upon which hangs every Christian crime committed "in the name of God."

Corporate Christianity supports its separatist agenda by claiming that Jesus came not to bring peace on Earth, but "division" (Luke 12:51). *His division was never about dividing Christians from non-Christians, but about dividing the Spiritful from the Spiritless.* He is the Shepherd that shall divide the Selfless "sheep" from the selfish "goats" (the "sheep" tread The Way of the Spirit, the "goats" do not; Matthew 25:31-46).

Jesus is the Way, the Truth, and the Life of Selfless Love and Good Works. No one shall come to the Father but through Jesus, meaning that no one shall enter the Body of God but through Oneness with His Mind, *His Message of the Spirit*. As your mind grows in Oneness with His Message, so too shall your "tree" (of life) naturally produce Good "fruit" (Selfless Works), thereby justifying and magnifying your soul's Good Spirit, moving it towards Eternal Oneness (Salvation).

Salvation does not come from the vain, outward idolatry of the name "Jesus," nor from the billions of man-made, false, graven images of Him, nor from the many verbal confessions of Him as Savior. Redemption and Salvation comes inwardly, through "Him," *the Christ Within*, effected only by conducting God's Good Spirit.

Acts 2:38 says, "Repent, and be baptized every one of you in the name of Jesus Christ for the remission of sins, and ye shall receive the gift of the Holy Ghost." Here, we are told that those who repent of their selfishness and live in the Spirit (those who live in the Spirit have the *Baptism Within*, the Baptism "in the name of Jesus Christ") shall be cleansed of their anti-Spirit ("remission of sins") and shall know Salvation ("gift of the Holy Ghost"). In short, building the Light Within naturally diminishes your soul's darkness and leads to Salvation. God is Love and All-Good, and what He desires from us is the same in return, *joyfully*.

Romans 12:21 (authored by Apostle Paul)
21. Be not overcome of evil, but overcome evil with good.

THE GREAT COMMANDMENT

Jesus tells us that the entirety of the Bible ("all the law and the prophets") boils down to the Great Commandment to love God (the Invisible Spirit of All-Goodness) with all your heart, soul, and mind (Matthew 22:37-38). Then Jesus defines Good and evil in His second Great Commandment, which instructs us to *love thy neighbour as thyself* (Matthew 22:39; Leviticus 19:18). Naturally, we would all agree that *that which is not Good* include all the things we would not want others to do to us. Selfless Goodness is to freely give unto others all the Good things you would want given unto you (respect, forgiveness, peace, kindness, love, etc.).

All the Commandments are, *before all else*, about your "personal relationship" with the Selfless Spirit of God. Proverbs 30:5 states, "Every word of God is pure: He is a shield unto them that put their trust in Him," meaning that the entire Bible is One with the Spirit, and that God is with those who *hold fast* to its Spirit (those who do not trust the Spirit interpret the Bible selfishly, their Spiritless minds seeing only selfish messages).

The following examination of the Ten Commandments shows how they all boil down to One Commandment.

The 1st Commandment is the Great Commandment, as given above. The remaining nine are born of the first (if you live by the first, you will not break the rest).

The 2nd Commandment tells us to have no idolatry (no worshiping anything over the Spirit), but to serve the Good Spirit first. We are not to create and/or serve graven images, and yet a leading news story in America, in August, 2003, revolved around the removal of a Ten Commandments monument from an Alabama courthouse. The Ten Commandments is not about honoring things (like monuments), but about *living its Message.*

The 3rd Commandment tells us not to speak His name in vain, or without worthiness (for example, those who speak, "I confess Jesus Christ as my Savior," but deny His Spirit, are using His name in vain. How easy it is to declare love for Christ, yet deny His Spirit of Selfless Love in favor of separatist, selfish religion).

The 4th Commandment to honor the Sabbath Day is a directive to do God's Will every day (John 5:16-17). *In the Old Testament*, the Sabbath Day is the seventh day, the day of rest following six days of labor, a day devoted to God's Will. *In the New Testament*, Jesus is "Lord even of the sabbath day" (Matthew 12:8), making Him the Lord over every day of the week, even Sabbath Day. Every day is the Lord's Day, *the Sabbath Day*, in the lives of those devoted to His Good Spirit.

The 5th Commandment tells us to honor "father and mother" so that we are not eternally damned (that we do not "die the death," Matthew 15:4). Honoring "father and mother" is not about biological parents, but about our True Father and Mother: the Source of Life, the Male-Female Spirit of God (Genesis 1:27). If "father and mother" was about biological parents, Jesus would not have revealed that those who are His "mother" are those who do His Father's Will (Matthew 12:50). Honoring "father and mother" is about making the Spirit of the Creator your life's first priority above all things created.

The 6th Commandment tells us not to kill. You are not to "kill" Goodness with evil, as doing so depletes the Spirit Within, weakening your bond to God. The Bible repeatedly speaks of the shedding of "innocent blood." The Innocent Blood represents Jesus Christ, who was Pure and One with the Spirit. The Innocent Blood represents the Light Within you, *the Mind and Spirit of God Within your being, the Christ Within.* Living to produce selfishness (anti-Christ) over Selfless Love (Christ) drains your soul of its Innocent Blood, killing the Christ Within you. [Christians who talk about Christ, but deny His Spirit, "crucify" the Christ Within their souls, moving their souls towards eternal separation. All who live in the Spirit, *Christian or not*, build the Christ Within, moving their souls towards Eternal Oneness.]

The 7th Commandment tells us not to commit adultery. There are two end-all marriages: the marriage to God (the "marriage supper of the Lamb," Revelation 19:9); and the marriage to satan (the "supper of the great god," Revelation 19:17). "Thou shalt not commit adultery" is about remaining true to your marriage to the Spirit. Unlike human marriages, marriage to the Spirit is up to you alone, justified by your devotion to Selfless Goodness. Deny the Spirit and you have committed adultery against God.

The 8th Commandment tells us not to steal. We are not to "steal" from God Within, *or rob our souls of Goodness*, but we are to build Goodness, magnifying God Within. To take of the Spirit that has given us Life without giving Life to the Spirit in return is to "steal" the Spirit ("Light-takers").

The 9th Commandment tells us not to bear false witness, an instruction to live in Truth (the Spirit is Truth).

The 10th tells us not to covet, an instruction to abstain from selfish, idolatrous thoughts.

The "cornerstone" Truth of God's Instruction to us is His First and Great Commandment. Those who do not break the first shall not break the rest.

GOD'S GRACE

First, let's examine two Biblical passages key to understanding the issue of God's Grace.

Ephesians 2:8-10 (authored by Apostle Paul)

8. For by grace are ye saved through faith; and that not of yourselves: it is the gift of God: [You are saved by God's Grace through your faith in Him. His Grace is the Governing Power of His Righteous Justice ('as you sow, so shall you reap'), by which all souls shall be judged of themselves, of their hearts and motivations. His Righteous Justice is His Spirit of the Law, the Law of Promise which promises that all who live and grow in His Spirit shall come to Salvation. Faith in His Spirit is justified through Selfless, Good Works ('faith without works is dead,' James 2:26), through which we are saved by His Grace. We are directed to live in His Spirit, as follows: *"Forasmuch then as Christ hath suffered for us in the flesh, arm yourselves likewise with the same mind"* (First Peter 4:1); *"live according to God in the Spirit"* (First Peter 4:6).]

9. **Not of works, lest any man should boast.** [Be not prideful of your Good Works, as it is not your Good Works that save you. It is God, *the Good Spirit*, that brings Salvation to those devoted to His Good Spirit.]
10. **For we are his workmanship, created in Christ Jesus unto good works, which God hath before ordained that we should walk in them.** [The "workmanship" of God are souls built upon the Selfless Mind and Spirit Within ('Christ Jesus' Within) unto Good Works. God instructs us to "walk" in Good Works.]

Titus 3:5-8 (authored by Apostle Paul)

5. **Not by works of righteousness which we have done, but according to his mercy he saved us, by the washing of regeneration, and renewing of the Holy Ghost;** [We are not saved by "works of righteousness" (Good Works), but according to God's Mercy, which is the Governing Power of His Righteous Justice. A tree is known by its fruit (Matthew 12:33). If you are a "tree" of His Spirit, you will naturally produce Good "fruit" (Selfless, Good Works), which naturally justifies your faith in His Spirit. It is by your faith in His Spirit that you are saved by His Merciful Justice of "as you sow, so shall you reap." *The "washing of regeneration and renewing of the Holy Ghost" is the cleansing process of redemption through "as you sow, so shall you reap."* Every time you overcome a measure of your selfishness (anti-Spirit) with Spirit, you purify a measure of your tainted soul, strengthening His Spirit Within... *this is the "washing of regeneration, and renewing of the Holy Ghost Within you.*]
6. **Which he shed on us abundantly through Jesus Christ our Saviour.** [God shed His Good Spirit upon us abundantly through the Savior-Spirit of His Word made flesh ('Jesus Christ our Saviour' is the 'word made flesh' that lives within those devoted to His Message of Selfless Love and Goodness).]
7. **That being justified by his grace, we should be made heirs according to the hope of eternal life.** [That being justified by His Grace ('as you sow, so shall you reap'), we should come to Salvation.]
8. **This is a faithful saying, and these things I will that thou affirm constantly, that they which have believed in God might be careful to maintain good works. These things are good and profitable unto men.**

Without the Grace of God's Righteous Justice, there would be no way to Salvation. There would be no way to build the Light Within, cleansing your soul of its darkness. Living in His Spirit would account for nothing.

Galatians 6:7 says, "Be not deceived; God is not mocked: for whatsoever a man soweth, that shall he also reap." God's Grace is effected through His Righteous Justice of "as you sow, so shall you reap," for as you sow to His Spirit, so shall you reap of His Spirit.

Why didn't God's Righteous Justice apply to Jesus when He was crucified? Jesus, who was One with God, *having sown no evil*, reaped crucifixion. How could this awfulness have happened? *Because of sinful humankind.* It is because of the selfishness alive within humans that Jesus was crucified (Mark 14:41), causing Him to reap what He had *not* sown (Matthew 25:26), but what idolatrous humans had sown. He overcame sin unto death and, in so doing, overcame the "fruits" of sin: death and hell. Consequently, He holds the "keys of hell and of death" (Revelation 1:18), and has become the Open Door to Salvation to all who tread His Way of the Spirit.

Jesus died for our sins on the cross (Romans 5:6, 5:8; First Corinthians 15:3; Second Corinthians 5:15), meaning that He died because of the selfishness (sins) of human souls. Were you taught that when Christ died He *literally* took your sins away? Had He taken away the sins of your soul upon His death, your Pure soul would now be in Heaven. He died so that you "should live unto righteousness" (First Peter 2:24), and that you "might be made the righteousness of God" (Second Corinthians 5:21).

Jesus did not have to die on the cross. He had the power to come off the cross and heal, but it was God's Will that He die (Mark 14:36), that He willingly release His Soul (He obeyed, and "gave up the ghost," Mark 15:37). When faced with death, He did not surrender to selfishness by saving Himself [He did not submit to the desire to keep His body alive (self-preservation)], but chose the Spirit, showing us The Way to Salvation. We are to follow His Way, sacrificing "self" (selfishness) for God's Good Spirit.

Second Corinthians 5:15 (authored by Apostle Paul)

15. **And that He died for all, that they which live should not henceforth live unto themselves, but unto Him which died for them, and rose again.** [He died for all, that we should not live for self, but live for His Selfless Spirit.]

SIN

All sin rises from human selfishness, and is relative. Selfishness sown by those lacking knowledge of the Spirit *shall reap lesser consequences* than selfishness sown by those having knowledge of the Spirit.

Luke 12:47-48 (spoken by Jesus; authored by Luke, disciple with Apostle Paul)

47. **And that servant, which knew his lord's will, and prepared not himself, neither did according to his will, shall be beaten with many stripes.** [We who know that God's Will desires true and faithful devotion to His Good Spirit, but do not prepare ourselves thusly, nor follow His Will, shall suffer great sufferings.]
48. **But he that knew not, and did commit things worthy of stripes, shall be beaten with few stripes. For unto whomsoever much is given, of him shall be much required: and to whom men have committed much, of him they will ask the**

more. [But we who have done things worthy of sufferings, and do not know The Way of His Spirit, shall suffer less sufferings. Those who have reaped much of the Spirit shall be required to sow much of the Spirit. And those who have committed much to the Spirit will seek even more of the Spirit.]

Life, as you know it, is your "world," perceived uniquely through your mind's understandings. Good and evil are the two spiritual powers upon which the structures of your mind's understandings are built. What you define as being sin may not be sin *in the construct of another person's Good Conscience.*

Our lives, minds, and lessons are unique. Even so, we all have one thing in common: we are living souls, bound by God's Spirit. This Truth is often eclipsed by outward labels that can serve to divide us, such as men vs. women, whites vs. blacks, straights vs. gays, Protestants vs. Catholics, pro-lifer's vs. pro-choicer's, etc. *God does not care how you define yourself outwardly, but knows you by your devotion to His Spirit.* God identifies us by our Good Spirit, not by our worldly labels. *Identify with others likewise.*

THE ONE TEMPLE

In the Old Testament, God instructed Moses to build One Temple, called the "Tent of the Congregation," a structure that speaks to the three-part nature of God's Temple and the human temple: body, mind, and soul [the human temple is in the "image" and "likeness" of God (Genesis 1:26), not meaning that we look like our Invisible God of Good Spirit, but that our substance is of God, and that we are living "gods" over our own respective "worlds" (Psalms 82:6; John 10:34)].

The Tent of the Congregation was the Temple structure where the Israelites gathered to worship God (Exodus, Chapters 26-40). It consisted of the Outer Court, the Inner Court, and the Holy of Holies. In the center was the Tent, *or Temple proper*, partitioned by an embroidered curtain, where one side was the Inner Court and the other side the Holy of Holies (wherein the Spirit of God dwelt, in the Ark of the Testimony). Surrounding the Tent was the Outer Court, a rectangular area enclosed by large, curtain "walls." The Outer and Inner Courts were areas for physical cleansing (via wash basins) and spiritual cleansing (via offerings and sacrifices).

The Temple of God has an Outer Court (Father; Body of God) that houses the Inner Court (Son; Mind of God) and Holy of Holies (Spirit; Soul of God). Likewise, the temple of flesh has a body (Outer Court) that houses the mind (Inner Court) and soul (Holy of Holies).

The Inner Court represents the mind. It was through Jesus, *the Mind of God in the flesh*, that God's Message of the Spirit was delivered to us. It is only through your mind that His Message can be "heard." *Your mind is the builder of your identity, of who you are and what you will become.*

The Holy of Holies represents God's Spirit Within your soul. Historically, it was through the Holy of Holies that the High Priest received Enlightenment from God. Before this could occur, purification rituals were performed in the Outer and Inner Courts through sacrifices, offerings, and physical cleansing. Similarly, your "High Priest" (Good Conscience) must be cleansed through sacrifices (sacrificing selfishness for the Selfless Spirit) in your body (Outer Court) and mind (Inner Court) to receive Enlightenments from God Within (Holy of Holies; the Kingdom Within).

The Tent of the Congregation, built of God's Divine Measurements, is a structural message to us about:

1. The nature of God's physical Temple, wherein His Spirit temporarily dwelt. [His Temple is of Father (Body; Outer Court), Son (Mind; Inner Court), and Holy Spirit (Soul; Holy of Holies).]
2. The nature of the human temple, wherein His Spirit temporarily dwells. [The human temple is of body (Outer Court; Father), mind (Inner Court; Son), and soul (Holy of Holies; Spirit).]

The message of the Tent of the Congregation instructs you to be true to the Good Spirit, like God Himself. The Temple of God is not a church system, but is you. You are the Temple of the Living God when you embody His Spirit. In the end, you will not be judged by what group you belonged to, but by your devotion to the Spirit. His Church is not a worldly structure of buildings, and His Congregation is made up of all souls devoted to exemplifying His Good Spirit.

It was Peter who received that zenith of Enlightenment about Jesus, *that He was the Christ.* That Enlightenment came from the Spirit Within Peter. Jesus revealed that His Church (not churches) shall be built upon Peter, *not upon Peter literally* (the Pope's Throne is directly above what they believe to be Peter's bones), but upon the Spirit Within Peter.

Matthew 16:15-19 (spoken by Jesus; likely authored by Apostle Matthew)

15. He [Jesus] **saith unto them** [His Apostles], **But whom say ye that I am?**

16. And Simon Peter answered and said, Thou art the Christ, the Son of the living God.

17. And Jesus answered and said unto him, Blessed art thou, Simon Barjona [Peter]**: for flesh and blood hath not revealed it unto thee, but my Father which is in heaven.** [Enlightenment comes from the Father Within (the collective Spirit Within; the Heaven Within), as this is where God lives ('the kingdom of God is within you,' Luke 17:21)]

18. And I say also unto thee, That thou art Peter, and upon this rock I will build my church; and the gates of hell shall not prevail against it. [So great was Peter's devotion to the Good Spirit that God enlightened only him to Jesus' Identity. Jesus revealed that His Church would be built upon "this rock," not referring to Peter, *the person*, but to Peter, *the one of greatest faith in His Spirit.* Jesus renamed Simon Barjona to "Petros" (or Peter, meaning the 'rock'). Peter's faith represents the "rock foundation" of The Good Way. Satan and hell shall not overcome those who have such a faith as Peter's. (Note: Christianity defines Jesus' 'Church' as being its man-made churches, but His Church is built Within those true to His Spirit. Matthew 27:51 revealed that upon Jesus' death, the 'veil of the temple was rent in twain,' a reminder to us that God's Spirit does not live in man-made temples. Your 'Church of Christ' is not a building or a worldly system of corporate religion, but is the Invisible Good Spirit Within that, through your free will, only you can ultimately build or destroy).]

19. **And I will give unto thee the keys of the kingdom of heaven: and whatsoever thou shalt bind on earth shall be bound in heaven: and whatsoever thou shalt loose on earth shall be loosed in heaven.** [It was Peter to whom Jesus gave the keys to the Gates of Heaven (Peter repeatedly denied God, but always realized his transgressions and overcame, growing even stronger in the Spirit. Peter is 'Everyman's Saint.' Those of us sinful souls who overcome, living and growing in the Spirit, shall be greeted by Peter at the Gates of Heaven). Peter's soul was so filled in Spirit that when he prophesied a blessing (a 'binding' to the Spirit) or a curse (a 'loosening' from the Spirit), they were true prophecies born of Enlightenment Within, born of the Spirit (those who strengthen the Spirit Within shall be strengthened in the Spirit-gift of prophecy).]

After the Israelites' entrance into the Promised Land, the portable Tent of the Congregation was replaced by the permanent structure of Solomon's Temple, built in Jerusalem from 964 to 957 B.C.. But, *once again*, the Israelites turned to idolatrous worship, making of their Temple a self-serving business. They grew so idolatrous, *abandoning God's Spirit*, that the Spirit of God abandoned them in 586 B.C., the year when the Temple was utterly destroyed by the Babylonian King, Nebuchadnezzar. The Ark of the Testimony (God's Presence) was removed from the Holy of Holies and never seen again. *No man-made temple since has been Glorified by God's Presence.*

The Israelites' enslavement in Babylon came as a spiritual lesson, teaching that sowing idolatry leads to enslavement to greater idolatry (they sowed idolatry, and so they reaped enslavement to the more-idolatrous Babylonians). During their enslavement, they restored their commitment to God's Will and, as a result, were set free by the Babylonians. Upon returning to Jerusalem they began to rebuild a temple over the ruins of Solomon's Temple, completed in 520 B.C. and referred to as the Second Temple (a temple not sanctified by God's Presence, unlike Solomon's Temple). Nearly 500 years later, when in ruin, it was rebuilt.

The Second Temple, in grave disrepair, was largely destroyed and rebuilt by King Herod in 24 B.C., who made it into a grander version of Solomon's Temple, *which I refer to as the Rebuilt Second Temple.* Herod created it specifically to be the center for the business of idolatrous worship. In was in this temple that Jesus threw out the merchants and the moneychangers, calling it a "den of thieves" (Matthew 21:12-13). At the moment of Jesus' death, the curtain-portal into its Holy of Holies tore in half (Mark 15:37-38), a dramatic reminder that God does not live in man-made temples of idolatrous religion. In the summer of the year 70 A.D., the Romans burned much of Jerusalem, destroying the Rebuilt Second Temple, *which was of zero consequence to God, because it had always been a "dead" temple (without His Presence).*

The Temple of God is not a building, but the Spirit Within you (John 2:19-21; Mark 14:58).

THE MUSTARD TREE

The Bible speaks of the EXALTED force of selfishness (anti-Spirit) versus the quiet, meek force of Selflessness (Spirit), as seen in terms of: MOUNTAINS vs. valleys and deserts; TREES vs. grasses; and EARTHQUAKES vs. a "still small voice" (First Kings 19:12).

Consider Psalms 23:4: *Yea though I walk through the valley of the shadow of death, I will fear no evil: for thou art with me; thy rod and thy staff they comfort me.* We know that every valley is naturally flanked by hills or mountains that cast shadows. The valley with its "meek" landscape represents the Spirit. The mountains that cast the "shadow of death" signify the EXALTED landscape of the anti-Spirit. Both the "rod" and the "staff" represent God's Divine measuring stick of "as you sow, so shall you reap," which is His Righteous Justice. [There are many examples of the "rod" and "staff" used in the deliverance of God's Righteous Justice. Both were protective tools used by shepherds to help herd their sheep and drive away wolves.]

Spiritually interpreted, Psalms 23:4 reveals: Though I walk The Way of God's Spirit (The Way of the Light; "through the valley") in a world overshadowed by anti-Spirit (darkness; human selfishness; "shadow of death"), I will not fear, for God is with me (God is "with" those who are "with" Him, *or who live and grow in His Selfless, Good Spirit*), and His Righteous Justice comforts me (regardless of human justice, God's Justice will be met).

Consider a field sown with mustard seeds when it has come into season. It is a field of tall, slender herbs (1 to 8 feet), their green stems tipped with small golden flowers and seeds. Its green stem signifies healthy growth (growth in the Spirit) that comes into maturity when its tips produce clusters of "golden flowers" (symbolizing purity) and healing seeds (fruits of the Spirit; The medicinal properties of mustard have been known for over 2,000 years; Mustard has been used internally and externally for such aliments as arthritis, rheumatism, toothaches, digestive disorders, and cardiovascular problems). The "mustard seed" is the Seed of Promise, *the One Spirit that is The Way to Salvation.* "Mustard herbs" symbolize individuals growing in the Light of the "field" (Earth) of the Lord, *devoted to the Spirit.*

Jesus' Parable of the Mustard Seed illustrates that corporate Christianity (the self-confessed "Kingdom of Heaven" on Earth) is like a mustard seed grown into a tree. As there is no such thing as a "mustard tree," this unnatural form refers to a man-made structure. The Mustard Tree symbolizes the vast system of corporate religion that uses the Good Spirit to exalt its selfish agendas over the souls of humankind. The great corporate system is a *soul-less thing* that loves the world over the Spirit. The Great Tree provides much "shade" (idolatry; darkness), shielding many from the Light.

Because the upcoming Parable of the Mustard Seed is about the corporate temple vs. the individual temple, let us quickly review the various temples we have covered thus far.

1. Heaven - the Eternal, Incorruptible Temple. [The Kingdom of God, wherein the Source of His Spirit dwells eternally.]
2. Human Beings - mobile, corruptible temples, wherein God's Children, *the souls of humankind*, dwell. [The collective Light within a human soul is its Spirit Within (God Within; Heaven Within; Kingdom Within).]
3. Tent of the Congregation - a mobile, corruptible temple. [The One portable Temple that God instructed the Israelites to build, which was replaced by the One "permanent" Temple: Solomon's Temple. God's Spirit lived within the Tent's Holy of Holies.]
4. Solomon's Temple - an immobile, corruptible temple. [The One permanent Temple that God instructed Solomon to build in Jerusalem. Though God's Spirit lived within its Holy of Holies, many Temple priests and worshipers grew idolatrous and, consequently, God's Presence departed and has never sanctified another man-made Temple since.]
5. Second Temple - an immobile, corrupted temple. [Built upon the ruins of Solomon's Temple, the Second Temple was the first unsanctified temple, as God's Spirit did not live within its Holy of Holies. The Second Temple was even more idolatrous and self-serving than Solomon's Temple.]
6. Rebuilt Second Temple - an immobile, corrupted temple [King Herod had the Second Temple rebuilt to serve as a center for the big-business of idolatrous worship. The Rebuilt Second Temple was the second unsanctified temple, and even more corrupt than its predecessor.]

God would not have ordered the Israelites to build any temple whatsoever had they not been stiff-necked idolaters. In their exodus from bondage in Egypt, they personally witnessed how God, *the Invisible Spirit*, freed them of enslavement to their idolatrous, Imperialistic Egyptian slaveholders. Even after so many up-close-and-personal miracles, many Israelites refused to trust their Invisible God of Spirit. Why? *Because they could not see Him! They wanted a God they could idolatrously worship, that they could touch and see. They wanted to bow before man-made things.* And because they would not deny their idolatry, they forsake God and made a "golden calf," worshiping before the monstrosity. Because of their selfish desire to have to see and touch Him in order to have faith in Him,

God ordered them to build the Tent of the Congregation, so that they might never turn to idolatrous worship again.

The Tent of the Congregation was the only Temple Period during which the Israelites, *as a whole*, succeeded in becoming true and faithful to God's Spirit. By the time of Solomon's Temple, they had turned back to idolatry. Finally, the last and most corrupt Temple Period of the Rebuilt Second Temple, created by King Herod (a Roman sympathizer), was a full-fledged business of self-serving, religious idolatry structured to wield power and control over the masses. After the Romans destroyed it in the year 70, followed by nearly 250 years of persecution towards the Jews and Jesus' followers, Imperialistic Roman opportunists wrested control over Jesus' Gospel and the Bible for selfish gain, *for money, power, and control over the masses*. The Temple corruption under King Herod's Romanesque regime would pale in comparison to Emperor Constantine's Roman "Catholic" (worldwide) Church.

It was Imperialist Romans who, *do not forget*, had sought to kill the infant Jesus and had brutalized and murdered Jesus' followers for centuries. In the early 4th century, the Roman citizenry grew so sick and tired of the merciless slaughtering of the early Judeo-Christians that they began sympathizing with them. This, *combined with the Empire's rapidly crumbling power*, led Emperor Constantine to make a brilliant political move. He supported and defended the Christian faith, having massive churches built, enabling the biggest religious business in history: the Roman Church.

Constantine's Universal ("Catholic") Roman Church was a man-made, unsanctified, corporate structure of religion, built by and for Imperialist minds to secure power and control over the increasingly popular religion of the early Judeo-Christians. Catholics regard Constantine as a Holy Christian, but was he not a "heretic" pagan and a tyrant? One of Catholicism's beloved stories is that of Constantine's "holy" vision of a flaming cross before battling at the Milvian Bridge in 312, an event that "called" him to support the Christian religion. If truly "called" by Christ, why didn't he seek Peace instead of war? Historically, the all-powerful and "Divine" Roman Emperors were notorious for using "gods" and "miracles" to legitimize their power over the masses.

Constantine's "vision," invented or not, helped unite his collapsing Empire, strengthening his "Divine" and "Holy" status (he remained a pagan ruler until, near death in 337, he was baptized). How "Holy" is a man who built, *upon the backs of slaves*, the biggest business of idolatrous dogma on Earth? How "Holy" is a man who, in 326 (per the *Epitome* of Aurelius Victor), had both his eldest son (Crispus) and wife (Fausta) killed?

So, three-hundred years after Jesus' death, Imperial Rome, *which had failed to conquer Jesus' followers through brutality*, finally conquered them by seizing control over His Gospel. The Emperor "stole" the Good Spirit of the Gospel to use for his benefit, fusing Church and State, securing for himself enormous power and control over the masses (the Roman Church was built by usurpers of the Word, or "Light-takers").

The self-confessed "Kingdom of Heaven" on Earth is the man-made system of corporate Christianity, which Jesus refers to as a Mustard Tree that houses the "birds of the air." [The "birds of the air" are creatures (creations) of the "prince of the powers of the air" (the anti-Spirit; Ephesians 2:2) that symbolize every manner of idolatry. This interpretation is confirmed in Revelation 19:17-21, where we see the birds of the air eating of the flesh of the anti-Spirit (the 'fowls that fly in the midst of heaven' that feed upon the body of the anti-Christ).]

Jesus specifically speaks of a Mustard Tree because He knows there is no such thing in the natural world, which means that He is referring to a man-made thing. The Mustard Tree represents a man-made thing upon Earth that rises over masses of individual temples ("mustard herbs"). The Great Tree and its many branches (sects) tower in supremacy over individual souls. Those in the shade of the Tree shall be tempted and comforted by darkness.

Matthew 13:31-33 (spoken by Jesus; likely authored by Apostle Matthew)

31. **Another parable put he forth unto them, saying, The kingdom of heaven is like to a grain of mustard seed, which a man took, and sowed in his field:** [the Kingdom of Heaven is of One Spirit, like a "grain" (not 'grains'), which Jesus sowed upon the Earth ('which a man sowed in his field').]
32. **Which indeed is the least of all seeds: but when it is grown, it is the greatest among herbs, and becometh a tree, so that the birds of the air come and lodge in the branches thereof.** [The Spirit is the "least," not only because it is One, but at the time Jesus spoke this parable, His true and faithful followers of The Way were the least of all religious groups in Israel. But when The Way of the Spirit has grown popular, it is the greatest among the people, and shall become a man-made structure, so that idolatrous religion ('birds of the air') shall settle within and make a home.]
33. **Another parable spake he unto them; The kingdom of heaven** [corporate Christianity] **is like unto leaven** [idolatry], **which a woman** [idolater] **took, and hid in three measures of meal** [the Message of the Three-in-One God], **till the whole was leavened.**

In Verse 33, Jesus reveals that corporate Christianity is like idolatry, because its builders (idolaters; "woman") took and blended idolatry into the Message of the Body, Mind, and Soul of God until the whole of God's One Message was mixed with idolatry (the "woman" is "whore of Babylon" . . . the idolator of "MYSTERY" that feeds and breeds selfish religion, and is drunk upon worldly wealth, power, and control; the "woman" is the anti-Spirit that has corrupted corporate Christianity; Revelation 17:3-6).

The Mustard Tree of corporate Christianity is a soul-less thing that has no individual mind, but is headed by an elite few to rule over the masses. Every corporate religion that holds itself the "way" to Salvation, making of itself a "Holy Mediator" between God and its individual members, is a false religion (the One Mediator between your soul and God is His Mind and Spirit *alive in your flesh*; the Christ Within; the "man Christ Jesus," First Timothy 2:5).

The corporate mindset rejects, fears, *even damns* those who refuse to submit their minds and souls to <u>its</u> groupist mentality, often defining outsiders as "heretic" or "hellbound." Jesus' Gospel cautions the "sheep" not to follow any "shepherd" but His Spirit, *the Good Shepherd Within*, warning us that there are many who will claim they know The Way, but they do not, being "wolves in sheep's clothing."

Know that corporate Christianity can serve a Good purpose, as it can be steppingstone to greater Enlightenment about God. If you choose to bind your soul to a man-made, corporate religion, use it as a stepping-stone, *to help you upon The Good Way*, but let it not become a stumbling-block, *enslaving your soul to any of its idolatrous dogma.*

"LOVE THE SINNER, HATE THE SIN"

How would you feel if someone said to you, "I love you, but you're going to hell?" Maybe you have heard Christians say, *on one hand*, "We love the abortionist (or homosexual, or non-Christian, etc.), but we hate their sin," then go on to casually add, *on the other hand*, "God says that all abortionists (or homosexuals, or non-Christians, etc.) are going to hell."

Corporate Christianity's most widely-accepted message is that only Christ-believing sinners are "saved" and all other sinners are going to hell. This being so, their mantra, "Love the sinner, hate the sin," is bogus, because it only applies to Christian sinners, as only they are "saved." *Aah... but why should only Christian sinners be "saved?"* Because Christian churches are filled with Christian sinners! *What is corporate Christianity's wellspring of money, power, and control?* Christian sinners! How better to firmly secure a cultist mentality than by insisting that only members are "saved" and all others are "damned." The nature of this cultist mindset, *in its extreme*, rejects all who refuse to bend to <u>its</u> will, labeling them as "heretics" and "hellbound."

How can someone love you and, with the same mouth, condemn you to hell, the worst condemnation EVER? How can you have love and hate in the same Temple of Spirit?

In the Book of Revelation, Jesus commends Apostle Paul's church in Ephesus, telling them, *"But this thou hast, that thou hatest the deeds of the Nicolaitanes, which I also hate"* (the Nicolaitanes were idolatrous religionists; Revelation 2:6). Jesus is not promoting hatred, nor is He revealing that He has an emotional hatred for the Nicolaitanes. With Jesus, everything that denies the Good Spirit is *naturally* repulsive to the Spirit, or "hated." Christians who say they "love" abortionists, non-Christians, and homosexuals, then condemn them all to hell are "hated" by Christ Himself for denying His Spirit.

Jesus said, *"If any man come to me, and hate not his father, and mother, and wife, and children, and brethren, and sisters, yea, and his own life also, he cannot be my disciple"* (Luke 14:26). Jesus is not telling you to hate yourself, your parents or your family, but instructing you to love the Creator-Spirit over all things created, to put Selfless Love first.

If God's Kingdom is Within, and if He is the Invisible Spirit of All that is Good, and if the entirety of the Bible boils down to loving the All-Good Spirit with the fullness of your being, then aren't the separatist fears and superstitions of corporate Christianity *naturally exposed* for being self-serving, idolatrous obstacles upon the One Way to God? *You bet.*

The Good Spirit transcends all worldliness, especially humankind's selfish, exclusive groups. But regardless of how you label yourself, either you live to Glorify the Good Spirit or you don't. No one can ultimately sow and reap the Good Spirit into your life but you. It is an individual process built upon personal responsibility. Only those sowing Good reap God. That's the One Way. *That just the way it is.* Once this concept is proven to your satisfaction, all your worldly labels and systems of selfishness will start falling away. Here is the Truth about being "born again."

Treading God's Way is the Wisdom of Spirit over self. As given in Revelation 10:9, the Bible is sweet to the taste, but bitter to the belly, *that is, the Wisdom of Good over evil is wondrous to speak of and desire, but difficult at times to absorb, or truly exemplify.*

Fearful, superstitious, selfish humans build greater selfishness upon Earth by conditioning, drilling, and enslaving others, *especially children*, in their "mysterious" religious idolatries. God repeatedly reveals this weakness about human nature... *about how easy it is to fall prey to idolatrous religion.* He tells us that the One Way to overcome is always, ultimately an individual trek that requires an ever-growing devotion to living in His Good Spirit, through which one's Good Conscience is polished to a higher brilliance.

Fear not the selfishness of others, nor think yourself able to make them change, but show yourself a beacon of Light that, *by your example,* they might see and follow.

Chapter 1

SALVATION

#2 - Breese, Dave (August 8, 1999)

Salvation is not by works of righteousness which we have done, but according to His Mercy (quoting from Titus 3:5). That's how He saves us. Why is it so difficult for people to believe the simple proposition that the Gospel of Grace and Salvation is by saying "Yes" to Jesus Christ, and Everlasting Life comes to all who will believe? Everyone has been atoned for by that awful set of events on Calvary's cross. People do not go to hell because they are wicked. It's because they refuse to receive Christ. People do not go to Heaven because they live a righteous, commendable life. There's no such a person. They go to Heaven because they have said "Yes" to Jesus and trusted Him as their personal Savior.

Dangerous is the lie that people can be "saved" without justifying their soul's Spirit through Selfless Works. Why bother having a Good Conscience if all you have to do to get to Heaven is submit to idolatrous, vain, verbal confessions of Jesus as "personal Savior?" Jesus makes it clear that He does not care if you say that you believe in Him, but that you live in His Father's Spirit. Your personal Savior is the Spirit Within that only you, *of your life's works,* can Glorify or crucify.

Though it is correct that none are saved by their Good Works, faith in God is "dead" without them (James 2:20), and without faith there is no Salvation by God's Grace. As a tree is known by its fruit, a soul treading The Way of the Spirit naturally produces Selfless, Good Works.

God's Mercy is not about saying "Yes" to Jesus. God's Mercy is His Righteous Justice, without which there would be no opportunity for the Salvation of our impure souls.

If "works of righteousness" have nothing to do with Salvation, then why does corporate Christianity insistently teach that you do its "works of righteousness": **1)** Publicly confessing your belief in Jesus; **2)** Gifting 10% of your annual income to the Church system; and **3)** going to church regularly?

Matthew 7:21 (spoken by Jesus; likely authored by Apostle Matthew)

21. **Not every one that saith unto me, Lord, Lord, shall enter into the kingdom of heaven; but he that doeth the will of my Father which is in heaven.** [Not everyone who verbally confesses Jesus shall enter Heaven, excepting those who live in the Spirit.]

Matthew 10:32-33 (spoken by Jesus; likely authored by Apostle Matthew)

32. **Whosoever therefore shall confess me before men, him will I confess also before my Father which is in heaven.**
33. **But whosoever shall deny me before men, him will I also deny before my Father which is in heaven.** [Man-made, ritualistic, verbal confessions mean nothing if you have not the *Confession Within, or Baptism Within* (pages 54-55), justified only through devotion to God's Will. True confession is not justified by words, but by the Spirit of our works (Matthew 15:17-20).]

Matthew 12:31-33 (spoken by Jesus; likely authored by Apostle Matthew)

31. **Wherefore I say unto you, All manner of sin and blasphemy shall be forgiven unto men; but the blasphemy against the Holy Ghost shall not be forgiven unto men.**
32. **And whosoever speaketh a word against the Son of man, it shall be forgiven him: but whosoever speaketh against the Holy Ghost, it shall not be forgiven him, neither in this world, neither in the world to come.** [Jesus reveals that all our sins and blasphemies, *even if we speak against Him,* shall be forgiven, establishing that rejecting Him is of no consequence in the lives of those who do not deny the Spirit (denying the Spirit is of greatest consequence, because those who do so shall suffer the consequences of their sins and blasphemies).]
33. **Either make the tree good, and his fruit good; or else make the tree corrupt, and his fruit corrupt: for the tree is known by his fruit.** [The Spiritful "tree" shall naturally generate Spiritful "fruit," or Selfless, Good Works. The Spiritless "tree" shall naturally generate Spiritless "fruit," or selfish works. We are known to God by the nature of our works, as they are proof of our devotion to His Spirit or not.]

John 5:29 (spoken by Jesus; authored by Apostle John)

29. **...they that have done good, unto the resurrection of life; and they that have done evil, unto the resurrection of damnation.** [This verse confirms the all-importance of the nature of one's works.]

Romans 5:1 (authored by Apostle Paul)

1. **Therefore being justified by faith, we have peace with God through our Lord Jesus Christ.** [Being justified by faith (faith is justified through Good Works), we have Oneness with God through His Spirit Within (Oneness through 'our Lord Jesus Christ' Within).]

John 3:16 (spoken by Jesus; authored by Apostle John)

15. For God so loved the world, that He gave His only begotten Son, that whosoever believeth in Him should not perish, but have eternal life.

Literally interpreted, John 3:16 is used to judge all non-Christians as hellbound. *Spiritually interpreted,* it reads, "For God (the Invisible, Good Spirit) so loved those of us in the world that He gave His only begotten Son (the Mind and Spirit of God alive in the flesh), that whosoever lives as He lived ("believeth in Him") should not perish, but have Eternal Life (faith in Christ does not come via idolatrous, verbal confessions, but by walking The Way of His Spirit).

Second Peter 3:9 (authored by Apostle Peter)

9. The Lord is not slack concerning his promise, as some men count slackness; but is longsuffering to us-ward, not willing that any should perish, but that all should come to repentance.

God is not willing for <u>any</u> to perish. *No one goes to hell for simply denying Jesus' name.* You can shout your belief in Christ from the rooftops, but it will mean nothing to Him if you live to deny His Spirit.

A soul that lives in the Spirit will be chosen by Christ (those without the Spirit do not have Christ, Romans 8:9). Those who are chosen are those who have chosen to live in His Spirit.

Revelation 17:14 (authored by Apostle John)

14. ...he is Lord of lords, and King of kings: and they that are with him are called, and chosen, and faithful. [Those who are called and chosen are those who have sought (called) and chosen His Way.]

John 15:16 (spoken by Jesus; authored by Apostle John)

16. Ye have not chosen me, but I [Jesus] **have chosen you...**

■ ■ ◆ ■ ■

#21 - Kennedy, D. James (May 16, 1999)

The resurrection of Christ has been proved more thoroughly than any ancient event in history by the greatest of minds. The evidences for the inspiration of Scripture are monumental, and the only people who question either of those are the ignorant, who have never made a study of the matter at all.

Jesus doesn't care if you question His literal Resurrection, but that you understand what it means. It means that all souls devoted to the Spirit shall be quickened unto Salvation by the Spirit, the same Spirit that resurrected Jesus (Romans 8:11).

■ ■ ◆ ■ ■

#9 - Finley, Mark (January 2, 2000)

Salvation is a free gift of God. You don't do any work for it. It's simply claimed by asking. Anyone watching this program can be saved right now by saying, in effect, "God save me."

Salvation does not come by speaking the words, "God save me," but by God's Grace through devotion to His Spirit.

■ ■ ◆ ■ ■

#8 - Falwell, Jerry (on *The Factor* with Bill O'Reilly; November 30, 2001)

Bill O'Reilly: There are some Christians around the world who believe that unless you accept Jesus Christ, that you can't go to Heaven. So, all the Jews, all the Muslims, all the Hindus, all the Buddhists, they're toast, they ain't goin'. Alright? It's an exclusionary faith. You see? Unless you, unless you think that Jesus is the Savior or believe that Jesus is the Savior, you're not going to Paradise. Now, in the Islam religion, there's a strain of that as well: "If you're not with us, you're an infidel." You see the two parallels?

Jerry Falwell: I do, but the difference is Christianity doesn't encourage killing the infidels, but encourages evangelizing...

Bill O'Reilly: But do you believe that unless you accept Jesus you're not gettin' in (to Heaven)?

Jerry Falwell: Bill, I believe outright that, as an evangelical Christian, and I grew up with a father who was an agnostic, a grandfather that was an atheist, but from hearing a radio broadcast when I was a Sophomore in college fifty years ago, I came to believe there is a God in Heaven who has a Son named Jesus Christ, who died for the sins of the world, mine included, and I was born again in January of '52, and I believe John 14:6, Jesus said, "I am the way, the truth, the life, no man cometh to the Father but by me," but I don't believe that's vindictive or in any way bigoted, I believe that's all-inclusive, and that's why I've spent fifty years sharing that Gospel with the world.

Bill O'Reilly: Okay, but if I'm a Jewish guy, and I don't believe that Jesus is God, can I go to Heaven?

Jerry Falwell: I don't believe anyone can go to Heaven, Gentile, Jew, black, white, red or yellow, whatever, without knowing Christ as Savior, and that's what your Catholic Church, basically, doctrine believes, and that is exactly what Billy Graham preaches.

Bill O'Reilly: No, no, no, they don't. No, they've got a little loophole here. And I, believe me, I know the finest Catholic scholars in the world, and the loophole, here's the loophole if you want to hear it. It's very interesting, and I believe this, I believe this to be true. The Catholic theologians, not all of them, but the ones that I respect, say that if you lead a life that mirrors the life of Jesus, in the sense that you love God, whatever God, above all things, and you treat your neighbor as yourself, that's enough to get you into Heaven or Paradise, whatever you want to call it, because that's Jesus' philosophy. So, maybe you don't acknowledge that Jesus is God but, by living The Way that He did, that's enough to get you there, and I believe that.

Jerry Falwell: You'll never get Pope John Paul II to "Amen" to that, and you won't get Billy Graham to "Amen" to that.

Bill O'Reilly: Maybe I won't, but I think that's an inclusionary religion, and that's a religion for all mankind.

Hooray! A "loophole." Per Jesus, the entirety of the Bible boils down to loving the Good Spirit with all your being. Those devoted to the Spirit above all else will be saved, *no matter their gods*, for the Good Spirit IS God. To know this is to know that God is not exclusively the God of Catholicism or any other Christian sect, but the God of all devoted to His Way of the Spirit. If this Truth were to be suddenly believed by all Christians wholeheartedly, they would free themselves from all the fears, superstitions, and rituals of idolatrous Christianity. The Truth that makes you free (John 8:32), *exalted in this book*, is denied by Christian leaders, as the Truth of the Spirit might lead the masses away from their Spiritually-asphyxiating "world" of seductive, separatist, idolatrous religion.

I was a non-religious child in a Catholic school in the 1960's in Japan, where I was repeatedly taught that all non-Catholics were going to hell. I have since learned that the Catholic Church found that it was acceptable, *by their Nicene Creeds*, for non-Catholic Christians to also enter Heaven. But these are the same Creeds used to judge all non-Christians "hellbound." Still, the Catholic Church (with its "direct link" to God through its Papacy) defines itself as the "Mother Church" and believes that nearly two-thirds of Earth's population is *heretic* and *hellbound.*

■ ■ ◆ ■ ■

#2 - Breese, Dave (May 30, 1999)

The following excerpt is a voice-over at the onset of the program. The remaining excerpts are from the sermon itself.

The Bible says, "Believe on the Lord Jesus Christ and thou shalt be saved." But once that's done, there arise serious and important questions. "What do I do next?" "How can I grow as a Christian?" "How can I avoid falling in with the wrong crowd?" "What privileges are mine as a child of God?"

"Believe on the Lord Jesus Christ and thou shalt be saved" is irrelevant if you do not live in the Spirit. True "belief" is justified through action, not thought.

Judging others as "the wrong crowd" denies the Spirit. The only "wrong crowd" is in yourself, crowded with wrongness for making such judgments.

Regarding a Christian's "privileges": What privileges? A believer's life is of devotion to the Spirit, which includes accepting that all our sufferings come for a reason (ultimately, all things unfold for the Good, for the Glory of the Spirit; Second Corinthians 1:6).

(43 seconds later)

But because we have so many millions of new Christians across the world, there is a question that's rather persistent between people who know the Lord, and that question is, "What now?" I've come to know Christ as my personal Savior. What then does He want me to do? What now will the future bring to pass in my life?

Christians asking "What now?" are not awakened to the Message of the Spirit or else they would not ask. If the Message of the Spirit was taught, they would know the answer to that question.

(3 minutes, 32 seconds later)

One of the best things I have known in life is to get in a conversation with someone, and that conversation answers a question that I've been pursuing, and it becomes a terrific, albeit short experience. Learn to know other people who are Christians, and I want to tell you: <u>their opinion, their understanding of the word of God, will be a blessing to you</u>. And I'll tell you something else: they too are looking for Christian fellowship, and your presence and your power with them will be a very singular blessing indeed.

Others' opinions of the word of God are of zero worth if they do not uphold The Way of His Good Spirit.

■ ■ ◆ ■ ■

#11 - Graham, Billy (*Billy Graham Classics;* aired January 12, 2002; recorded live in Portland, OR, 1992)

In all these centuries, the way of salvation is still the same. "Neither is there salvation in any other, for there is none other name under Heaven given before men whereby we must be saved," in Acts 4:12. John 14:6 says, "I am the way, the truth, and the life, no man cometh to the Father but my me."

Acts 4:12 is referenced, examined as follows.

Acts 4:11-12 (spoken by Apostle Peter; likely authored Paul's disciple, Luke)

11. **This is the stone that was set at naught of you builders, which is become the head of the corner.** [The "stone" that was rejected by the builders of Israel's faith was the "rock" Way of the Spirit of Jesus, which has become the cornerstone of faith in God ('head of the corner').]

12. **Neither is their salvation in any other: for there is none other name under heaven given among men, whereby we must be saved.** [The One Way to Salvation is through Jesus Christ (by any name, 'Jesus Christ' was the Mind and Spirit of God alive in the flesh, *and is the Mind and Spirit of God alive Within all who live and grow in Selfless Love and Good Works*).]

(3 minutes, 45 seconds later)

He (Jesus) can give you total assurance that your sins are gone, and that God will never hold you accountable for them again. They're forgiven. And He receives you with open arms. And He'll do it tonight if you'll let Him, and I'm going to do something we saw hundreds of people do last night. I'm going to ask you to get up out of your seat and come and stand in front of this platform and say, by coming, "I want Christ to come into my heart; I want Him to take all of me; I surrender my life to Him," and say "Lord, Jesus, I am willing to repent of my sins and turn, by faith, to you, and put my total confidence and my total faith in you." He died on the cross and shed His blood for you, and certainly you can come and take a stand here for Him. <u>He said if you're not willing to acknowledge me publicly before men, I'll not acknowledge you before my Father which is in Heaven</u>.

Salvation does not come through idolatrous, ritualistic confessions. True "acknowledgment" of Jesus in public comes by exemplifying His Good Spirit before others. Confession in Him is not about saying, "I believe in Jesus," but about living in His Spirit. There are countless millions of non-Christians who "acknowledge" Jesus everyday through their devotion to Selfless Goodness.

■ ■ ◆ ■ ■

#39 - Swaggart, Jimmy (November, 1998)

He (God) once dwelt in a building, but when Jesus died, he cleared the record, and he took my sins away. Hallelujah. Glory to God. I said, "He took 'em away." Jesus, by His death, gave us a spotless righteousness, a perfect pardon, a great Salvation, and He came to live in our hearts and lives. Others may leave you, but He'll never leave you.

If Jesus took our sins away upon His death, clearing our sins and granting us a spotless righteousness, a perfect pardon, and a great

Salvation, then why would we, *at present*, be impure souls suffering sin and death on Earth? Why are we not enjoying our Salvation? *Because only by living and growing in the Spirit are we promised spotless righteousness and Salvation* (Hebrews 9:15, James 1:12, 2:5).

Those who claim Salvation for themselves and their congregations are effectively claiming Holiness over others.

What does the Spirit tell us about Jesus' crucifixion?

- He knew that His death was imminent, and He feared. [Hebrews 5:7; He "feared" not for Himself, but for us. He did not want to leave us, not for His benefit, but for ours. He wanted to continue to teach us through His Message and Way of the Selfless, Good Spirit.]
- Though Jesus had the power to heal the wounds of His crucifixion, it was God's Will that He "give up the ghost." [Mark 15:37]
- Faced with death, He did not choose self-preservation over God's Selfless Spirit. [He did not surrender to His desire to live (self-preservation), choosing not to preserve and honor His flesh, but to preserve and honor His Spirit.]
- Jesus sacrificed the "flesh" for the Spirit, showing us The Way to Salvation. ["I am the way"; John 14:6]
- The Way is through self-sacrifice. [Salvation comes to those who overcome their evil with Good, *who sacrifice their selfishness for the Selfless Spirit*].

Those who love the Spirit above selfishness are New Creatures (Second Corinthians 5:17) having the New Consciousness that speaks with a New Tongue (they think and speak in the nature of the Good Spirit over their own selfishness).

The statement that Jesus will "never leave you" is false, proven as follows (in verses 22-23, specifically).

Colossians 1:19-23 (authored by Apostle Paul)

19. **For it pleased the Father that in him should all fulness dwell;** [It was God's Will that the Spirit should dwell fully in Jesus.]
20. **And, having made peace through the blood of his cross, by him to reconcile all things unto himself; by him, I say, whether they be things in earth, or things in heaven.** [Having overcome death by His Spirit, it is thereby through His Good Spirit that all things can be redeemed (the 'blood of his cross' is His Selfless Spirit, the power of Redemption and Salvation).]
21. **And you, that were sometime alienated and enemies in your mind by wicked works, yet now hath he** [Jesus] **reconciled**
22. **In the body of his flesh through death, to present you holy and unblameable and unreproveable in his sight:**
23. **If ye continue in the faith grounded and settled, and be not moved away from the hope of the gospel, which ye have heard, and which was preached to every creature which is under heaven;** [We are unblameable if we resolutely

continue in the Spirit, treading The Way towards Salvation ('hope of the gospel'). This definitively proves that the Good Spirit of Jesus will depart those who deny His Spirit, *naturally*.]

■ ■ ◆ ■ ■

#11 - Graham, Billy (*Billy Graham Classics;* aired March 9, 2002; prerecorded live from Cleveland, OH)

I have broken the law, the laws of God: the Ten Commandments; the Sermon on the Mount. I haven't lived up to the Sermon on the Mount, and I haven't kept all the Commandments, and the Scripture says if you've ever broken one Commandment, you've broken them all (referring to James 2:10). So, I'm guilty of all in the sight of God, and so are you, and the result of that breaking of the law is death.

James 2:10 is referenced, examined as follows.

James 2:8-13 (likely authored by James, Jesus' brother)

8. **If ye fulfil the royal law according to the scripture, Thou shalt love thy neighbour as thyself, ye do well:** [The Royal Law is the Great Commandment, *the Spirit of the Law,* the totality of the Bible's Message.]
9. **But if ye have respect to persons, ye commit sin, and are convinced of the law as transgressors.** [If you respect the created over the Creator (if selfishness comes before the Spirit), you have sinned, and are proven a sinner by the Spirit of the Law.]
10. **For whosoever shall keep the whole law, and yet offend in one point, he is guilty of all.** [Whoever is Sinless, yet commits one sin, is "guilty of all." *But what does this really mean?*]
11. **For he that said, Do not commit adultery, said also, Do not kill. Now if thou commit no adultery, yet if thou kill, thou art become a transgressor of the law.** [If you do not break the 7th Commandment (thou shalt not commit adultery), yet break the 6th (thou shalt not kill), you are guilty of being a transgressor of the Spirit of the Law. This does not mean that a murderer is also guilty of adultery, or that an adulterer is also guilty of murder, but that doing either is a denial of the Spirit, *a denial of the Whole Law,* the Spirit of the Law.]
12. **So speak ye, and so do, as they that shall be judged by the law of liberty.** [Be as those who shall be judged by the Law of Liberty (the Law of Liberty is the Royal Law, the Spirit of the Law that liberates souls from their sins. Devotion to the Spirit redeems sins, cleansing the soul upon its path to its final liberation: Salvation).]
13. **For he shall have judgment without mercy, that hath shewed no mercy; and mercy rejoiceth against judgment.** [Deny the Spirit when judging others' sins and you shall, in the end, be denied the Spirit when judged of your own.]

It is incorrect to teach that if you have broken one Commandment you have broken them all, and guilty of all. To covet (breaking the 10th

Commandment) does not make you guilty of murder. Any one sin shall make you "guilty of all," because the "All" of the Whole Law is the Spirit. Either you are Pure in Spirit, like Jesus, or you are not. If not, you have, at some point, denied the One Spirit, the "All" Spirit of the Law. Be not deceived, those who sow greater sufferings and evils upon others shall reap greater separation from God, *naturally*.

There are countless deceived Christians running around planet Earth thinking their souls are saved simply because they have verbally confessed their belief in Jesus as their "personal Savior." Take that deceived mindset and teach it to believe that to sin once is to be guilty of having sinned every sin. If you program people to believe that God already considers them guilty of every sin imaginable, and that they are saved from all their sins (past, present, and future) because of their "confession" of Jesus as Savior, then what's to stop them from sinning right and left till they die? Why the need for a Good Conscience? Why bother living in God's Spirit when you've got man-made religions that give Free Admission into Heaven through idolatrous rituals?

America is reportedly 82% Christian and has the highest incarceration rate on the planet (percent of Americans who identified themselves as Christian in 2001was 82%, per pbs.org and adherents.com; see Internet References). Is it not reasonable to conclude that somewhere around 82% of the incarcerated are Christians? Is this not proof that something is wrong?

Yes, one sin does taint the soul, but the purity of one's soul is relative to one's sins, which are relative to one's heart and motivations. The more you sin, the more you deny (deplete) the Spirit Within, moving closer to the hell-goal.

(24 seconds later)

All the suffering, and the shame, and the disgrace, and the dishonor that you and I deserve, He bore for you. The Scripture says He was made a curse for you. The sin that you and I committed He took on the cross. He became guilty of your sins and mine. He became guilty of murder, of adultery. He had never committed a sin, and you can imagine what it must have been to have that on Him. "For He hath made Him to be sin for us, who knew no sin, that we might be made the righteousness of God in Him." Because of the cross, God offers forgiveness to you. He offers to place you before Him as though you had never committed a sin.

Jesus ended up on the cross because of selfish humans who put their sins upon the Sinless One when they feared, captured, and crucified Him. Jesus never, never became guilty of murder, adultery, or any sin whatsoever due to His dying on the cross. *Are we to believe He, at any time, was guilty of evil?*

Jesus reaped where He had not sown. He had never sown sin, but reaped suffering and death, the consequences of sin. By reaping what He had not sown when He suffered and died, His Selfless, Good, Sinless Spirit conquered the world of suffering and death and became the Open Door to Life Eternal for all who follow His Way.

When our impure souls finally reap Purity (Salvation), we too shall have reaped where we have not sown. Like the Sinless Jesus, *who reaped where He had not sown when He reaped the consequences of sin*, all sinners who ascend to Salvation shall reap where they have not sown when they reap the consequences of Sinlessness.

The Governing Law of the Spiritual Universe (the Realm of Eternal Life) is the Royal Law, *the Spirit of the Law*. In the Physical Universe (the Realm of Life and Death), it is *the Letter of the Law*. God reveals that He did not consciously create these Universal Laws, but that they were predestined before the creation of our souls and of the Physical Universe (Ephesians 1:3-14 and Romans 8:28-30, given in Chapter 7).

- *The Spiritual Universe says: Mine is the Power to reap where I have not sown, and sow where I have not reaped.* This is the nature of the Spirit, where "like attracts like," where Spirit attracts and builds Spirit. This is the Spirit of the Law, where the Spirit always conquers the anti-Spirit. This is why the Spirit is all Life, *Life Eternal.*
- *The Physical Universe says: Mine is the Power to reap where I have sown, and sow where I have reaped.* This is the nature of the Physical Universe, where "opposites attract" (for every action, there is an equal and opposite reaction). This is the Letter of the Law that allows anti-Spirit (death) to afflict and sometimes conquer the Spirit. This is why the Physical Universe has life and death.

Those who live to Glorify the Good Spirit shall be judged by the Spirit of the Law and shall have Salvation, reaping what they have not the power to reap on their own. Those who deny the Spirit shall be judged by the Letter of the Law, reaping the anti-Spirit they so-loved to sow.

(1 minute, 10 seconds later)

You don't know when your moment is going to come when you have to stand before God. And the sin that God cannot forgive, think of it, He cannot forgive this sin: He cannot forgive the sin of your turning Jesus Christ down. If you say "No" to Christ, He can't forgive it, because He's made that as the road to Heaven, by the way of the cross. The man and the woman who does not flee to the cross to accept the shelter that God offers is doomed.

God has already Judged through His Righteous Justice, by which each soul is responsible for its own final destiny. He has Judged, and the rest is ultimately up to you. When Judgment Day comes, God shall be eternally separated from all the idolaters, *from all who rejected His Spirit*. Saying "Yes" to Jesus and "running to the cross" is empty idolatry if you deny the One Way to Salvation: *Living in the Spirit*.

■ ■ ◆ ■ ■

#34 - Robertson, Pat (February 27, 2002)

We are living in a very, very dangerous world these days. It's much more dangerous than, I think, any of us realize, and bad things can begin to happen to people, but <u>we need the covering power of Jesus, and not only in this life, but in the life to come, because if we come to Him, we will not only have His Presence now, but we will be with Him forever in glory</u>. Now, if you would like to know the Lord, I want you to pray this prayer with me right now. Don't be afraid. Just bow your head and pray right now. Pray these words, "Jesus," that's right, pray with me, "Jesus, I know, Lord, that you died for my sins, and I know, Lord, that you rose again, that I might have everlasting life, so right now, Jesus, I turn away from sin and I turn to you, and I confess without you I have no hope, but with you I have all hope, so Lord come now into my heart. Restore what is in me that should be toward you. Give me a new life in Christ, and from this moment on, Lord, I'll live for you and I'll serve you all the rest of my days. <u>Thank you Jesus for saving my soul</u>. Thank you for dying for me. Thank you for rising again."

Like any good salesman, the corporate "mindset" first hypes affliction ("We are living in a very, very dangerous world these days"), immediately followed by the "cure," which is the "covering power of Jesus" that is yours through a prayer. Idolatrous religion teaches fear, followed by a prayer that, *behold*, "saves" your soul. But Jesus reveals that we all suffer afflictions, and that we are not to fear, but to meet our troubles with Selfless Love and Good Works, as this is His Way to Salvation.

■ ■ ◆ ■ ■

#39 - Swaggart, Jimmy (January 22, 1999)

There is no alternative. It's Jesus Christ or eternal damnation. Let's say it again: It's Jesus Christ or satan. It's God's Way or the way of darkness. Sorry, Buddhism has no in-between. Islam, no in-between. Mormonism, no in-between. Catholicism, no in-between. Apostate Christianity, no in-between. Hinduism, no in-between. Confucianism, Shintoism, no in-between. Only Jesus. "No man cometh to the Father but by me," He said.

Everyone is hellbound except Christians who are not Mormon or Catholic. In other words, only Christ-believing Protestants are saved. Here is

"Christianity" that condemns most of humanity to hell, *blatantly denying God's Good Spirit.*

■ ■ ◆ ■ ■

#5 - Crouch, Paul (February 20, 2002)

Just say, "Oh, God, I know you're there, and I feel you now, and I do believe that Jesus Christ came to be my Savior. I believe He died on the cross, shed His precious blood to forgive all my sins. Come into my heart, Lord Jesus. Be my Savior, now and forever. Amen." If you prayed that simple, little prayer and meant it with all your heart, the greatest miracle of all, healing is wonderful, but the Salvation of the soul is the most important thing that can ever happen on planet Earth, and you've just received Him. Get to the phone. Tell somebody about it. Confess with your mouth the Lord Jesus. If there's nobody around there, you don't have a phone, just say it out loud so the devil and the furniture can hear you, "I'm saved, I'm saved." Hallelujah.

Saying a prayer with "all your heart" does not make you "saved." Living in the Spirit is The Way.

■ ■ ◆ ■ ■

#13 - Graham Lotz, Anne (on *Hannity & Colmes* with Sean Hannity and Alan Colmes; December 11, 2001)

Alan Colmes: The terrorist victims of September 11th, those who are not Christians, will they go to Heaven?

Anne Graham Lotz: The Bible says Jesus said, "I am the way, the truth, and the life, and no one comes to the Father except through me." So, according to the Bible, there's only one way to God, only one way into my Father's house, and that's when your His child through faith in Jesus Christ.

Alan Colmes: So Jews, Muslims, anybody else who lost their lives, unless they accept Jesus Christ, they're not going to where you think you'd like to see everybody go.

Anne Graham Lotz: That's what the Bible says.

Alan Colmes: Are our enemies created in God's image, and do they have the same infinite value that every human being possesses?

Anne Graham Lotz: Absolutely.

Alan Colmes: Our enemies do? Bin Laden does?

Anne Graham Lotz: Yes. And that's, when God created the world, He created humankind. In Genesis, Chapter One, it says He created us male and female in

His image, and to be in the image of God doesn't mean that we just walk upright and whatever, but that we have a capacity to know our Creator in a personal relationship. And Bin Laden has that capacity to know God in a right, personal, internal relationship. But sin in Bin Laden, and in me, and in you is what separates us from God, which is why we need Jesus, who is our Savior who takes away our sins and brings us into a right relationship with His Father.

(1 minute, 26 seconds later)
Sean Hannity: What do you say, Alan asked just moments ago about Christians only getting into Heaven, [to] those who [have] accepted Jesus Christ in their heart? What do you say to those people when they hear that, they get angry at that, and you know for a fact that they do?

Anne Graham Lotz: They do and, you know, if there had been any other way that you and I could go to Heaven besides the cross of Jesus Christ, I believe God would have found it.

Sean Hannity: Does it have to be conscious? Could good people accept it and not even know what they've gone through?

Anne Graham Lotz: No.

Sean Hannity: Has to be a conscious decision.

Anne Graham Lotz: Has to be a conscious decision. But, you know something, God is the Judge, and God will determine what takes place in a person's heart.

The message is clear: Every non-Christian that died on September 11th went to hell, *the ones in the planes, in the buildings, and on the ground… even heroes*. Not wanting to stir public outrage with a direct answer, we get a softened, passive response that still says: *all non-Christians go to hell.*

Know that God's determining of "what takes place" in our hearts means, *for example*, that though we might deceive others, He knows our motivations. Know that He is Judge, and has already Judged us via His Grace (His Righteous Justice), whereby we shall be judged of ourselves, reaping what we have sown (page xvi).

■ ■ ◆ ■ ■

#31 - Paulk, Donnie Earl (January 22, 1999)

He (God) doesn't heal based on your conduct, He heals based on your faith.

Yes, we are healed by our faith, but our faith is <u>based</u> upon our conduct. Faith is "dead" if not justified by Selfless Works (a Spiritful "tree" naturally produces Spiritful "fruits").

James 2:14, 17, 20, 26 (likely authored by James, Jesus' brother)
14. What doth it profit, my brethren, though a man say he hath faith, and have not works [Selfless, Good Works]**? can faith save him?**
17. Even so faith, if it hath not works, is dead, being alone.
20. But wilt thou know, O vain man, that faith without works is dead?
26. For as the body without the spirit is dead, so faith without works is dead also.

■ ■ ◆ ■ ■

#38 - Schuller, Robert A. (son of #37; January 26, 2002)

And Jesus comes, and Jesus says, "I am the rock," translated in Greek is "petros." That is the Greek word for "rock." And Jesus, when Peter recognized who He was, 'cause Jesus addressed Peter and said, "Peter, who do men say that I am?," and the apostles said, "Oh, some think you're Elijah or Jeremiah or one of the prophets." And Jesus looked at the apostles again and He said, "But, who do you say that I am?" And with that, Peter stood up, and he proclaimed, "You are the Christ, the Son of the living God." And hearing that, Jesus changed his name from Simon Barjona to Peter. "You are petros," He said, "You are Peter, you are rock, and upon this rock I will build my church." So, we see the rock as a theme which starts in the very beginning of God with Abraham to the very present corner today as the foundation of this church. You and I, anyone who calls upon and recognizes that Jesus Christ is the Son of God becomes the rock upon which He builds His church.

(4 minutes, 48 seconds later)
The "rock" is real. It's open to everybody, because nobody is ever too bad to come in. Nobody is ever too good to stay away. It's open for everybody. Come in. Join the party. Enjoy the fun, the laughter, the joy, the excitement.

Here, we are taught that the "rock theme" of the "Church of Christ" belongs exclusively to Christian churches and Christ-believers. This is incorrect. Christ's Church is not a man-made structure, but is the Congregation of all devoted to Selfless Goodness. Furthermore, describing faith in Christ as being a party of fun, laughter, joy, and excitement is nothing more than the marketing of "feel good" corporate religion. *Come join us, our "way" is fun and exciting.*

■ ■ ◆ ■ ■

#39 - Swaggart, Jimmy (June 6, 1999)

The first Adam failed and lost it (lost Purity by surrendering to sin), but the second Adam (referring to Jesus, First Corinthians 15:45-47) will win it back, will purchase it back with His own precious blood.

(45 seconds later)

This magnificent plan, this great Salvation, God would become man, and let me try to make something clear to you: When God did this, all of Heaven became vulnerable. God reduced all of His power down into a man, Jesus Christ. The man, Jesus Christ. You're not getting what I'm saying. This was satan's opportunity: If I (satan) can get this man (Jesus) as I got the first man (Adam), then the whole thing falls down and evil triumphs. Everything was on the line. Not only the salvation of God's greatest creation, man, not only redemption, not only my salvation and your salvation, but every angel of Heaven, all of the New Jerusalem, all of the Glory of God was at stake. This is the love that you and I cannot even begin to fathom. And God reduced it even further. He reduced it down to Jesus Christ on the cross becoming a sin offering. And if His life had not been perfect, therefore to offer up a perfect, spotless body that would be an acceptable offering to God, because God can only accept perfection, well, then all of Heaven is lost, and mankind is lost, and redemption is down the tubes. So, it was reduced to that lone figure hanging on a wooden gibbet, bearing the whole sin of the world. And if the sacrifice had been in any way improper, God could not have accepted it, and Jesus could not have been raised from the dead, and the whole thing is damned, if you'll pardon the expression. Hallelujah. Somebody said, "Well, you now, that's nothing, because He was God, He couldn't fail." Yes, He was God, but He didn't hang there as God, He hung there as a man.

How can God "reduce all of His power" if He is Omnipotent? His Power is Infinite. If God ever reduced all His Power, the whole of Creation and the Universe would implode. *C'mon!*

Jesus' life on Earth was not satan's opportunity to overthrow God. His life did not put everything "on the line," risking the "Glory of God." There was never any risk that Jesus, *the Spirit and Mind of God in the flesh*, would have surrendered to satan. Heaven was never vulnerable.

As far as Jesus bearing the sins of the world while on the cross, those "worldly sins" were put upon Him by selfish humans when they hated, captured, and crucified Him. He does, though, bear (acquit; redeem) your "world" of sins when you repent and devote yourself to living in His Selfless, Good Spirit. *He did not literally bear the sins of your soul while upon the cross, otherwise you'd be in Heaven right now.*

Did Jesus die as a man, not as God? No. *He was both.* He was the Mind and Spirit of God alive in the flesh (Colossians 1:19) that could not be killed, but had to "give up the ghost" to die (Mark 15:37).

(5 minutes, 42 seconds later)

Not many Christians run to a cross. Most run the opposite direction from the cross, even though it's your answer.

The only Apostle who witnessed Jesus' crucifixion was John the beloved. All the rest deserted Him, *running away from the cross.* They were never forsaken for doing so, but received Salvation. Living in the Spirit is the answer, not idolatry of the cross. He died on the cross so that we might receive the Promise of Salvation (First Peter 3:18), the Promise that comes to only those who follow His Way (Hebrews 5:9).

■ ■ ◆ ■ ■

#16 - Huch, Larry (June 20, 1999)

I want us all to pray this out loud together. You that are watching by television, you pray it with us, and we're going to see Jesus do the greatest miracle since your salvation, and set the captive free. Everybody lift their hands. Now, everybody say this out loud together, say it out loud, and you that are watching by television, say it with us. Say this out loud church. Say, "Father, I come to you right now in the name and by the blood of Jesus Christ. I know that I've sinned. We've all sinned. But I know this, you love me." Say it again, "You love me so much, you sent Jesus to pay the price in full for my sins. Right now, I receive Jesus Christ as my Lord and my Savior in the name, by the blood of Jesus Christ. Satan, get out of my life, get out of my home, get out of my family, get out of my mind, get out of my body, get out of my spirit. I declare in the name by the blood of Jesus Christ, I am born again. Now hear me devil. Who the Son set free, and that's me. Who the Son sets free, that's my family. Who the Son sets free, is free indeed. Amen, and Amen." Now c'mon, give the Lord a big freedom-clap offering.

If the audience already has Salvation, *which they could not possibly have, as they are sinners on Earth,* then why plead for satan to stop afflicting their lives? How can satan be a threat to those who have Salvation?

■ ■ ◆ ■ ■

#2 - Breese, Dave (May 30, 1999)

What shall we involve ourselves in now that we have come to know Christ? One of the very best suggestions is what we have come to call "Christian fellowship." God has allowed certain things to take place across the world in our time, and one is the building of churches, churches that reach from here to the ends of the Earth and back. And those churches are groups of people who are assured of salvation. They encourage one other.

God never "allowed" the building of global corporate Christianity as some "certain thing" that had to take place upon Earth. *God gave us the free will to create and destroy all that we have chosen to create and destroy throughout history.*

Corrupt humans sabotaged the Bible and Jesus' Gospel for their own selfishness, forsaking His Spirit for separatism and idolatry. His is the Church Within, *the Church of the Spirit of Selfless Love and Good Works,* a Church that is built Within the souls of all who build the Church Within.

Regarding Christian Churches as being groups of people "assured" of Salvation: You can attend church every week, but if you do not live to Glorify the Good Spirit Within you, your church-devotion will have been for nothing.

If meeting others in churches and swapping encouragements helps you to live and grow in Selfless Goodness, *that's wonderful.* Even so, know that God's Presence lives not in soul-less buildings, *but Within all who live in His Spirit.*

John 4:23-24 (spoken by Jesus; authored by Apostle John)

23. But the hour cometh, and now is, when the true worshipers shall worship the Father in spirit and in truth: for the Father seeketh such to worship him.
24. God is a Spirit: and they that worship him must worship him in spirit and in truth.

First Corinthians 3:16 (authored by Apostle Paul)

16. Know ye not that ye are the temple of God, and that the Spirit of God dwelleth in you?

Second Corinthians 6:16 (authored by Apostle Paul)

16. And what agreement hath the temple of God with idols? [What agreement does God's Way have with idolatrous worship?] for ye are the temple of the living God; as God hath said, I WILL DWELL IN THEM, AND WALK IN THEM; AND I WILL BE THEIR GOD, AND THEY SHALL BE MY PEOPLE.

John 2:19-21 (authored by Apostle John)

19. Jesus answered and said unto them, Destroy this temple, and in three days I will raise it up.
20. Then said the Jews, Forty and six years was this temple in building, and wilt thou rear it up in three days? [The Jews responded: *But it took forty-six years to build this Temple, and you are going to destroy it and rebuild it in three days?*]
21. But he spake of the temple of his body.

Mark 14:58 (likely authored by Mark, disciple with Apostle Peter)

58. We heard him [Jesus] say, I will destroy this temple that is made with hands, and within three days I will build another made without hands. [Jesus will destroy Jerusalem's Rebuilt Second Temple, and within three days He will build a Spiritual Temple (referring to His Resurrected Being).]

Jesus did not *literally* destroy Jerusalem's Temple upon His death, but it was destroyed nonetheless, at least for those who had eyes to *see* and ears to *hear*. Upon Jesus' death, the curtain-portal into the Temple's Holy of Holies tore in half, accompanied by an earthquake (Mark 15:37-38; Matthew 27:51), a powerfully dramatic statement from God to the idolatrous Israelites, saying, *effectively*, "I do not live in your dead, man-made, unsanctified temple of idolatry." Three days later, the Temple was "rebuilt" in the form of Jesus' Resurrected Being, showing us that, *like Him*, The Way to our First Resurrection is through devotion to His Father's Spirit [the First Resurrection shall involve those who have ascended to Salvation, all of whom shall be resurrected shortly after Christ's Second Coming (Revelation 20:5-6)].

God is not about man-made, idolatrous churches, but is about the Spirit Within, this Truth evident through Jesus' Gospel, Crucifixion, and Resurrection.

■ ■ ◆ ■ ■

#28 - Parsley, Rod (June 20, 1999)

Father, in the name of Jesus, everybody pray with me: Lord Jesus, I cry out to you, a man in need. Oh God, today, let me receive Jesus Christ in fullness, in forgiveness, in power, make a new creature out of me. Change me from the top of my head to the bottom of my feet. Change me. Come in Lord Jesus. I confess I'm a sinner. I need a Savior. I cry out to you: Forgive me, and give me Eternal Life. Let me know I'm saved. I'm a Christian. Now, turn around and tell somebody, "I'm born again, I'm a Christian." Look 'em right in the eye. Tell 'em, tell 'em, "I'm a Christian." Tell 'em. Be a man. Tell 'em. Tell 'em, "I'm a Christian, I'm a Christian, I'm saved, I'm saved."

Just say a few words and, *presto-chango*... you're saved!

■ ■ ◆ ■ ■

#38 - Schuller, Robert A. (son of #37; August 8, 1999)

Yesterday afternoon, Steven (Note: I have withheld the name of this youngster, and refer to him as "Steven"). Steven was with another one of his friends and he was hearing these words, read from John 14, "Do not let your hearts be troubled. Trust in God. Trust also in me. In my Father's house are many rooms. If it were not so, I would have told you. I am going there to prepare a place for you. And if I go and prepare a place for you, I will come back and take you to be with me, that you will also be where I am. You know the way to the place where I am going." And hearing those words, Steven quit breathing. He went to be with Jesus. The question isn't why, but when. And when your time comes, <u>you can have the assurance of Steven that you have a place for you by simply saying a beautiful little prayer</u>. It's very simple. It's as simple as reaching out and accepting a gift when somebody gives it to you. It's not difficult, you simply reach out and you take it, and you say, "Thank you." And so is our prayer. Our prayer is: "Thank you Lord Jesus for saving me. Thank you Lord Jesus for giving me everlasting life with you. Thank you Lord Jesus for the beautiful gift of grace. Amen."

Might it be shameless to manipulate the audience's emotions via the tragedy of a young boy's death in order to drive home the idolatrous message that Salvation is yours by "simply saying a beautiful little prayer?"

Chapter 2

HOLIER-THAN-THOU

#39 - Swaggart, Jimmy (January 22, 1999)

The only thing that keeps these cities from being blown off of the face of the earth, considering the Light of the Gospel they have had, is the saints of God that's living in these places (pointing at the church's floor), saved, and full of the Holy Ghost.

Earlier, *in Chapter 1*, this preacher taught that only Christ-believing Protestants are saved. Now we learn that without Protestants, Earth's cities would be obliterated. Here is a holier-than-thou attitude that exalts Protestants over all non-Protestants, *over most of humanity*. How is it possible that the world's cities have managed to survive without Protestant Churches and worshipers? *How did cities survive before the birth of Protestantism in 1517?*

Matthew 23:12 (spoken by Jesus; likely authored by Apostle Matthew)

12. And whosoever shall exalt himself shall be abased; and he that shall humble himself shall be exalted [Whosoever lifts self above the Spirit shall suffer, but he that lifts the Spirit above self shall be Glorified.]

(3 minutes, 1 second later)

You, on the job, you may bemoan the fact that you're the only tongue-talkin', blood-washed child of God on your assembly line or wherever you work. Get that out of your mind. Put it in the positive. You're the only thing there that's got any Light to it.

Only Protestants have Light. Everyone else on Earth is without Light... *pure darkness... unregenerate evil.*

(2 minutes, 28 seconds later)

No airplane can fall with you on it, unless the Lord just wants to take you home and the rest of that rotten bunch.

Now, everyone but Protestants are "that rotten bunch." Protestants, *on the other hand*, are like lucky charms, but only until God wants one of them dead, as destructive events (plane wrecks, car crashes, wars, earthquakes, hurricanes, etc.) happen because it's time for one or more Protestants to go to Heaven. *Why not then rid the world of Protestants so that the rest of humanity could be safe from disaster?*

■ ■ ◆ ■ ■

#29 - Patterson, Gilbert E. (August 8, 1999)

The anointing of God, the empowerment of the Spirit to do a work for God, that's really what the anointing is. Now, in the Old Testament, the anointing was always symbolized by the pouring on of oil. The tabernacle, all of the vessels in the temple were anointed. Kings were anointed, priests were anointed, and that anointing was to make sacred by pouring or rubbing oil on. And this is why once somebody had the oil poured on them to be a priest, the oil had been poured upon this individual, and now he's the king, this person has been anointed, set apart, then nobody was to violate that individual, nor the vessels of the temple. Anything that was consecrated by the pouring on of the Holy Oil and set aside for the Master's use was nobody supposed to mess with it. That's why it says He reproved kings for that sake, saying, "Touch not mine anointed, and do my prophets no harm" (First Chronicles 16:22). <u>If we really understood what the anointing is about, we'd be careful how we treat those who God has anointed to do a work for him</u>. <u>We'd be especially careful about how we treat pastors, prophets, evangelists, apostles, teachers, people whom God have anointed to do a work for Him</u>.

Though the "anointing of God" is the "empowerment of the Spirit to do a work for God," know that the Anointing is not exclusive to corporate Christians. The Anointing of the Holy Oil represents the *Baptism Within*, the One Baptism that is possessed by those devoted to living and growing in the Spirit, *regardless of one's occupation or religious membership.*

Here, we are instructed to have respect for the "anointed" Christian clergy. But if truly Anointed, there is no need to teach any such self-serving instruction, because the Anointed know that God is no respecter of persons (Acts 10:34). The Anointed, having the *Baptism Within*, do not self-exalt or need "especially careful" treatment.

Romans 8:14 (authored by Apostle Paul)

14. For as many as are led by the Spirit of God, they are the sons of God. [Those who live by the Spirit are the "sons of God."]

Second Corinthians 11:12-13, 19-20 (authored by Apostle Paul)

12. But what I do, that I will do, that I may cut off occasion from them which desire occasion; that wherein they glory, they may be found even as we. [Paul will not involve himself with followers who exalt or judge, as they should be of equally devoted character as Paul himself, otherwise they have denied the Spirit.]

13. **For such are false apostles, deceitful workers, transforming themselves into the apostles of Christ.** [For such are idolatrous followers who deny the Spirit, yet strive to appear as faithful disciples of Christ (they are 'wolves in sheep's clothing').]
19. **For ye suffer fools gladly, seeing ye yourselves are wise.** [For you gladly submit to fools, thinking yourselves wise.]
20. **For ye suffer, if a man bring you into bondage, if a man devour you, if a man take of you, if a man exalt himself, if a man smite you on the face.** [And you shall suffer when you are in bondage to idolatry, and when you are used and "consumed" by religious predators (the 'wolf shall seek to devour the sheep'), and when you are "robbed" of The Way, and when you are treated as inferior, and when you are abused "in the name of God."]

■ ■ ◆ ■ ■

#39 - Swaggart, Jimmy (November, 1998)

I've had Him help me face every demon of darkness. And a lot of these spineless, jellyfish Christians will run, but He won't run. He's a helper. He'll help you in school, help you find a husband, and he (referring to the husband) won't be some good-for-nothin', two-bit lout, but he'll be a Christian.

Non-Christian men are good-for-nothin', two-bit louts.

■ ■ ◆ ■ ■

#28 - Parsley, Rod (May 16, 1999)

<u>I've already bound the devil before I came in this building</u>. He has no right to your life, and tonight the chains will fall off of you and fall around your feet, and you can run to freedom, and you can breathe free with assurance, the full assurance that you're assured for Heaven, as if you're already there. You can do that tonight. I want to give you the opportunity to do it, to say "yes" to God and "no" to the devil, "yes" to Heaven, "no" to hell. I'm not asking you to join this church. I'm asking you to receive Jesus Christ in the forgiveness of your sins and eternal life, so that you can live for eternity in Heaven instead of hell. That's the offer I make to you tonight. But since eternity waits for no one, I can't wait for you. I'm gonna count to "three," and when I say "three," if you want to go to Heaven and not hell, you shoot your hand up in the air. We're gonna pray a prayer. <u>At the end of that prayer, you'll be assured for Heaven as if you were already there</u>. Christians, are you praying? This is it. You can break the chains. Don't wait for tomorrow. You may be in hell tomorrow.

Only Christ has the power to bind satan (Christ holds "the keys of hell and of death," Revelation 1:18). This pastor self-exalts, lifting himself to Christhood, and warns that those who do not follow "may be in hell tomorrow." We are taught that by saying one prayer, you have Salvation "as if you were already there." *What does any of this have to do with The Way of the Spirit?*

■ ■ ◆ ■ ■

#23 - Mann, Gerald (June 13, 1999)

Love unconditionally. What separates Christians from others is the way they love.

Only Christians love unconditionally?

■ ■ ◆ ■ ■

#22 - Long, Eddie L. (June 20, 1999)

Do you want to know why I am where I am? It's because, watch this, listen, I've got some sons around me who will die to keep me alive. Listen. Not because they just love me, but they see God's hand on me, and they realize if I don't finish what God ordained for me to finish, they're finished, their children are finished, the children of others are finished. And because they recognize an anointing and a purpose, I might have just been called to die for them. How many men in here will die for the next generation?

How many will die for this preacher to ensure Salvation to their offspring and forthcoming generations? Here, we learn that if this preacher dies, some members of the audience and all their forthcoming generations will go to hell ("they're finished"). Is this preaching really an example of an "anointing and a purpose?" *To whose purpose?*

■ ■ ◆ ■ ■

#14 - Hagee, John and **#18 - Jakes, T. D.** (July, 1999)

John Hagee: This is the first time that we've had Bishop Jakes here at the Cornerstone Church, and we're honored to have him. Simply said, he's one of the greatest Gospel preachers in America today.

(30 minutes, 32 seconds later)
T. D. Jakes: When you get ready to come into the Presence of God, you have to come out of all titles and strip down. Oh, yes. You might have been somebody when you was out there, but when you gettin' ready to get into the

Presence of God, you got to humble yourself. Oh, yes. When you really gettin' ready to get up unto the anointing, you can't get up unto the anointing trying to impress people with how many degrees you got.

Are we not always in the Presence of God? And yet, we are taught the importance of humility before God, pointing out the need to drop any titles "when you gettin' ready to get into the Presence of God." Why, then, does this preacher carry the exalted title, "Bishop," and accept an exalted introduction? God is no respecter of persons (Acts 10:34).

■ ■ ◆ ■ ■

#3 - Bynum, Juanita (on #5's *Praise The Lord;* January 16, 2002)

He's (God's) grounding us in this season, and He's calling us to focus in on what's important, and <u>I believe that God called me on the set today to warn somebody that the enemy desires to sift you as wheat</u>. <u>He (the "enemy") desires that you be out there somewhere without a covering, without leadership</u>. And I'm talking the people in this audience. If you haven't found a pastor, you know what, you need to be on your knees fastin' and prayin', sayin', "God, is this where you have me? Is this the church that you have me in? Because if it is, then I want you to cause my spirit to begin to submit to authority, that I may receive an impartation for the end times, that my feet shall not slip."

Here, Christian churches and leaders are exalted as the "covering" and "leadership" that protects you from the "enemy." Be not deceived, the only Mediator between your soul and God is Christ, *Christ Within* (the Mind and Spirit of God alive in the flesh; First Timothy 2:5; Romans 8:26, 34).

■ ■ ◆ ■ ■

#32 - Paulk, Earl (September 26, 1999)

It's in the parable that you'll learn "harvest time" is coming. It's in the parable that you'll learn that reapers are angels. <u>Who are the angels of the church</u>? Read Revelation. <u>It's the pastors of the church</u>. They're the reapers that God sends out to... (sentence ends).

The Parable of the Tares of the Field (Matthew 13:36-44) is used to exalt pastors as the "angels" of "harvest time" who gather the believers to Heaven. Incorrect. The time of the "harvest" is Christ's Second Coming, when the unregenerate shall be gathered unto death by two reapers: Christ (Revelation 14:14-16); and one of His Angels (the Angel in Revelation 14:17).

■ ■ ◆ ■ ■

#25 - Meyer, Joyce (October 17, 1999)

Some of your friends may think you're crazy for taking your Saturday, maybe your only day off, and sittin' here and listenin' to some woman preach all day. I want to tell you, you are wiser than any of them. But next week they'll be gettin' in trouble and you won't. How many of you had somebody that was supposed to come to this conference with you and they backed out?

(2 minutes, 20 seconds later)

I just made a decision. From now on, every single one of these conferences that we do, I want you and the (word garbled, unable to transcribe) assessors prayin' specifically for weeks ahead of time for all the people that are supposed to be in these meetings that back out. We are not gonna leave them alone. We are gonna take authority over that mess, and they are gonna get here and get fixed.

We are taught that non-churchgoers are not as wise as churchgoers and will be "gettin' in trouble" for not going to church. This ministry pledges not to leave non-churchgoers alone, but to govern over their broken lives (they need to "get fixed").

Why exalt churchgoers over non-churchgoers? Why the need to drag "that mess" of unfixed people into church? Could it be that increased attendance in church translates into bigger dollars? Could it be that a lack of churchgoers leads to business failure? *Where's the Message of the Good Spirit that cares not about attending man-made churches, but only about teaching and embodying God's Good Spirit?*

■ ■ ◆ ■ ■

#33 - Ray, Harold (on #22's *New Birth Ministries;* November 14, 1999)

Now, I see you get in an attitude because you can't touch him (your preacher) personally every day and share your pity-party every day. What you need to do is wake-up and thank God that "I have a man of God in the set ministry that has already disrupted." Some want to call me at 9 o'clock, talkin' about "Can I come counsel with you?" I already been prayin', and rebuked that devil, and cast him out at 6 a.m. You just now rolling out of bed, baby, I done took care of your problem, and the old devil too. What you need to do is wake-up and say, "Lord, I thank you, 'cause I'm connected to an apostolic house, I'm connected to a prophetic house, and if I don't see pastor today, thank you that he's already disrupted this thing." You got to remember something, as long as you are connected, you're covered.

We are taught not to worry, because as long as you are with a church ("connected"), your soul will be saved ("covered"). Are we really to broker our souls through others, like preachers? No one, *not even preachers* have the authority to cast the "devil" out of your life. That authority lives Within you, and is strengthened through your devotion to the Good Spirit.

■ ■ ◆ ■ ■

#37 - Schuller, Robert (May 11, 2003)

Be respectful of others to have their opinion, but don't be rude, don't be sarcastic, don't be holier-than-thou, be humble.

(13 seconds later)

Don't be ashamed to say, "I am a Christian," and people won't be upset with you. They won't agree with you, they may not believe you, but you can get by with it today and fulfill your Holy calling.

Since when is our "Holy calling" fulfilled by saying, "I am a Christian?"

(7 minutes, 45 seconds later)

Light. A missionary light. The light of a movement. A movement that's telling the world that we've got to have a Lord, and it's got to be from God, and it's got to be Jesus Christ. So, here's where I'm at. I want you to embrace Jesus Christ as the light of the world for you, then let it shine, let it shine, let it shine. You're called not just to embrace it, but to show it off, and people will see you. They'll be impacted. The world will finally, only be changed by Christians who show it off, who live it with their words, their language, their behavior.

Here, he teaches that only Christians shall change the world, denying his earlier revelation that Christians should not self-exalt. The Truth of the matter is that God's followers are those devoted to exemplifying His Selfless, Good Spirit, *whether labeled "Christian" or not.*

■ ■ ◆ ■ ■

#28 - Parsley, Rod (October 21, 1999)

I was preaching about a place called Heaven. I was preaching about these old folks whose underpinnings had all gone out of them, and their silvery hair, their raven-black hairs turned silvery-gray, and their skin no longer taut on their face, and I talked about there was gonna come a time when they would leap like a (garble word, unable to transcribe) over the everlasting hills of God to suffer no more, to cry to more, to sigh no more, to die no more. I was trying to preach about the blessed hope, and they cut me off. Now, you excuse me, but I'm a preacher. I am the medium upon which the heart of God breaks into language, and through which the purpose of the Infinite is made to be heard.

and all the indignation which is proper to its outrage. I'm a preacher. They wouldn't hear me preach. Turned me off. They didn't want to hear nothin' about Heaven. Didn't want nothin' about no Rapture.

If you don't believe the blood, you're not my brother. If you don't believe the cross, you're not my brother. If you don't believe in holiness, you're not my brother. You don't believe in "straight and narrow," you're not my brother. You don't believe in Heaven, you're not my brother. You don't believe in hell, you're not my brother. Jesus said, I'll remind you, "he that is not for us is against us." There is a holy indignation which is proper to the outrage of God Himself.

If you don't believe in... *blah, blah, blah*... "you're not my brother." Is this the love of Christ? When Jesus said, "He that is not with me is against me" (Matthew 12:30), He was telling us that those without His Selfless, Good Spirit are not with Him (even if they call themselves "Christians").

Evidently, a preacher is a "medium" of God's heart who declares, "There is a holy indignation which is proper to the outrage of God Himself." *God, who is only Good, has outrage?* Outrageous! There may be a "holy indignation" proper to the "outrage of God" within some preachers, but not within those devoted to the Spirit. The only indignation we see from God in the New Testament is towards those who refuse the Spirit of the Law (Romans 2:8; Hebrews 10:26-27; Revelation 14:9:10).

(17 minutes, 21 seconds later)

The preacher does not deal in the merchandise of the surface and extremities. The Gospel preacher puts his hand on the heart of humanity and announces, "This is my mission." If I get the heart right, I get your heart right, you won't be coveting my wife. I get your heart right, I won't have to teach you how to give. I get your heart right, I won't have to teach you how to be healed. I get your heart right, I won't have to teach you how to pray.

No human has the power to "get" another person's heart "right." You can preach till your tongue falls out and still not have influenced some towards living in the Spirit.

(2 minutes, 52 seconds later)

I am not the guardian of your soul. These men are the guardians of your soul, these men, these men, these men (referring to the many preachers in the audience). They are your pastors, and God intends to do everything He does through the apostolic authority of the local church in this hour. These are the guardians of your soul.

Here, pastors are exalted as "guardians of your soul." Incorrect. There is no Guardian for you but the Good (God) Mind and Spirit Within, *which only you can ultimately embrace or reject.*

■ ■ ◆ ■ ■

#4 - Clark, Eugene (March, 2000)

Anyone who enters your home regularly is a strong influence on your child and, of course, you are. So, the very first thing you do is make sure that the people who come into your home are practicing Christians, good character, sweet and kind people [who will] deal with the child that way, and from whom they will never, ever hear a lowdown or unbecoming statement or action. That's very important. You, as an adult, may be with those people. There may be reasons why you must be with them. You may be related to them, but you make sure the children don't see very much of them. That takes a little doing, but that child is more important than your cousin. He's more important than your colleague in business. He's too sensitive at that age. You know, he absorbs, she absorbs everything, so therefore they know. Children will know a lowdown type if their language isn't proper, if they don't speak kindly to one another, if they're angry types, if they're drinkers. Whatever. Whatever. Things you don't want your child to see and what the child will admire. And he'll tend to admire anyone you bring into your home.

You also want to be careful of people who are terribly funny and breezy, but about the wrong things. You know. People think it's terribly funny to make jokes about everything. Well, a child can sense when a joke is unbecoming. He senses, probably in your reaction or in the person who's telling the story, so you have to be rather strict with people. If, for instance, people are forever talking about the marriage, remarriage, desertions in Hollywood, let us say, well, these are not good subjects for your child. If a person tells stories about peoples' failure and collapse and psychological disintegration and all that, you don't want your child listening to any of that. So, you really do, I say it with kindness, I hope, you have to exclude people from your home while the children are awake, and be very strict about it.

We talk about protecting your child from the culture. Well, what are we talking about? Well, first of all, we're talking about the popular American culture, which is now held captive by Hollywood. Hollywood wasn't so bad up until about twenty years ago, then it got a little racy, and now we have a very serious problem. It is absolutely secular. I'm sure you've probably noticed, but in dramas, situation comedies, nobody goes to church, nor is church ever mentioned except for a shoot-out, occasionally. So, what are they telling the child? That all these clever people, all these good-looking people, all these people who speak well, however they're doing it, they don't usually murder the English language in the role their playing, but they're accomplished people, their desirable people, their imitable. All these people never go to church.

This vision of "Christian" parenting is one of stifling overprotection and judgmentalism, fueled by fear. Where's God's love in this suffocation? Do these rules apply to poor Christians or to just middle-upper class, suburban types? How is a child to grow prepared for the real world if so sheltered? How does the parent see to it that this asphyxiating protection is delivered outside the home, especially in school?

Of course, parents consider their children special, but the most "special" in God's eyes are those who serve all others with humility and Selfless Love ("he that is greatest among you shall be your servant"; Matthew 22:11). Teach the children thusly.

Chapter 3

TITHING

#14 - Hagee, John (December 5, 1999)

And lastly, the financial curse of Malachi 3:7. The Bible says that the man who steals his tithes from God is cursed with a curse, for you have robbed me in tithes and offerings. I am too shy to say a thing like that, but it is in the word of God, Malachi 3:7-8, for those of you who would like to read it, it's there. I did not write it. I did not commission it to be written. It was there long before I got here.

Tithing is step-one to financial independence. When you tithe, God blesses you. You will live better on the ninety percent God blesses than the hundred percent in which God has said you're under a financial curse. When you refuse, God calls you a "thief." He then puts your mugshot on Heaven's bulletin board. Some of you came to church today driving stolen cars, wearing stolen clothes, and stolen jewelry. <u>You took God's money</u> and bought those things, and God is going to shut off your business, He's gonna let your car breakdown today on the loop going home, you're mother-in-law is going to move in with you, and the IRS is gonna want to inspect you back to the Civil War. You say, "I've never heard this before." You have heard it now. And it is the truth.

No, it's not the truth. There is no "God's money." What does God need with money? The "currency" of God is not corruptible dollars, but Incorruptible Spirit.

In the Old Testament, tithing was about bringing one-tenth of your annual harvest of meat and/or grain into the "storehouse" (chambers in Solomon's Temple; Nehemiah 10:38) to provide for the Levite priests and their families, who were the keepers of the Temple in which God's Spirit dwelt.

In the New Testament, tithing is never mentioned. Since Solomon's Temple, God's Spirit has not live in a man-made church because of corporate idolatry (page xx). *You are the Temple of the Living God.* Tithing is not about providing for corporate churches, but about providing for His

Spirit Within you, effected by pouring-out your Spirit as best you can, even as little as ten percent so as to magnify His Spirit Within by at least ten percent [as you give (sow) your Good Spirit, so shall you build (reap) the Spirit Within]. *Why does He ask for so little?* Because He knows that those committed to the Spirit, *even as little as ten percent of the time*, shall naturally grow in the Spirit and desire the Spirit even more (Luke 12:48).

In First Corinthians 16:1-3, Apostle Paul, *knowing that the followers in Jerusalem needed assistance*, instructed the followers in Galatia and Corinth to put aside an amount of prosperity (not necessarily money) every week to be transported to Jerusalem. This prosperity did not go to support corporate idolatry in Jerusalem, but went directly to Apostle Peter to help his followers of The Way in Jerusalem.

If collecting ten percent of one's annual income in the form of money was Paul's intent, then why is there no mention of this? Furthermore, if Paul's aide to the Jerusalem followers was an instruction for *all followers* to tithe ten percent of their annual income to corporate Christianity (a nonexistent entity at that time), then why give this instruction to only the Galatians and Corinthians? At no time are the followers in Colossae, Thessalonica, Philippi, or Ephesus given any such instruction.

Apostle Paul reminds us that we will reap what we sow, and instructs us to sow Charity according to our hearts, and to give freely and lovingly, not grudgingly or because of necessity.

Second Corinthians 9:6-7 (authored by Apostle Paul)

6. **But this I say, He which soweth sparingly shall reap also sparingly; and he which soweth bountifully shall reap also bountifully.**
7. **Every man according as he purposeth in his heart, so let him give; not grudgingly, or of necessity; for God loveth a cheerful giver.**

Tithing is about sowing the Spirit, not money, as God is made of Spirit, not money. It has nothing to do with what you give, *but how you give it. You are tithing when you are personifying Selfless Love and Good Works.* Tithing is God's Charity that manifests in countless ways. Instead, we are taught by this pastor that God curses those who do not tithe ten percent of their income, and that worldly gain shall be rewarded to those who tithe fully. *Apostle Paul instructs us to turn away from preachers who teach that "gain is godliness."*

First Timothy 6:3-5 (authorship unknown, possibly Apostle Paul)

3. **If any man teach otherwise** [if preachers teach not The Way of the Good Spirit], **and consent not to wholesome words, even the words of our Lord Jesus Christ, and to the doctrine which is according to godliness;**
4. **He is proud, knowing nothing, but doting about questions and strifes of words, whereof cometh envy, strife, railings, evil surmisings,**
5. **Perverse disputings of men of corrupt minds, and destitute of the truth, supposing that gain is godliness: from such withdraw thyself.**

Per the Bible, God brings financial wealth in the sense that, *because of His Spirit of Life,* we are alive and have the capability of gaining financial wealth. When the Bible speaks of wealth and riches in regards to God, it is referring to enrichment in His Spirit. Make no mistake, financial wealth can be gained selfishly (deceit, murder, stealing, etc.). The Message of His Spirit reveals that being rich does not make you Godly, as being poor does not make you ungodly.

First Peter 4:8 (authored by Apostle Peter)

8. **And above all things have fervent charity** [Selfless, Good Works] **among yourselves: for charity shall cover the multitude of sins.**

First Timothy 1:5 (authorship unknown, possibly Apostle Paul)

5. **Now the end of the commandment is charity out of a pure heart, and of a good conscience, and of faith unfeigned.** [The entirety of God's instruction to us is that we give life to our Good Spirit through Selfless, Good Works.]

Luke 11:42 (likely authored by Luke, disciple with Apostle Paul)

42. **But woe unto you, Pharisees! for ye tithe mint and rue and all manner of herbs, and pass over judgment and the love of God: these ought ye to have done, and not to leave the other undone.** [Woe to you Pharisees (Pharisees were the idolatrous religious scholars and teachers of Jesus' time who denied the Bible's Spirit of the Law). Woe to corrupt religionists because they tithe by the Letter of the Law and not by the Spirit of the Law. Their tithing is idolatrous and for want of worldly rewards. Such tithing shall know no Heavenly rewards, having served selfish motivations.]

Malachi 3:7-8 is used to support this pastor's teachings on tithing, examined as followed.

Malachi 3:7-11 (authored by the prophet Malachi)

7. **Even from the days of your fathers ye are gone away from mine ordinances, and have not kept them. Return unto me, and I will return unto you, saith the Lord of hosts. But ye said, Wherein shall we return?** [God tells the nation of the Israelites that He has left them because they have denied Him, and that He will return to them if they return to Him. The Israelites, knowing their sins, had incredulously asked God, "How do we return to you?" (At this point in the long-running history of the Israelites' rebelliousness to God's Spirit, they know very well that God wants them to repent and follow His Will).]
8. **Will a man rob God? Yet ye have robbed me. But ye say, Wherein have we robbed thee? In tithes and offerings.** [God tells them that they have robbed Him in tithes and offerings of the Spirit. Their lives prospered from His Good Spirit, but they have given little to no Spirit in return.]
9. **Ye are cursed with a curse: for ye have robbed me, even this whole nation.** [It is not God that has cursed them, but rather they have cursed themselves through their denial of His Spirit.]

10. Bring ye all the tithes into the storehouse, that there may be meat in mine house, and prove me now herewith, saith the Lord of hosts, if I will not open you the windows of heaven, and pour you out a blessing, that there shall not be room enough to receive it. [Build the Spirit into the temple of your being ('storehouse') that there may be the substance of the Spirit ('meat') wherein God lives. Those who sow to the Spirit shall reap abundantly of the Spirit.]
11. And I will rebuke the devourer [satan] for your sakes, and he shall not destroy the fruits of your ground; neither shall your vine cast her fruit before the time in the field, saith the Lord of hosts. [Devotion to the Spirit brings Redemption and Salvation.]

First Corinthians 16:14 (authored by Apostle Paul)
14. Let all your things be done with charity.

The following Biblical excerpt, known as the "Parable of the Talents," is about investing measures of Spirit, not measures of money, or "talents" (a talent is a large coin, but can also be a measurement of weight, one talent weighing anywhere from 82 to 95 pounds).

Matthew 25:14-30 (spoken by Jesus; authored by Apostle Matthew)
14. For the kingdom of heaven is as a man [Jesus] travelling into a far country [Earth], who called his own servants, and delivered unto them his goods.
15. And unto one he gave five talents, to another two, and to another one; to every man according to his several ability [Unto three of Jesus' followers was given a portion of Spirit according to each one's faith in the Spirit]; and straightway took his journey.
16. Then he that had received the five talents went and traded with the same, and made them other five talents. [The follower possessing the greatest faith made use of all the Spirit he had gained, his soul gaining that much more Spirit Within.]
17. And likewise he that had received two, he also gained other two. [Likewise, the second follower made use of all the Spirit he had gained, his soul gaining that much more Spirit Within.]
18. But he that had received one went and digged in the earth, and hid his lord's money. [But the follower with least faith did not make use of the Spirit he had gained and, instead, hid it.]
19. After a long time the lord of those servants cometh, and reckoneth with them.
20. And so he that had received five talents came and brought other five talents, saying, Lord, thou deliveredst unto me five talents: behold, I have gained beside them five talents more.
21. His lord said unto him, Well done, thou good and faithful servant: thou hast been faithful over a few things, I will make thee ruler over many things: enter thou into the joy of thy lord. [Here, it is revealed that those who use their Spirit fully shall be increased in Spirit fully, and shall have the power of the Spirit in many things, and shall Commune in the Joy of the Lord.]

22. He also that had received two talents came and said, Lord, thou deliveredst unto me two talents: behold, I have gained two other talents beside them.
23. His lord said unto him, Well done, good and faithful servant; thou hast been faithful over a few things, I will make thee ruler over many things: enter thou into the joy of thy lord.
24. Then he which had received the one talent came and said, Lord, I knew thee that thou art an hard man, reaping where thou hast not sown, and gathering where thou hast not strawed:
25. And I was afraid, and went and hid thy talent in the earth: lo, there thou hast that is thine.
26. His lord answered and said unto him, Thou wicked and slothful servant, thou knewest that I reap where I sowed not, and gather where I have not strawed:
27. Thou oughtest therefore to have put my money to the exchangers, and then at my coming I should have received mine own with usury. [The follower of least faith is told that he should have, minimally, used some of the Spirit he had gained to, in turn, reap more of the Spirit.]
28. Take therefore the talent from him, and give it unto him which hath ten talents. [Here, it is revealed that those who deny the Spirit in any measure shall lose that measure of Spirit from their souls, further separating their souls from God.]
29. For unto every one that hath shall be given, and he shall have abundance: but from him that hath not shall be taken away even that which he hath. [Those who give of their Good Spirit shall grow in the Spirit abundantly, but those who hide and deny their Good Spirit shall continue to deplete the Spirit Within until, finally, they become unregenerate. These unregenerately selfish souls are the "unsaved" who have, of their own choices, failed their many opportunities for Redemption.]
30. And cast ye the unprofitable servant into outer darkness: there shall be weeping and gnashing of teeth. [Those who live to deny the Spirit shall be separated from God eternally.]

■ ■ ◆ ■ ■

#29 - Patterson, Gilbert E. (July 4, 1999)

There are so many believers in Christ who are presently between local church homes. For some reason you had to leave the church where you were, and you are now just somewhat traveling and not placed by God into a new church home. Why don't you pray about tithing to this ministry until the Lord places you in a local assembly. I know that once you are a part of a local assembly, then certainly your tithing belongs at your local church, but you might just pray about sending a generous love offering.

If it is your desire to worship in a corporate system of religious buildings... *fine.* Having free will, that's your choice. But what about those who do not worship that way? Have they been abandoned by God, that they have not been "placed" into a church? Isn't His Church the Spirit Within? Don't all who dwell in Selfless Love dwell in Him?

First John 4:16 (likely authored by Apostle John)
16. God is love; and he that dwelleth in love dwelleth in God, and God in him.

■ ■ ◆ ■ ■

#17 - Huch, Tiz (wife of #16; January 21, 2002)

When Larry and I first got married, our first year, I wasn't working, Larry made $4,200 that year. We gave $2,500 to the church that year. So, somehow we lived on less than $2,000 that year. Never had a late payment. We bought a little trailer, a funky little one-bedroom trailer, but it was home. Just stay out of the windstorms. We bought a little truck, it needed a lot of prayer, but it was ours. We never had a late payment, but we knew how to give to God. We sowed, we received. We sowed, we received more. We sowed, we received more. And for twenty-four years we've been sowing and reaping, and sowing and reaping, and God has brought a hundred-fold return in our life. And I'm going to teach you how to have that happen in your life. But the key is to keep sowing, to keep investing in God, and He keeps bringing a greater return in your life. Are you with me?

The key to financial prosperity is to keep giving your money to churches, no matter how poor you are. But wait…

(34 seconds later)

The Bible tells us in Hebrews 11:3 that the world was literally framed by the word of God. Now, God didn't go in there and say, "Okay, I need me a hammer, saw, some two-by-fours," you know, and begin hammering out a world. He didn't get a potter's wheel and start shaping something. All He did was think it, conceive it, and speak it, and it was formed, just like that. That same power lives in you and I. That same creative power is in you and I. You know, if we really believed that, we wouldn't even be sitting here having this conversation.

If you had the same creative power as God, effected by "really believing," then why not just psych yourself up and speak money into existence? The Truth is that you are not God, but have the ability to effect a measure of His power through faith, which is not about "really believing," but filling your life with Selfless Love and Good Works, trusting that this is His Way to Salvation amidst life's afflictions.

(9 seconds later)

If we really believed it, how would that change the way that you prayed? How would that change the way that you speak over your life? Do you realize that when Jesus cursed the fig tree, He didn't get down, put His hands together, "Oh God, in the name of Me, I curse this fig tree." It wasn't an official prayer. He walked by, He saw it wasn't producing fruit. No longer. He cursed it, just in His conversation, and the thing was dead. It wasn't an official prayer. So, what you say in the course of a day is so absolutely critical, because you are speaking that into your life. You are literally creating that in your life.

The notion of an "official prayer" is incorrect. Truest Prayer with God is Oneness with His Spirit, *no matter what you are doing.*

It is correct that words are power, but it is not what you speak that is "absolutely critical," but rather your heart and motivations. How easy it is to *appear* Selflessly Good through words, but be driven by selfish motives.

(continuing)

That is why my children have never, in their life, heard the words, "We can't afford it, we have no money for that, we're flat broke." Never in their entire lives have they heard those words spoken in our home. My daughter, oldest daughter, is 21-years-old, and you can ask her. Never. And I'm telling you, there were days that, in reality, we were flat broke. But we would not speak those words over our life. We would not allow that to be spoken and created into our life. We always lived our life in the spiritual dimension that God has promised. The reason we're where we're at today is because of prayers over the last twenty-four years, because of seeds planted over the last twenty-four years, because our finances are tied into a spiritual realm, not just to the economic system of this world. And so, the words that you speak, you know, you can be praying twenty hours a day, you could be interceding twenty hours a day, but if the other four hours of the day you're saying, "Well, I don't think this is going to work for me, I gave my tithes, I ain't seen nothin' happen yet," or the kids come and ask for a new bicycle [and you respond], "No, we don't have any money for that, how many times do I have to tell you there is no money for a bicycle." I've heard people say that. I mean, I've walked through the grocery store and I've listened to, "Mommy, I want some of this and this and this," [and the mother replies], "We don't have any money for that." Oh, man, it just makes me cringe inside, because they're speaking that destiny. Saved or unsaved, the laws of God work, and you're speaking that destiny into your life.

Ever since Jesus left us with His Gospel, humans and their Christ-based religions have clouded His Truth with superstitions and lies. Here, the spoken word is exalted, *idolatrously worshiped,* as if the spoken word was the Invisible Spirit of God Himself. Though the spoken word has power, its power lies in the Spirit with which it is spoken *and heard.*

Why fear the truth? If your children cannot have some things because you cannot afford it, why lie? Why not explain that mommies and daddies all over the world live on a budget? There are very few people on this planet with the wealth to buy almost anything. Most of us have to live on a budget and do without certain things. What is the shame in that? This preacher teaches struggling parents to give their hard-earned, much-needed $$$ to the church, then wants them to deny their children the truth about not being able to afford certain things.

Tithing to the Spiritual Realm is about joyfully giving your Good Spirit unto all for want of no worldly rewards. It is not about giving monies to man-made churches so as to gain financial prosperity in return. We are instructed to withdraw ourselves from those who suppose that gain is Godliness (First Timothy 6:5).

■ ■ ◆ ■ ■

#14 - Hagee, John (July 4, 1999)

Tithing is giving ten percent of your income. You say, "Preacher, do you expect me to give God ten percent of my income?" No, I don't, but God does. I'm in sales, He's in management. He controls your income, He controls your health, He controls your next breath, and if you want to tick Him off, go for it.

At no time does God define tithing as giving ten percent of your annual income to the unsanctified, man-made system of corporate Christianity. Teaching that God controls your income, health, and next breath denies that you have any control over your own life, and denies His Righteous Justice ("as ye sow, so shall ye reap"). Furthermore, threatening the audience with God's displeasure ("if you want to tick Him off") is nothing more than the age-old tradition of fear-mongering.

Preachers often tell of the sin of smoking cigarettes, but if God controls our health, then why be concerned that cigarettes might bring ill health? If God controls health, why are many preachers obese? According to medical specialists, being overweight is not healthy. Are we to believe that all fat preachers are living proof of God's displeasure?

God is All-Good and does not bring dis-ease. We bring dis-ease into our own lives. It is the darkness we have sown into our own souls through selfishness that eventually reaps sufferings (illness, divorce, bankruptcy, etc.) and death. Dis-eases and afflictions are not without cause, but ultimately come for the "greater Good," to Glorify the Spirit (page xii).

(1 minute, 16 seconds later)

"Oh well, pastor, I send my tithes to Dr. Superdoc." Fine, when you get sick in the hospital, you call Dr. Superdoc and have him come see you. Don't call our church. When you need counseling, you call Dr. Superdoc. Don't call this church. Don't call us, because that's how we pay the bills around here. That's how we pay the light bill. That's how we pay the employees that serve you here in the kingdom of God, and it is unfair and it is unreasonable for you to go here week after week, month after month, year after year and absorb all of the wonderful benefits this church gives, and never give a dime to make it happen. That's wrong.

In the "Dr. Superdoc" example, tithing is equated with payment to a doctor. Patients do not tithe to their doctors, but pay for services rendered per a legally-binding agreement.

Are we to believe that tithing to corporate Christianity is tithing to the Kingdom of God? Per God, His Kingdom is not some Earthbound, man-made, corporate structure run by impure humans that need money to pay the bills.

Most disturbing is that all non-tithers are warned not to come to this particular church and ask for assistance if they need it. Here we see the centuries-long tradition of corporate religion persecuting those who do not obey their exclusive, idolatrous vision of God. Christian or not, what church *alive in the Spirit* would turn anyone away?

If you are one whose churchgoing *helps you* to grow in the Spirit, *then you should give back,* cheerfully. Giving back is not about money, but about contributing your Good Spirit according to the purpose in your heart.

Luke 10:30-37 (likely authored by Luke, disciple with Apostle Paul)

30. A certain man went down from Jerusalem to Jericho, and fell among thieves, which stripped him of his raiment, and wounded him, and departed, leaving him half dead.

31. And by chance there came down a certain priest that way: and when he saw him, he passed by on the other side.

32. And likewise a Levite [Levites were God's appointed priests and guardians of Solomon's Temple], **when he was at the place, came and looked on him, and passed by on the other side.**

33. But a certain Samaritan [the Israelites regarded the Samaritans as sinners, and unholy before God], **as he journeyed, came where he was: and when he saw him, he had compassion on him,**

34. And went to him, and bound up his wounds, pouring in oil and wine, and set him on his own beast, and brought him to an inn, and took care of him. [The "pouring in oil and wine" represents the Samaritan's Holy Anointing (the pouring-out of his Selfless, Good Spirit upon the sufferer).]

35. And on the morrow when he departed, he took out two pence, and gave them to the host, and said unto him, Take care of him; and whatsoever thou spendest more, when I come again, I will repay thee.

36. Which now of these three, thinkest thou, was neighbour unto him that fell among the thieves?

37. And he said, He that shewed mercy on him. Then said Jesus unto him, Go, and do thou likewise.

(continuing)

Why tithe? Because God commends it. And refusing to obey God is rebellion. Why tithe? Because you live under a financial curse. God says, "I will curse you with a curse" (Malachi 3:9). And when you live under God's curse, you will not have sufficiency.

(52 seconds later)

Malachi 3:11, "I will rebuke the devourer, which is satan, for your sake." God will hold satan on a leash and will not allow him to attack you or your family or your business when you give the Lord the tithe and the offering. He will hold him. And let me tell you something, in this world you need Almighty God holding the devil off of you, because the devil's assignment is to rob, to kill, and to destroy. You think you're in good hands with Allstate? You're not nearly in as good hands as you think you are. You're not in good hands until you're in the nail-pierced hands of the Son of God.

God does not curse us. Our sufferings come because we curse ourselves when we deny the Spirit (Malachi 3:9). But here we are taught that God unleashes satan upon those who do not give their money to man-made churches. To teach that God will exempt only money-givers from illness and other sufferings is to teach that "gain is godliness" (First Timothy 6:5). Every one of us, no matter how faithful, shall have sufferings unto death, as our souls are impure in some measure.

As is taught in the Parable of the Good Samaritan, we see that God loves the "heretic" that magnifies His Spirit and rejects the "Holy and Righteous" priests and religionists that deny His Spirit. This Parable further supports what has already been proven... *that God does not care about your religion or social status, but that you give life to His Good Spirit.*

■ ■ ◆ ■ ■

#7 - Dollar, Creflo (January 16, 2002)

I'm tellin' you right now, your prosperity is in my hands. Your deliverance is in my hands. The Bible says I watch for your soul. I'm just tellin' you the truth right now. The living words that come out of my mouth that minister to your ears, that bring you faith, it's in my hands. When I speak a word over your life, it is in, it is in the hands of the brother (referring to the pastor). And if you don't trust me, your prosperity has been hindered, and I love you enough to tell you to go to another church where you can find somebody that you do trust, because you not gonna' prosper in any area until you learn how to trust your man of God. You can forget it. You can forget it and, you know, I don't want your money. You can forget it. It ain't gonna happen. And that's why the devil put the slogan, "All preacher's want is your money." He tryin' to stop the prosperity. Psalms 10:15 says, "How can they preach except they be sent." Now, for years we thought that was talkin' about bein' called by God. That ain't talkin' about (sentence ends). The original Greek says, "How can they preach except you send them." Send them how? In financial support, like Paul talked about. I mean it's all over the, all in the Scripture.

Only the Selfless, Good Mind and Spirit Within you is Mediator between God and your ultimate "prosperity": *Salvation.* To believe that some other impure human named "preacher" is the Mediator of your soul ("your deliverance is in my hands") is idolatry.

God never sanctified corporate Christianity, so why would He instruct His followers to financially support it? The financial support of corporate Christianity is not "all over the, all in the Scripture" (Psalms 10:15 is referenced to prove this, but Psalms 10:15 was probably meant as Romans 10:15: "And how shall they preach, except they be sent").

"And how shall they preach, except they be sent" is not about financially supporting corporate Christianity, but about spreading the Good Spirit. *And how shall the Good Spirit be realized, except through those who conduct the Good Spirit.*

(3 minutes, 1 second later)

And you know what, you know what the devil's tryin' to stop. Let me show you what he's tryin' to stop. Let me show you what he's after. He's tryin' to stop evangelism. He's tryin' to stop souls from being saved. And if he can stop you from receivin' the message, and if he can stop you from trustin' your prophet (referring to the minister), and if he can stop you from knowing that this is your rights, he stopped evangelism. It takes money to tell people about Jesus.

No, it does not take money to "tell" people about Jesus, *to be a living beacon of Jesus' Spirit.* God's followers are not corporate mindsets who relentlessly demand money, but are those devoted to His Selfless, Good Spirit.

■ ■ ◆ ■ ■

#18 - Jakes, T. D. (December 5, 1999)

If I were to take a census of the men that are watching me around the country behind prison walls right now, seventy percent of them are in jail right now for the lack of money. Either stealing or robbing or selling drugs or writing bad checks or people who are desperately trying to get in on some American dream that they felt exempted from and thought they couldn't get to, and because there's such a "wall" in Wall Street, they got on the backside of the wall and tried to create some economic revenue so that they could feed their children and, see, and they wanted to buy a car for Mama and they didn't figure they'd ever get one, so they stole one, and desperate people do desperate things, and I'm not excusing them, but I think that, sooner or later, instead of spending billions of dollars on building bigger prisons, we need to spend some money in this ministry to help people to be delivered by the power of the Holy Ghost, and I'm not afraid to say so.

Here, corporate Christianity blames corporate America for the many thieves and others in prison, citing that it is the "wall in Wall Street" that keeps these breakers-of-the-law from financial success. *It is not lack of money that turns people into thieves and drug dealers, but lack of Spirit.*

So, what solution is offered? Give money to this church, as it will "help people to be delivered by the power of the Holy Ghost," resulting in less crime. America is 82% Christian and has the highest incarceration rate on Earth. Why throw more $$$ into the bottomless coffers of corporate Christianity to stop crime when it teaches idolatrous worship over Christ's Message of the Good Spirit?

■ ■ ◆ ■ ■

#18 - Jakes, T. D. (December 26, 1999)

How many thousand women are off welfare, but all for what? If we don't start teaching economic empowerment, we're gonna have to stop dancing a few minutes and prepare ourselves so that we can begin to understand that faith moves Heaven, but money moves Earth. That's why the Bible says, "Money answereth all things" (quoting from Ecclesiastes 16:19). I can assure you we didn't get (rent) this MCI center by speaking in tongues.

(27 seconds later)

They (referring to the owners of the convention center) don't care if I talk "hopscotch" as long as I pay the bill when it's over. They didn't rent me this building because they believe in my ministry. They rented me this building because the check didn't bounce. And I can have it from 2 to 5, and Farrakhan can come in and take it from 7 to 11, and it will make them absolutely no difference, and Hari Krishna can come in behind him, and it makes no difference what you do. If the check is good, they'll let you do it, because "money answereth all things."

Why should the owners of the convention center care about those who rent their venue as long as they get paid? Isn't the goal of any money-making business to make money? Isn't this ministry also a business that wants to make money?

Plucking the phrase "money answereth all things" from the Bible, then using it in conjunction with a story about money-for-services effectively reminds the audience that they need to pay-up when the plate is passed around. But money does not answer all things except in weak, ineffectively ruled countries (and businesses) overcome with discontent and corporate selfishness, examined as follows.

Ecclesiastes 10:16-20 (likely authored by King Solomon)

16. **Woe to thee, O land, when thy king is a child, and thy princes eat in the morning!** [Woe unto the land which is ruled by an irresponsible, immature, unwise king, where the first business of the day is not to attend to the matters at hand, but to feast.]
17. **Blessed art thou, O land, when thy king is the son of nobles, and thy princes eat in due season, for strength, and not for drunkenness!**
18. **By much slothfulness the building decayeth; and through idleness of the hands the house droppeth through.** [Governmental (and corporate) corruption increases unemployment, the poor getting poorer.]
19. **A feast is made for laughter, and wine maketh merry: but money answereth all things.** [The corrupt system, *rich and powerful,* can do anything through money.]
20. **Curse not the king, no not in thy thought; and curse not the rich in thy bedchamber: for a bird of the air shall carry the voice, and that which hath wings shall tell the matter.** [Under such corrupt rule, do not speak against the ruler or the thriving rich, not even in private, because someone shall surely *tattle on you,* which may prove injurious, even fatal.]

(minutes later)

God is a businessman. He invests in people and things that return a dividend. Why should God pour into you when you don't even tithe? What benefit is Heaven getting out of blessing you? You bless the mall, you bless the hotel, you bless everything else, why should God keep giving to you when you can turn the wealth of the righteous over to the hands of the wicked.

God is the Invisible Good Spirit, *not a businessman.* What He pours into us is His Spirit. What He wants in return is that we return His Spirit in like kind, otherwise our Spirit Within grows meaningless and shall depart (as given in the Parable of the Talents).

Evidently, paying for merchandise is to give a blessing unto the "wicked" merchant. Are we to believe that consumer transactions are not legal, business-as-usual transactions, but blessings? If a merchant lies to get your money, that would surely be wicked, but aren't preachers also merchants, "sellers" of God's word? Do they not ask for money for their services? Do they not use God to further self-serving, idolatrous worship?

■ ■ ◆ ■ ■

#18 - Jakes, T. D. (July 24, 1999)

You're supposed to affect whatever it is, whatever, whatever, whatever, whatever it is. God sent you. God didn't put you on that job for you to make money. God could have given you money anywhere. <u>Money's no big deal to God</u>. You are on a mission.

If "money's no big deal to God," then why, *in the previous excerpt,* were we taught that "money answereth all things" and that "God is a businessman?"

■ ■ ◆ ■ ■

#37 - Schuller, Robert (October 17, 1999)

I need to know that I have value. So do you. A lot of people feel little: "I'm just a little person, I don't have big money to give to any charities." <u>That's why we have created a statue</u>, never done before in Christianity to my knowledge, the bronze statue of the poor widow whose dropping her two mites ("two mites" is a farthing, approximately one-fortieth of a penny), and Jesus spots her and says to the Apostles, "See here, she's giving more than anybody else." <u>And that bronze statue salutes the single largest collection of financial supporters this ministry has had: poor widows</u>. <u>We don't know their names</u>.

Though the word "tithing" is not used, here is a plea for money by way of an idolatrous statue that exalts givers, a reminder of the importance of giving money to the church.

Surprisingly, *even though it is admitted that "poor widows" have contributed more financially than anyone else in the audience,* we learn that their names are not known. Is it true that this ministry really doesn't know the identities of the many widows who have willed their fortunes, *some even forsaking their own children by willing their entire estates?*

Here is a church that, every week, pleads for money, yet sees no problem with building an expensive, self-serving (but otherwise utterly useless) statue that works to "remind" the flock of how they should give $$$ to this church like generous widows.

Mark 12:38-44 was referenced, examined as follows.

Mark 12:38-44 (likely authored by Mark, disciple with Apostle Peter)

38. **And he [Jesus] said unto them in his doctrine, Beware of the scribes, which love to go in long clothing, and love salutations in the marketplaces,** [Jesus warns us of the "scribes," or false religionists (like the Saducees and Pharisees), who appear publicly in distinguished, religious attire, and love the reception they receive, ...]
39. **And the chief seats in the synagogues, and the uppermost rooms at feasts:** [...and love their exalted status, which brings them many worldly benefits:]
40. **Which devour widows' houses, and for a pretence make long prayers: these shall receive greater damnation.** [So wanton is their greed that they demand for even widows (women without an income, living off their savings) to give monies to their churches, devouring their estates. Their sermonizing is all for show. Such false teachers shall know greater sufferings.]

41. **And Jesus sat over against the treasury, and beheld how the people cast money into the treasury** [Jesus observed the treasury containers of the Temple, into which offerings and Temple-taxes were put]**: and many that were rich cast in much.**
42. **And there came a certain poor widow, and she threw in two mites, which make a farthing** [about one-fortieth of a penny]**.**
43. **And he** [Jesus] **called unto him his disciples, and saith unto them, Verily I say unto you, That this poor widow hath cast more in, than all they which have cast into the treasury:**
44. **For all they did cast in of their abundance; but she of her want did cast in all that she had, even all her living.**

Like the Parable of the Talents, the Parable of the Poor Widow is not about money, but about Spirit. The widow's last farthing is of no importance compared to her devotion to God's Spirit. Unlike the rich who gave much, her charity was *born of the Spirit,* making her tiny contribution of greatest value.

In Matthew 21:12, Jesus kicked out the moneychangers and merchants in the Rebuilt Second Temple, as they had fallen into the "business" of idolatry and selfish gain, making of the Temple a "den of thieves" (Matthew 21:12-13).

■ ■ ◆ ■ ■

#16 - Huch, Larry (October 17, 1999)

Now, we don't know that Jesus is coming right now. We don't know that. I don't know. But what if, all of a sudden, an angel stood here, and he said, "You've got 45 minutes. You've got 45 minutes." Would anything change in your life? Would you get more serious about getting your child saved? Would you get more serious? <u>Would you start throwing your tithes up and saying, "I don't want to be left behind 'cause of my tithes</u>?"

Earlier, *in Chapter 1,* this ministry taught that only Christ-believers are saved. Now we learn that tithing is the key to Salvation. *Which is it?* Neither, *of course,* as The Way is tread by those who choose Spirit over selfishness.

■ ■ ◆ ■ ■

#38 - Schuller, Robert A. (son of #37; January 16, 2000)

We want to love God. <u>We want to prove that we love Him more than anything else, but something always gets in the way and we think, "You know, if only that bill hadn't come in, shucks, I can't fulfill my pledge today</u>." And one thing after another. We can always find a reason why we need the money more than God. And we never fulfill the desires of our hearts. We never have the means to somehow make it happen. We remain in a toxic financial crisis, because the blessings of God just don't happen. "Love the Lord your God with all your heart" begins with a desire, a hope, a wish, a want to do it. And if you can love the Lord your God with all your heart, then you can begin to love the Lord your God with all your soul, with your breath, with your life, with your actions. You have to realize that God will empower us if the desire is there, if we come before Him in prayer and if we continue to share with Him that somehow, someway there's got to be a way.

Here, the Great Commandment of loving God with all your heart, soul, and mind is equated with giving money to corporate churches, once again exalting $$$ over the Spirit.

(continuing)

My wife and I love cats. We had four of five kittens. Unfortunately, not a single one ever celebrated their first birthday. We live in an area which is very beautiful. The only problem is there is also lots of coyotes. And so, as soon as the cats would get about 9-10 months old, they would become as fast as lightening, and we would open the door and they would dart outside, and we couldn't keep them in the house, and then they'd venture a little further, and a little further, and a little further, and it was just a matter of weeks once they got outside before they never returned. And it was really sad.

So, one day my wife comes home with this beautiful Persian kitten that was so cute, and I was so angry. I said (wife's name deleted), "You spent all this money on this beautiful kitten and you know it's not going to see its first birthday, how can you do it to this poor cat?" She said, "But Robert, they guarantee me it's an inside cat." And do you know what, she has celebrated her first birthday and soon she's gonna be two. She has never gone outside the house. Isn't that amazing?

What's amazing is: *Where's the owner's responsibility?*

All domestic kittens can be trained as indoor pets, *always*. If you acquire a cat that had roamed freely outdoors, it can be difficult, *even impossible* to train it to become an indoor creature. It will most likely tear up your home and urinate everywhere but in the litter box. But when domestic kittens are not allowed outside and trained to use the litter box and, *of course*, given lots of love, they will be happy, well-adjusted indoor pets that can, at a later time, be let outside into an enclosed yard *with supervision*. As far as pets "darting out" when an outside door is briefly opened... who is in charge of the door? At what point does the owner become mindful to open the door cautiously, shooing away the animals so that they have no chance to escape?

So, why this awful story? To reach its end, where, after 4-5 lost, *probably dead kittens*, we learn that it is "amazing" that there's such a thing as an "indoor" cat.

The kittens did not repeatedly escape, but were allowed to escape. Any person having lost one kitten to the coyotes and claiming to "love cats" would be acutely aware to be cautious when opening an outside door. But the kittens were allowed to repeatedly escaped, each time progressively trekking further away until, finally, *no more kitty*. How many "beloved" pets perish due to human selfishness, ignorance, and/or negligence?

How many sheep blindly follow blind shepherds?

Chapter 4

IDOLATRY

How is it that adults fall prey to charismatic preachers like David Koresh and Jim Jones, giving them their love, loyalty, money and, in the end, their lives? We now know that these particular Christian-based cults were lethal, headed by self-serving preachers who denied God's Spirit. Cult members are vulnerable people who, through repetitive drillings, grow lost in religion that denies the Spirit, breeding separation, *even isolation* from others who disagree with their Spiritless, *sometimes extremist* vision of the Bible.

What's the difference between fringe Christian cults and mainstream Christianity? In principle, nothing, except that the latter is acceptable to the masses. Big-business Christianity is the king of cults, where the brainwashing most-often begins in early childhood, provoking a lifelong submission to corporate "traditions" that put separatism and idolatry before God's Spirit. Such selfish agendas have been sown into human minds for so long that masses of people actually believe that their souls and lives are nothingness without the "covering" of corporate Christianity.

An extremely effective way for an elite few to control the masses is through religion. Indoctrinate people to believe that separatism and idolatry is God's "way," convincing them that they are otherwise hellbound, and you've got a growing army of souls that can be led to persecute "outsiders," *even kill them* for the sake of some selfish, man-made dogma.

Religious cults are obsessed with the fear of damnation, *but the Spirit fears nothing*. Many are so fearful that, to feel less fearful and better about *their* lives, they try to "fix" everything judged by their cult as being "broken," but see not that the "fixing" they need to do is *Within themselves*. Having been programmed to believe that they are "saved" through idolatry breeds a holier-than-thou mentality that permits blaming others for the world's problems. Their us-versus-them perception denies the Spirit, perpetuates blame, and further strengthens the cult mentality.

Why give your precious soul over to one of the many cults of corporate religion? Why let some soul-less entity act as "Intermediary" between your soul and God? Your soul is ultimately your responsibility, not the responsibility of man-made religions that claim they can "save" you if you join them. Why unite with corporate religions fraught with idolatry, thievery, enslavement, and bloodshed? Why define yourself through another? They are not The Way of the Spirit. The Way is in you, and is your responsibility to embrace or deny. You are to walk the One Way of the Good Spirit before any of the ways of the idolaters, for they are "blind" to the Spirit. Be not among the blind who follow the blind, nor among the dead who are buried by the dead" (Matthew 8:22, 15:14).

James 1:26-27 (likely authored by James, Jesus' brother)

26. **If any man among you seem to be religious and bridleth not his tongue, but deceiveth his own heart, this man's religion is vain.** [Those who seem religious, but are not careful to speak the Truth of the Spirit, are self-deceived, and their religion worthless.]
27. **Pure religion and undefiled before God and the Father is this, To visit the fatherless and widows in their affliction, and to keep himself unspotted from the world.** [Pure, undefiled religion before God is to pour your Selfless Love upon sufferers (like the Good Samaritan did) and to keep yourself aligned with the Good Spirit, not selfishness.]

The Spirit instructs us to internalize God, building His Spirit Within (John 4:23). We are not to externalize God through idolatrous worship, as this tempts and breeds greater idolatry. Yet centuries of corporate religionists have somehow forgotten the story of the "golden calf" (Exodus, Chapter 32) by making one of Jesus Christ through their idolatrous worship of His name and image over His Spirit. So idolatrous has corporate Christianity grown that, *for example,* there are white Christians repulsed by black Jesus icons and black Christians equally repulsed by white Jesus icons. Both forsake the Spirit in their idolatrous love of *plastic Jesus.*

Second Peter 2:1-3 (authored by Apostle Peter)

1. **But there were false prophets also among the people, even as there shall be false teachers among you, who privily shall bring in damnable heresies, even denying the Lord that bought them, and bring upon themselves swift destruction.** [There are false religionists among the masses who teach and tempt idolatry, denying the Spirit in their teachings, the very Spirit that gave them life in the first place. In doing so, they "kill" a measure of the Spirit Within their souls, building a measure of death, *of eternal separation.*]
2. **And many shall follow their pernicious ways; by reason of whom the way of truth shall be evil spoken of.** [And many shall follow them, for they make their lies appear as truth.]

3. **And through covetousness shall they with feigned words make merchandise of you** [And through idolatry shall they manipulate God's word to make "merchandise" of you (they deceive through idolatry in their lust for members, power, control, and money)]**: whose judgment now of a long time lingereth not, and their damnation slumbereth not.**

■ ■ ◆ ■ ■

#8 - Falwell, Jerry (on *Rivera Live* with Geraldo Rivera; March, 2000)

Geraldo Rivera: When you think back to the 19th century, I'm sure that people considered the church of the Latter Day Saints, the Mormons, to be a cult. Now you have the Scientology group, you have the Moonies, many charge that they are cults. Where does religion stop and cults begin?

Jerry Falwell: Well, it's very complex Geraldo. A cult leader is almost always a religious extremist, and he believes or she believes "Every one is wrong but me," demands total submission from the followers, allows no room for debate or argument or disagreement, expels all dissenters, and preys upon the insecure and the unloved, the unwanted. But the caution is that strong beliefs alone are not a danger sign. No one would accuse Billy Graham of being a cult leader, and yet he has strong beliefs, and millions of evangelicals agree with him or Pope John Paul II.

How is it that the definition of "cult" applies not to Protestantism and Catholicism? Yet both global titans are exclusionary, doomsday cults that judge most of humanity as hellbound. Both have gained their power through centuries of preying upon the weak through idolatry, fear-mongering, threats, and unthinkable brutality (slavery, rape, torture, murder).

Though corporate Christianity finally stopped its wholesale slaughtering of "heretic" tribes and peoples, and though it no longer stands behind violence, *generally speaking*, it breeds violence by embracing separatism and intolerance, *the seeds of all manner of evils and wars*. Be not deceived by idolatrous churches that call themselves "peaceful" when all the while they feed and breed the seeds of war.

■ ■ ◆ ■ ■

#37 - Schuller, Robert (December 26, 1999)

You know, I spent hours last week in four long visits with the Grand Mufti in Damascus, Syria. We found a kinship of spirit that was instant and immediate. And he said something that was profound. He said, "Religion comes like rain, fresh, clean, all life needs it, but then the extremists come and they pollute the waters until the waters are dangerous to drink." That's what's happened. Its happened in all of the religions that claimed the name of Jesus

Christ, and I call upon all of us today to focus, in the next millennium, on cleaning up the pollution in religion, whatever that religion might be. We're cleaning up the pollution in the air, and we're cleaning up the pollution in the water, and we're cleaning up the pollution in the oceans and, my God, we will clean up the pollution in religion and in our faiths. Yes. How do we do that? We go back to square-one. We go back to where it all started. We get away from the dogmas and the creeds and the theological books, and we go to a manger in Bethlehem, and we simply look into the face of innocence and holiness, and you cannot look into the face of Jesus without becoming a beautiful believer in the God of love, and that is what will change the world.

Finally, it is taught that corporate Christianity is polluted with false religion. *Yes!* But how to eliminate it? *Simple...* just go to Bethlehem and look into some idolatrous rendering of the face of baby Jesus. Let's all just forget about the evident truth that He lived and died some time ago, and that we do not know His actual birthplace, birth date, or image.

(1 minute, 24 seconds later)

Tonight, I want to share with you, who watch me here and around the world, a story I shared with my people last week in the church, because, you see, it's time for religions of the world to stop competing with each other. Don't try to convert me. I won't try to convert you. Let's just all try to find faith. And let's find it by following Jesus Christ. And then, let's lock arms and help each other to create the world of peace and live out God's promise and bring peace to the world.

"Don't try to convert me," and yet religions are asked to stop competing, *that none should press conversion,* but that all should find faith by "following Jesus Christ." *Need I say more?*

■ ■ ◆ ■ ■

#39 - Swaggart, Jimmy (January 22, 1999)

This God-forsaken, hellbound, two-fold child of the devil called Baton Rouge, Louisiana. The news media would like to put this church out of business and have done everything they know to do to do it, when they're so too-stupid they don't know the prosperity of this city is because of this church and others like it in this city. Ha-kay-kay-hel-ah-boo-hun-da-rub-ba-ba-la-ba-ba-si-tay-mah-kay-kay-hel-la-ba-ba-hun-da. Glory to God.

Baton Rouge is a "God-forsaken, hellbound, two-fold child of the devil," a city whose news media is stupid and ever-trying to put this ministry out of business, a city whose prosperity is to be credited to only its Protestant churches. What does any of this have to do with teaching Jesus' Spirit?

Per the Bible, speaking in tongues, or *glossolalia*, can be proof of holiness. But how Holy is speaking in tongues during services that teach blaming and separatism?

The Bible reveals that the tongues of stammerers shall speak plainly by the Spirit (Isaiah 28:11, 32:4). The "stammerers" are those whose tongues speak of the Spirit, yet trip over the Spirit with idolatry, interpreting Scripture by the Letter of the Law. Those who lift the Spirit of the Law over the Letter of the Law shall stammer no more, speaking with a "new tongue" (Mark 16:17).

The Bible reveals that *speaking in tongues* is speaking the language of one's ancestors, a true language that the speaker never learned (Acts 2:1-11). This happened to Jesus' Apostles forty days after His Ascension, when the Holy Spirit descended upon them, empowering them to speak in the languages of their ancestors. In an another instance, Apostle Paul was enabled by the Spirit to speak "with the tongues of men and angels" (First Corinthians 13:1). Obviously, "tongues of angels" would be languages not known to man.

Is "Ha-kay-kay-hel-ah-boo-hun-da-rub-ba-ba-la-ba-ba-si-tay, mah-kay-kay-hel-la-ba-ba-hun-da" from any language? If not, then this string of syllables must be the language of angels. Regardless, if the preaching is Spiritless, the tongue-talkin' is false, *probably staged*, and not proof of Holiness.

Corporate religionists exalt the Bible as "the inerrant word of God," yet somehow ignore the revelation that instructs us *not to speak in tongues in church* unless there is an interpreter.

First Corinthians 14:9, 19, 27-28 (authored by Apostle Paul)

9. So likewise ye, except ye utter by the tongue words easy to be understood, how shall it be known what is spoken? for ye shall speak into the air.

19. Yet in the church I had rather speak five words with my understanding, that by my voice I might teach others also, than ten thousand words in an unknown tongue.

27. If any man speak in an unknown tongue, let it be by two, or at the most by three, and that by course; and let one interpret.

28. But if there be no interpreter, let him keep silence in the church; and let him speak to himself, and to God.

■ ■ ◆ ■ ■

#28 - Parsley, Rod (May 30, 1999)

I want everybody in this building on your feet and I want you to praise Him for the next 30 seconds, right now. I want you to praise Him. I want you to praise Him. I want you to praise Him. Ye-en-doe-doe-bo-ya-vish-grome-vo-do-vo-mrash-sha-da. C'mon, you can speak mysteries. Leh-bro-vo-do-va-bra-da-va-keesh-kee-vra-va-da-va-ba-vra.

To the Enlightened, there are no mysteries about God (Matthew 13:11; Mark 4:11; Luke 8:10), being stewards of wisdom that the unenlightened call "mysteries" (First Corinthians 4:1). Per Jesus, "MYSTERY" is idolatrous (self-ish) religion, *the lover of illusion*, the "mother" of all abominations (Revelation 17:5).

First Corinthians 14:2 (authored by Apostle Paul)

2. **But he that speaketh in an unknown tongue speaketh not unto men, but unto God; for no man understandeth him; howbeit in the spirit he speaketh mysteries?** [Those "in the Spirit" do not speak mysteries.]

■ ■ ◆ ■ ■

#28 - Parsley, Rod (January 22, 1999)

Audience members have just been invited to come to the stage and "receive" the Holy Spirit. With energetic music playing, some come up dancing and shaking uncontrollably, others come up and lay on the floor, quaking and "speaking in tongues." Hands are "laid" upon the ecstatic, followed by:

God just told me if you shout in your Holy Ghost language (in your glossolalia), He'd give you a brand new language and baptize you fresh in the Holy... (sentence ends).

(5 minutes, 3 seconds later)

I want to welcome America to the outpouring of the Holy Ghost. You have joined a Holy Ghost outpouring in process. Warning, if you don't want a fresh touch of power, turn the channel now.

The pastor now prepares to pitch, *like a baseball*, the "Holy Spirit" into the audience.

(1 minute, 3 seconds later)

Are you ready? My God, I've never felt an anointing like this. Cancers are about to fall out of peoples' bodies, blind eyes are about to pop open, arthritis is gone, deafness is healed, the Holy Ghost is falling, get ready to speak with other tongues, in the name of Jesus, on "three," shall receive ye the Holy Ghost. One..., two..., three...

The "Holy Spirit" is now "pitched" into the audience, with human-ordained "promises" that audience members will receive the healing powers of the Holy Spirit. Here, the Holy Spirit is mocked via a theatrical stunt that denies the Truth that the Spirit is God's to pour into our souls (He pours His Spirit into those who pour-out His Good Spirit unto others). *God's Spirit will never be "pitched" to the masses by the pitching-arm of an impure human called "pastor" who uses the Spirit to falsely promise anointings and instantaneous healings.*

Mark 1:8 (likely authored by Mark, disciple with Apostle Peter)

8. **I** [John the baptist] **indeed have baptized you with water: but he** [Jesus] **shall baptize you with the Holy Ghost.** [It is by your devotion to the Spirit Within (the Christ Within) that you have the Baptism of the Holy Ghost, *the Baptism Within*.]

Galatians 5:6 (authored by Apostle Paul)

6. **For in Jesus Christ neither circumcision availeth any thing, nor uncircumcision; but faith which worketh by love.** ["Circumcision" was the Old Testament's ritualistic baptism. Here, we learn that Christ does not care about ritual baptisms, but that the source of your faith is Selfless Love.]

Ephesians 4:4-6 (authored by Apostle Paul)

4. **There is one body, and one Spirit, even as ye are called in one hope of your calling;**
5. **One Lord, one faith, one baptism,** [Not two baptisms. Ritual baptism means nothing without the *Baptism Within*.]
6. **One God and Father of all, who is above all, and through all, and in you all.**

John 4:24 (spoken by Jesus; authored by Apostle John)

24. **God is a Spirit: and they that worship him must worship him in spirit and in truth.** [Confirming, once again, that the Baptism is Within.]

(23 minutes, 32 seconds later)

During our recent "Raise the Standard, Pastors and Church Leaders" conference, the Lord led us into a time of repentance, repentance for our sins, the sins of our loved ones, and the sins of our entire nation. Many of you sent in your prayer needs on a piece of cloth to be prayed-over during this great national day of repentance "sackcloth burning" service.

A bin, filled with pieces of cloth sent in by viewers, is set ablaze (upon each cloth was a written request or prayer). The cloths are ignited and prayed-over for the repentance of sins.

Repentance is not effected through idolatrous, man-made rituals. Repentance is the internal process of changing, *of turning your selfishness into Selfless, Good Works.*

God never instructed us to make a "great national day of repentance," but did give us the Day of Atonement (Yom Kippur) that, per Christ, is every day that you live in the Spirit.

■ ■ ◆ ■ ■

#19 - Jones III, Bob (on *Larry King Live* with Larry King; February, 2000)

Larry King: Bishop Pike once said in an interview, the late Bishop Pike, "All Christians are Jews, many of us forget it."

Bob Jones III: That's a strange statement.

Larry King: Do you ever think of yourself as Jewish?

Bob Jones III: No.

Romans 2:25-29 defines two categories of humans: the "Jews" and the "Gentiles" (the "sheep" and the "goats," respectively, in Matthew 25:32-46). Jews and Gentiles are not defined by ancestry or religious membership. *By God's definition,* all devoted to the Spirit are "Jews." They are the Chosen Ones, chosen by the Spirit because they *have* chosen the Spirit. The not-chosen ones are, *by God's definition,* the "Gentiles," even if ancestrally Jewish (Per Romans 9:6, there are hereditary Jews who are "Gentiles"; Gentiles are not chosen by the Spirit because they have not chosen the Spirit).

Regardless of religious beliefs, we are known to God by our devotion to the Spirit, by which we define our eternal souls as either "Jew" or "Gentile."

Romans 2:25-26, 28-29 (authored by Apostle Paul)

25. **For circumcision verily profiteth, if thou keep the law: but if thou be a breaker of the law, thy circumcision is made uncircumcision.** [Ritual baptism has value if do not break the Spirit of the Law, but otherwise it is valueless (the 'law' is the Royal Law, the Spirit of the Law; James 2:8-13).]
26. **Therefore if the uncircumcision keep the righteousness of the law, shall not his uncircumcision be counted for circumcision?** [Therefore, if you are one who is not ritually baptized, but lives in the Spirit, shall not your lack of ritual baptism be counted as ritual baptism?]
28. **For he is not a Jew, which is one outwardly; neither is that circumcision, which is outward in the flesh:** [You are not a Jew by way of outwardly things (such as ancestry or religious membership), nor are you baptized through outwardly things (such as ritual baptisms).]
29. **But he is a Jew, which is one inwardly; and circumcision is that of the heart, in the spirit, and not in the letter; whose praise is not of men, but of God.** [You are a Jew if you are one inwardly, *that is, if you are true to His Good Spirit.* Baptism is not a ritual, *as per the Letter of the Law,* but is Within, *as per the Spirit of the Law.*]

We are not defined by our outwardly labels and rituals, but defined by our inwardly commitment to the Spirit. Just as there are Christian Jews and Gentiles, so too are there non-Christian Jews and Gentiles. *Not all Christians sinners are necessarily saved, and not all non-Christian sinners are necessarily unsaved.* Only the Spiritful shall know Salvation.

Ages upon ages of unnecessary sufferings caused by the hatred between the Abrahamic religions (Judaism, Christianity, Islam), and for what reason? Because of religionists who deny the Spirit in order to see *their own agendas* realized.

History is filled with Christians who have bullied their way through life to have *their* wants met, steamrolling over the Spirit with deceptions, threats, hatred, intolerance, and separatism. Some are so protective of their false religion that, when compromised with the Truth of the Spirit, they will seek to silence those who seek to expose their Spiritlessness. They are the true deniers of God's Spirit, *the true Atheists*, the Gentiles.

The Truth about the *Baptism Within* and about God's definition of Jew and Gentile clarify the issue of being "born again." Being "born again" is not a baptism sanctified through man-made rituals, but a *circumcision of the heart and mind*. A person who proudly says, "I'm a born-again believer," may be nothing more than an idolatrous, self-deceived Gentile.

When confronted by selfish souls, pour-out your Spirit, that they might see your Spirit Within and choose to Glorify *their* Spirit Within. If they grow too offensive, repaying your Goodness with selfishness, depart, peacefully and respectfully (you do not have the power to make others respect the Good Spirit).

■ ■ ◆ ■ ■

#36 - Rutler, George (August 8, 1999)

Saint Basil said [that] the only reason we have a sense of justice, the only reason we say. "it should not have happened," is because we have seen the man (referring to Jesus). We know justice, because justice has been revealed to us in the perfect man. Only the Christian can cry out fully in indignation against justice because the Christian has seen the full revelation of human dignity. The Pagan does not object to injustice. He may speak of injustice, and he may speak of justice, or when justice fails, the Pagan will shrug his shoulders and say, "Well, life is absurd anyway." Our culture is being seduced by that Paganism. It has begun to think that suffering itself is absurd, that the offering of a cloth (referring to a scapular) is a curse. And that is why we hide from the truth. Anything unpleasant we cannot understand, any evidence of the complexity of the human order we tend to shy from. We look for pop-philosophers, gurus, self-help experts, and government assistance, even drugs, to hide.

Here, we witness holier-than-thou teachings that exalt Christians over all others, this time on the subject of justice. Evidently, only Christians know the difference between justice and injustice.

This Catholic "mindset" is so catechized in lies that it does not see that its own Church was built upon Paganism.

Here, Paganism is blamed for teaching "our culture" that scapulars are a curse (a scapular is a piece of cloth blessed by ritual, investing it with "protective powers"). *Scapulars are Paganism.* They are nothing more than idolatrous talismans, like crosses and crucifixes. There are people who will not go anywhere without wearing or carrying their cross or crucifix, superstitiously believing that their "Holy and Protective" idol will keep them from evil. *So, why have they not heard that the Comforter lives Within, and not in man-made things?* Because of idolatrous religion. Consequently, many believers have become unwitting idolaters, having been brainwashed to hold man-made fears and superstitions over and above the Good Spirit Within.

The following, from *Revelation Earth,* is an overview of the historical rise of false religion in Christianity.

> The power of satan is the power of false religion, a power that can mislead us from God's Will. The false religion in Christianity has its roots in the false religion of Babylon.
>
> It was in Babylonia that descendants of Noah built the tower of Babel, a structure built upon their lack of faith in God. Nimrod, a great-grandson of Noah, was ruler of Babylon during the tower's construction. The Babylonian's religious beliefs, or Babylonianism, grew out of Sumerian mythology.
>
> The Babylonians worshiped Ishtar, the creator of mankind and the mother of the gods. She was the goddess of sexual love and was often depicted nursing a child (the people worshiped the image of mother and child). She was responsible for having her brother and lover, Tammuz (the god of vegetation), killed and resurrected. This myth served to explain the annual "death and rebirth" of vegetation.
>
> Thereafter, the people worshiped Tammuz' resurrection during the yearly festival of Ishtar to honor the "rebirth" of vegetation and crops [devotion to Tammuz is a great abomination (Ezekiel 8:13-15)]. Tammuz gave his people a symbol, "T," that they should worship before it in remembrance of him, and the people placed the symbol in their homes and upon their altars. The "T" was even used to dispatch Tammuz' enemies. This particularly cruel method of death was crucifixion.
>
> The false religion of Babylonianism included:
>
> - absolution
> - Holy water
> - a realm of atonement between Heaven and Earth [later indoctrinated by the Roman Church, known as "purgatory"]
> - worshiping mother and child [referring to the worship of Ishtar, the mother-goddess often depicted nursing a child, later seen in the Roman Church as the idolatrous worship of Mary and Jesus]

- the establishment of the queen of heaven [the title given to Ishtar; later seen in Christianity as the title for Mary; there is no queen of heaven in God's Kingdom; those who worship the queen of heaven are practicing false religion (Jeremiah 44:15-23)]
- the festival of Ishtar [celebrating the resurrection of Tammuz; later instituted into the Roman Church in the sixth century and renamed Easter, celebrating Christ's Resurrection (the term 'Easter' entered the Bible in 1611, in Acts 12:4, replacing the word, 'Passover')]
- the festival of the Sun-god, celebrated around December 25th [the great annual festival to honor the "return" of the sun, or the lengthening of daylight following the shortest day of the year; later instituted into the Roman Church and renamed Christ Mass, or Christmas, celebrating the birth of Jesus (Jesus, who represents Light and New Life, is thought to have been born in Spring, *the season of new life*, yet His unrecorded birthday is celebrated in the dark, dead of Winter)]
- the cross [Tammuz' sacred symbol "T," later used by the Romans to crucify Jesus (this great symbol of idolatrous religion would eventually become the global symbol for corporate Christianity)]

When the Babylonian civilization perished, its false religion continued to thrive in Egyptian, Greek, and Roman mythologies. Julius Caesar was the first "Supreme Pontiff of the Babylonian Order," a title which the Roman Emperors held until Emperor Gratian refused it in 376. Two years later, the title was given to the Bishop of the Roman Church, Damascus, making him the Supreme Pontiff (High Priest) of Babylon, "marrying" corporate Christianity to Babylonianism.

The Roman Church began adopting more and more of the seductive false religion worshiped by the Babylonians, attracting throngs of Pagans into the Church, enlarging membership and, *of course*, gaining more money and power for the Church.

In Revelation 17:1-5, the "whore of Babylon," whose name is "MYSTERY," is the anti-Spirit, the feeder and breeder of false religion, the lover of illusion (mystery, fear, idolatry) over Truth. Corporate Christianity is "in bed" with political leaders and peoples of the Earth ('fornicating' with the kings and peoples of Earth), its "life" abundantly fueled through the Good Spirit Within the souls of its masses of followers ('drunk with the blood of the saints').

Matthew 15:7-9 (spoken by Jesus; authored by Apostle Matthew)

7. **Ye hypocrites, well did Esaias** [Isaiah] **prophesy of you, saying,**
8. **This people draweth nigh** [near] **unto me of their mouth, and honoreth me with their lips; but their heart is far from me.** [They preach about Jesus, but do not live in His Spirit.]
9. **But in vain they do worship me, teaching for doctrines the commandments of men.** [They worship Christ in vain through idolatry, *through man-made beliefs, rituals, and superstitions.*]

Second Corinthians 1:24 (authored by Apostle Paul)

24. **Not for that we have dominion over your faith, but are helpers of your joy: for by faith ye stand.** [Paul reveals that teachers of the Gospel do not have dominion over your faith, but are to help you grow in the Spirit. It is through your faith that your standing before God is determined (faith is justified by Selfless, Good Works, page xv).]

■ ■ ◆ ■ ■

#1 - Mother Angelica (May 9, 1999)

I guess I'm just not for sports, but I just hope at some point you could see somebody on the field (referring to a player on the baseball field) making the sign of the cross, just to ask God's help (to ask God's help for a homerun). He wants to help us in everything, whether it's football, baseball, whatever it is.

(8 seconds later)

What an example, though, he would be if, before he got up to bat, he would just make the sign of the cross.

God never instructs us to make the "sign of the cross."

(16 minutes, 36 seconds later)

Every time you go to communion, you just don't receive a piece of bread. That's the body, blood, soul and divinity of Jesus. What a great gift from God.

No, it's just a sip of wine or juice to wash down a thin, round wafer of bread-like material. Jesus' teachings at the Last Supper, *grossly misunderstood,* is why the false ritual of transubstantiation exists (transubstantiation is the man-made, Catholic ritual that "turns" wine and bread into, *respectively,* the blood and flesh of Christ).

The Spiritual Message of the Last Supper instructs you to bless with the Spirit all the things you "eat," which is not primarily about food, but about all the things "absorbed" into your soul's experiences. His Last Supper is an instruction to stay true to God's Spirit, and when you do, you "eat of the Last Supper."

Those who "eat of the Last Supper" (who internalize the Spirit, living and growing in Selfless Goodness) shall have the Eternal Supper of the Lamb (Revelation 19:9). You are to "eat of the Last Supper" every day, *as if tomorrow were your last.* Stay faithful... tomorrow may very well be your last (Revelation 3:2).

First Corinthians 10:31 (authored by Apostle Paul)

31. **Whether therefore ye eat, or drink, or whatsoever ye do, do all to the glory of God.** [Conduct the Good Spirit in everything you do.]

First Corinthians 10:16-18 (authored by Apostle Paul)

16. **The cup of blessing which we bless, is it not the communion of the blood of Christ?** [The cup (vessel) is your soul. The Cup of Blessing is your soul's Spirit (the Christ Within), which is the truest Holy Grail. We bless (Glorify) our Christ Within through Selfless Love, which is the Communion of the Risen Spirit of Jesus ('blood of Christ'; the power of Redemption and Salvation).]
17. **The bread which we break, is it not the communion of the body of Christ?** [The flesh ('bread') being broken is one's selfish ways being "broken" (conquered) by the Spirit, which is the Communion of the Risen Body of Jesus (the Power of Redemption and Salvation).]
18. **For we being many are one bread, and one body: for we are all partakers of that one bread.** [The One Bread and One Body is the One Spirit. We who are the many partakers of the One Spirit are of that One Spirit.]

Matthew 26:26-28 (spoken by Jesus; authored by Apostle Matthew)

26. **And as they were eating, Jesus took bread, and blessed it, and brake it, and gave it to the disciples, and said, Take, eat; this is my body.**
27. **And he took the cup, and gave thanks, and gave it to them, saying, Drink ye all of it;**
28. **For this is my blood of the new testament, which is shed for many for the remission of sins.** [The bread and wine, after being dedicated by and for God's Good Spirit (the Christ Within), is ready to consume as "food" for the soul. We are to bless with our Spirit all things that come before us so that, by doing so, we are blessed by the Spirit. We receive the blessing of the Spirit when we *give* our blessing of the Spirit. Bless with the Spirit, especially in times of sufferings, and so shall you be Glorified by the Spirit (the Last Supper was a time of suffering for Jesus, who knew His death was imminent).]

How can transubstantiation be harmful? Because many Catholics are taught that if they do not partake in this ritual, they are not fully bound to God. God's Spirit reveals that we are bound to Him not by idolatrous rituals, but by personifying His Selfless, Good Spirit.

(59 seconds later)

And God has such mercy on all of us. He (Jesus) gave us His mother (Mary) to be our mother. We don't understand that one, do we? But it's true. Mary is our mother. <u>I could go to her anytime and ask her for anything</u>. If it's not good, she's like all mothers, she's not going to pray for us, 'cause she loves me, she loves you.

There is no other Mediator than the Christ Within (the Spirit Within). We are instructed not to worship the created (like Mary, the Angels, and the Saints) over the Creator: the Life-giving Spirit of God (Revelation 19:10, 22:8-9).

First Timothy 2:5 (authorship unknown, possibly Apostle Paul)

5. **For there is one God, and one mediator between God and men, the man Christ Jesus.** [The One Mediator between you and God is the "man Christ Jesus" (your 'man Christ Jesus' is the Mind and Spirit of God alive in your flesh).]

Matthew 10:37 (spoken by Jesus; authored by Apostle Matthew)

37. **He that loveth father or mother more than me is not worthy of me: and he that loveth son or daughter more than me is not worthy of me.** [Those that love the created (idolatry) more than the Creator are, by their own doing, unworthy of Salvation.]

(11 minutes, 10 seconds later)
Caller: I was reading Chapter 3 in Matthew today, and it talks about baptism in water and baptism with the Holy Spirit and with fire, and I want to know the difference between both and how you know you've got the baptism of the Holy Spirit, and if you don't, how do you get it?

Mother Angelica: Well, baptism of the Holy Spirit is baptism, period. When you're baptized in the church, in the Catholic Church or in any church for that matter, we hold all real baptisms that they are legitimate and real, but when you're baptized, your whole being, your whole, all your faculties change, [they're] no longer what they were, and that's through the power of the Holy Spirit. When you're baptized, it's not an initiation, it's not that you belong to this big club. Baptism means that the Father, the Son, and the Holy Spirit come and live in you. I mean, that's awesome. So, you are baptized in water. It is though the water and the Priest [and] the Altar Christus (the "Altar Christus" is the altar in a Catholic Church that is worshiped as the Presence of Christ) that the Spirit comes and lives in you, but He's not alone, He brings with him the Father, the Son, and the Spirit, and all three Persons live in you. And then, when you're confirmed, that Presence is made more active and you receive something else. You receive the seven gifts of the Holy Spirit. Why? You need them. At confirmation, you receive the fear of the Lord, that's the filial love for God, His Father. You receive piety, that relationship between the Father and you. You receive fortitude, the gift to persevere in your lifetime. You receive the gift of counsel, that's discernment. You've got to discern every day in your life, whether you're dealing with the Holy Spirit, the evil spirit, or the human spirit. If you don't discern, you're gonna be in trouble. And then, you receive three contemporative gifts. These are active gifts. And that's knowledge. You understand?

Here, this Catholic "mindset" teaches that it is only by ritual baptism that your being is invested with God, and it is through the ritual of confirmation that you receive the fear of the Lord, piety, fortitude, counsel, and knowledge. Here is idolatry which denies the Truth that the wisdom and gifts of the Spirit only blossom within souls that live to conduct the Good Spirit, *regardless of ritual baptism.*

(10 seconds later)

What is the one thing necessary? That I know, love, and serve God. It's a kind of detachment from the things of the world. Then comes understanding. I just can't read this book (the Bible) like a newspaper. I got to know it. I got to understand what I'm reading. That's the gift of understanding. Then there's the greatest gift of all. It's wisdom. Wisdom is not being smart-aleck. Wisdom is to know and share in the very wisdom of God. You don't see things the way people see 'em through only human eyes, you see 'em through supernatural eyes. All that is gifts of the Holy Spirit. It isn't something you can get by doing anything. It's something that comes to you directly from God at baptism and confirmation. If you're not baptized, then I'd take instruction. If you are baptized, you cannot be baptized again, so there's no use soakin' yourself in a river somewhere, you're only gonna get wet. I can guarantee you nothing else is gonna happen. You're either baptized or you're not. You can't get baptism five times. Once, and that's it. So, that's how it works.

Spiritual understanding and wisdom does not come via man-made rituals. If it did, the Catholic Church would never have committed its many atrocities towards humanity, and never have enslaved its masses to idolatrous worship.

(40 seconds later)

Caller: I just wonder why our kids aren't being given this blessed gift from the Blessed Mother, the scapular? It's hardly known.

Mother Angelica: Well, honey, I think the scapular went away of all things, like so many devotions, which is one of the most unfortunate that ever happened. It's not a scrupulosity. It's not a superstition. It's something Our Lady's asked for. A scapular is just a tiny, little cloth that's blessed by (garbled, unable to transcribe), and we wear it. Why? It's a protection. And Our Lady has put a lot of graces and gifts along with that, and I don't know why. One day, I think, if that morning ever comes (most-likely referring to the day of Christ's Second Coming), there won't be enough scapulars in the world. I figure you all are going to have to be scared to death again to get 'em. Now, this rosary, this rosary doesn't seem like much, [it's] really made out of glass. I got it at (garbled, unable to transcribe). But you know what Our Lady said about this rosary, every rosary? That the whole world would change if everybody said it. Now what is it? Tell me, what is this rosary that it should change the world? The whole world. Well, I don't know. It's the life of Jesus, I know. It's a mini-Scripture, and I pray it every day. I don't need to know why or how it's gonna work. If my Mother says, "Say it," I am going to say it. Isn't that simple? Why do you have to know why?

(34 seconds later)

But, now, this rosary and the scapular are very powerful. Why? Because God said it.

(24 seconds later)

God willed it so. He willed that we wear a scapular. He willed that we say this rosary.

God instructs us not to worship idols, which means that we are not to honor "things created" over the Spirit of the Creator. To honor and accept the "protective" powers of a scapular is to dishonor and reject your one and only True Protector: *The Spirit Within.*

God's eternal "protection" is His Spirit Within, which cannot be Glorified through superstitious idolatry.

(34 seconds later)

Caller: I want to ask you about our tabernacles that are being changed to the side altars, and to the, on the side, we don't even see them. Why can't our Pope demand our churches to bring back our tabernacles to the center altar. Sister, I am so upset. Why don't we do something about it?

(1 minute, 57 seconds later)

Mother Angelica: And I'm sure, I'm sure, I'm sure, I'm sure the Holy Father would like it changed. And I think, more and more, churches are doing that. But remember this little thing I just told you: When you go to God's house, you have a right to see God. Why else would you be there?

(2 minutes, 23 seconds later)

You know what amazes me about God (referring to the church's tabernacle), a priest can put Him (the "altar Christus") wherever he wants to put Him. He never says a word. If He could be with you, He'll go wherever they put Him. I have a sneaking suspicion that the Eternal Father is not at all happy with where you put Him. That's His Son, and He wants His Son up front.

Catholicism defines the Altar Christus as the Presence of Jesus Christ within their churches. *God does not live in furniture.* Yes, man-made things can be "holy" reminders, but do not look for comfort in worshiping before things, because the True Comforter is the Spirit Within (John 14:26).

■ ■ ◆ ■ ■

#37 - Schuller, Robert (October 17, 1999)

Let me tell you a story, you may remember this. When Pope John Paul was ordained as the new Pope in Rome, maybe you saw on the television the lineup of royalty, and power-people, all the big-league people, including somebody who was probably in your league, a little woman, dressed in very modest clothing. She didn't look like she belonged in that group, but she did as all others did, as appropriate Catholics that knelt and kissed his ring, he now wears the papal ring, she kneels and kisses the ring, and then she does something which is shocking. She lifts her left hand, where there is a wedding ring, and she says to the Pope, "Now, you kiss that ring, because if it hadn't been for that ring, you wouldn't be wearing your ring." She was his mother.

A humorous, interesting story about the most-exalted religious seat of Catholicism, but a denial of Jesus' Gospel of the Spirit. Kissing the Papal ring is just another idolatrous, man-made ritual. The Pope, *like the rest of us*, is one who has sinned, yet he is called the "Vicar of Christ" and is the center of fervent adulation by Catholics worldwide.

The super-exalted image of the "infallible" Pope is that of a man living amidst luxury, dressed in the finest robes, his foot upon a religious sea of priceless gems, jewelry, statuary, paintings, churches, and souls. *Is this how Jesus presented Himself to the world? Is this how He wanted us to worship the Spirit?*

Vatican City's 108 acres is the richest plot of dirt on Earth, showcasing the world's grandest monuments and articles of Christian idolatry. So unbelievably wealthy is the Catholic Church, yet millions of Catholics in predominantly Catholic regions (South America, Philippines, Mexico) are still miserably poor, even after centuries of supporting the Church financially. Instead of building more grandiose churches in these nations, *why not return all the riches "stolen" from these nations and peoples?* Even if all the riches were returned, can the Church's immeasurable oppression and brutality heaped upon the ancestors of peoples and nations ever be reconciled before God? Can its ages of teaching false religion ever be reconciled?

Consider the false ritual of confession. Confession does not build the self-discipline of repentance, because it effectively removes the sting of sin from the sinner. How does one build Good Conscience if one lacks self-discipline? Many are trapped in the cycle of sinning and confessing, then, after confession, return to sinning, only to confess again, caught up in the false belief that God has forgiven them. The false ritual of confession nurtures selfishness, because all you have to do to be officially absolved of wrongdoing is ritually "confess."

Redemption of sin can only be granted by God, effected through His Merciful, Righteous Justice of "as you sow, so shall you reap." If you do not repent, you shall know no "remission of sins," because forgiveness is justified only through repentance, and repentance is justified only through faith, and faith is justified only through Selfless, Good Works.

Here is just one example of the depth of the false nature of confession. On April 26, 2002, ABC's 20/20 presented a segment about accused pedophile Father Marciel Maciel, the powerful Catholic leader and founder of the "League of Christ," an organization where Catholic boys, aged 10 or older, are trained to become priests and servants of the Pope. One of Father Maciel's eight sworn accusers, Juan Vaca, was responsible for bringing certain boys into Maciel's room at night for sex, sometimes two at a time. Then came a point when young Mr. Vaca confessed to Father Maciel that he believed this sexual activity was sinful, saying, "But, Father, I think I committed a sin." Father Maciel replied, *"Don't worry. I absolve you for your sin in the name of the Father and of the Son and of the Holy Spirit. Go in peace. Don't worry about it. Forget about it."* [The eight accusers informed the Vatican, but after years of no response, went public in 1997, shortly after which the Pope elected Father Maciel as his representative at a principal meeting of Latin American bishops, openly opposing these victims.]

The false ritual of confession, *like magic,* wipes away one's sins. Confession is a powerful tool in the hands of those who seek to manipulate and control. Is it any wonder that this ritual destroys personal responsibility and breeds corruption? Is it any wonder why the Catholic Church and its Hierarchy is fraught with immoral, unethical, and criminal activity? No one has to take responsibility. No one has to repent. All it takes is "official absolution" via idolatrous, ritual confession.

Another idolatrous ritual is beatification, which is when the Catholic Church, after a "formal investigation," informs the public that some dead Catholic is worthy of idolatrous veneration. And if that dead Catholic is found to be especially exemplary, canonization follows, creating a new "Saint." At no time does God instruct corruptible, impure humans to "beatify" and "make Saints" of dead humans. Who knows if any of them actually made it to Heaven? Did we live their lives, that we should know their hearts and motivations? If any of these sinners did become Saints in Heaven, then every one of them is as repulsed as Christ Himself at having been made into a Spiritless idol for an idolatrous people.

We are all at different levels of Spirit-growth and, surely, there are many Catholics who live in the Spirit. Nevertheless, idolatry is a tempting "crutch." If you feel you need to partake, then, *per Jesus,* "hold fast" to the Good Spirit before all else (Revelation 2:25), and beware that idolatry tempts even greater idolatry. *Know that you can, trusting your Spirit Within, throw the crutches away and rise and walk without them.*

Colossians 2:16-19 (authored by Apostle Paul)

16. **Let no man therefore judge you in meat, or in drink, or in respect of an holyday, or of the new moon, or of the sabbath days:** [Let no one judge you via rituals, ceremonies, or holy days…]
17. **Which are a shadow of things to come; but the body is of Christ.** […which are without substance ('shadow'; without Spirit); however the substance ('body') is of Christ, *the Mind and Spirit of God alive in the flesh* (alive in *your* flesh).]

18. **Let no man beguile you of your reward in a voluntary humility and worshipping of angels, intruding into those things which he hath not seen, vainly puffed up by his fleshly mind,** [Be not led away from Salvation ('reward') through another's humility or worshiping of angels or false revelations, for this person is self-deceived and of a worldly mind,]
19. **And not holding the Head, from which all the body by joints and bands having nourishment ministered, and knit together, increaseth with the increase of God.** [And not upholding the Mind of God (not 'holding the Head'; the Christ Within), which nourishes "all the body" relative to one's empowerment of Its Spirit (Matthew 25:16-17).]

■ ■ ◆ ■ ■

#37 - Schuller, Robert (December 27, 1998)

Innocence is so angelic. It comes from God. It is the Spirit of God within you and within me. So at Christmastime, we're invited to witness innocence in the virgin, in the baby, in the angels. Yield to that compulsion to touch innocence. It is a call to living life with a higher level than the pure greedy, sexual, sensual, sinful, cynical world in which we have to live. There's a beautiful world out here. God is in the center of it. Christ is the Lord of it. Most of you are living in it. And you respond to what I'm saying because you relate to this. <u>You love the truth</u>. And what is truth? It is knowledge that is innocent of error.

What does Truth have to do with Christmas idolatry?

Galatians 4:8-11 (authored by Apostle Paul)

8. **Howbeit then, when ye knew not God, ye did service unto them which by nature are no gods.** [How is it that when you did not know God, you worshiped gods of nature that were not gods? For example, Christmas was born of an ancient holiday that celebrated a natural celestial event representing the birth of the Sun-God. This ancient, Pagan holiday was 'stolen' for the idolatrous worship of the birth of the Son of God.]
9. **But now, after that ye have known God, or rather are known of God, how turn ye again to the weak and beggarly elements, whereunto ye desire again to be in bondage?** [Now, after you have known God and know that He is watching, how is it that you worship the created, desiring enslavement to worldly things?]
10. **Ye observe days, and months, and times, and years.** [You observe your man-made holidays and seasons (Sundays, Christmas, Easter, Lent, Ash Wednesday, Good Friday, All Saint's Day, etc.).]
11. **I am afraid of you, lest I have bestowed upon you labour in vain.** [Paul is alarmed by these Spiritless souls, concerned that his exhaustive teachings have been worthless.]

■ ■ ◆ ■ ■

#16 - Huch, Larry (May 30, 1999)

I can see in my spirit, right now, your families, your children. I can see them. I can't see their faces, but I can see younger children, older children, moms and dads. I'm putting my hand on your family right now and I'm covering them. Come in agreement with me. Father, I cover our children, our grandchildren, our family with the blood of Jesus. I cover them. Folks, I can see like a bubble of protection that no bullet, no bomb, no violence, no satan, no devil can penetrate right now. Say with me, "I cover my family with the blood." Say it, "I cover my family with the blood." And mom and dad, let me, let me encourage you. Jesus shed his blood, grandma and grandpa, on His hand, so that everything we put our hands to, on His feet, so that every place He puts the sole of His feet. I want to challenge you, as we're doing here in Portland (Oregon), to march around your school. Now, you don't have to do it when, do it when they're closed. Put your hands on those schools and say, "I plea the blood of Jesus." We put a barrier of the blood of Jesus around these children, around our school and, devil, you cannot trespass on blood-bought property.

Every soul, being impure, shall be subjected to suffering unto death. Jesus prophesied that, before His Second Coming, the Spiritless ("Gentiles") would grow more corrupted, during which time the Spiritful ("Jews") would suffer greater sufferings (Matthew 24:5-9). Instead, we are taught about some magical, *Instant Protection* from evil via idolatrous beliefs and rituals.

■ ■ ◆ ■ ■

#14 - Hagee, John (October 24, 1999)

This book (the Bible) is a miracle. it's the only book that's ever been written that can change your life. You can read Shelley, Keats, Byron, Shakespeare, and Longfellow, and it will not change you. But when you read Matthew, Mark, Luke, and John, it will make you a new creature. It will give you a new attitude. It will give you a new name written down in the Lamb's book of life (those in the Book of Life have Salvation, Revelation 21:27). It will change your disposition, for this book is alive. It is the living, eternal, sovereign word of God.

Evidently, God's Spirit is not alive in books other than the Bible, the only book that will "give you a new attitude," even Salvation. You can read the Bible every day, but it won't mean a thing if you don't "get" its Message of the Spirit. Though recommended, reading the Bible is not the end-all to your Salvation.

(1 minute, 4 seconds later)

When I quote the atomic Scripture that's located in this divine book, every demon in hell begins to tremble. The gates of hell are conquered. Disease retreats. Fear is gone. Depression must surrender to joy unspeakable and full of glory. Worry and anxiety surrender to the peace of God that surpasses all understanding. This book has the answer to every question you're ever going to have. I am what this book says I am. I am a child of the King, my sins are forgiven, they're buried in the deepest sea, never to be remembered against me anymore. I have everlasting life. The royal blood of Heaven is flowing in my veins. I am Prince John Hagee. I am created a little lower than the angels. I am loved by an everlasting God. I can charge the gates of hell with a water pistol and win, because of the power of this book.

If the spoken Scripture of this "prince" conquers hell and rids the world of disease, fear, depression, worry, and anxiety, *then why are we all still suffering on Earth?*

(23 minutes, 53 seconds later)

I can have what the Bible says I can have. I can do what the Bible says I can do. I have authority to lay hands on the sick and expect them to get well, and so do you. I have authority to cast out demons with the word.

How can any impure soul, preacher or not, claim "authority" to heal the sick and *expect* them to get well? Surely you have heard of Christian parents who have refused medical treatment for an ill child, causing the child a slow, agonizing death. Could it be that such parents were blindly following this kind of preaching? Has it ever occurred to such zealots that it is through God's Life-giving Spirit that humanity possesses ever-growing understandings of healing through medicine? *Medicines are miracles!* God does not instruct us to refuse medicines and surgeries.

■ ■ ◆ ■ ■

#37 - Schuller, Robert (December 19, 1999)

The greatest gift you can give someone is to invite them to your house. <u>I want to give you a gift</u>. I want to give you a blessing. I can't come to your home, but we've had a beautiful gift made. <u>In this gift, spiritually, I want to be in it, come to your home, in your living room, and give you a blessing</u>. In my mind, I honestly promise you it's worth a lot more than ninety-nine dollars, and yet we can take almost that entire ninety-nine dollars and use it to pay the television bills which keeps this program alive.

When you send your year-end gift of ninety-nine dollars, I have a truly magnificent, beautiful, masterful, brilliant way of saying "thank you." We have created an original porcelain work of art of Jesus with his hand up, raised, pronouncing, "Peace be still." Makes a fabulous Christmas gift to anyone, young or old, rich or poor. Remember, it's new, it's never been offered anywhere before. Yes, and for a gift of only one-hundred-fifty dollars, we can send you two of these beautiful "Peace be still" porcelain statues, one for you and another one maybe to a student in school or a child that's getting married. Someone needs it. They need a blessing today. You need a blessing today. Let me send you blessing. We need to hear from you with your special year-end gift today.

The greatest gift you can give someone is to invite them to your house? The greatest gift is Selfless Love, always. So, why this statement? To segue into peddling. Most do it, selling medallions, statues, books, seminar tapes, music, etc. The need for your money is usually always about paying the television bills, but where else does all that money go?

The audience is told, "I want to give you a gift," followed by a sales pitch. The word "payment" is not used, yet the customer is to give a $99 "gift" for the product. *Yes, you, who loves this preacher, can have him in spirit, in your home, in the form of a Jesus statue. You, for $99, can buy a blessing.*

Whether a priceless antique or an assembly-line, cheesy-looking ceramic, Jesus statues are graven images that tempt idolatry. Why do people allow themselves to be suckered-in to parting with relatively large amounts of money via such peddling? What does this say about many of today's churches and their members? When someone gives money to get something back, that's not Charity, that's just business, *in this case, the big-business of corporate Christianity.*

■ ■ ◆ ■ ■

#40 - White, Paula (May 26, 2003)

Aren't you sick and tired of being sick and tired? Today's the day of divine, supernatural intervention. I speak it, and I take authority over every weapon the enemy has used to form against you. It will not prosper this day. It is over. I am prophetically speaking to you right now in the name of Jesus. Tomorrow, about this time, God can supernaturally turn your situation around [and] take you from poverty to wealthy, take you from sickness to health, take you from down-and-out to up-and-in, because He is El Shaddai, the God that is more than enough. I expect it. If you believe it, your faith hooked up with my prayer is going to turn the situation around in the name of Jesus. That's why you need to get these tapes. You need to hear the word of God over and over...

Here, *once again*, you are instructed to broker your soul unto God through a false mediator. The True Mediator lives Within you and has infinitely more power than any church ritual or "sanctified" assistance from a pastor. No one can effect your healing and Salvation but ultimately yourself, by your devotion to the Spirit. People who claim the power to heal and save you are not teaching The Way of the Spirit, but are self-exalting (holier-than-thou) with their "special powers." Be not deceived. You hold the power to your Salvation, not them.

This minister is so sure of her *holy link* with God that she "expects" from God. How can any of us *expect* anything from God for someone else when, according to God, every person shall reaps what he/she sows?

(3 minutes, 12 seconds)

I believe in you. I believe that God, that we serve, has great things ahead for you. You know, I want you to write me with your prayer request. It is so important that you put that down on paper and that you write me. Why? Because we'll have a point of contact where we can lay our hands on it. We have intercessors that pray every single day. We bombard Heaven and petition God on your behalf. And, listen, I am a woman of faith. I know how to reach Heaven. I know how to hear from God.

Why not just teach the Truth that there is only One Intercessor... *the Spirit and Mind Within you*, governed by your Good Conscience? You can have a million people "laying on hands" and praying "on your behalf," but that will reap nothing if you yourself have not sown the Good Spirit into your soul. You shall reap what you sow, not what others sow. Do not be like the deceived, falling prey to the "mysteries" of man-made, religious rituals that promise healing and Salvation, but know that the power is Within you, strengthened only by your devotion to Glorifying His Good Spirit.

■ ■ ◆ ■ ■

#37 - Schuller, Robert (January 19, 2002)

We're unveiling a statue of the prodigal son. We're giving it the title, "Coming Home."

At the helm of this mega-corporation's image is its high-holy Christmas extravaganza, its over-the-top glass cathedral, and its grounds full of statuary. What does all this grandiosity and idolatry have to do with teaching God's Spirit Within?

■ ■ ◆ ■ ■

#37 - Schuller, Robert (January 9, 2000)

I never thought I'd live to see the world the way I saw it on New Year's Eve Day, 1999. The celebrations in China, the celebrations in the Kremlin Square, the celebrations in the world that wouldn't have allowed it five, ten, fifteen years ago. We're enjoying a peace and a freedom beyond anything ever experienced by human beings on planet Earth before. You think there's no God, and He doesn't keep His promise? Go back to New Year's Eve Day, 1999, and it was God putting on a big show, where there was peace on Earth, good will to men. Hallelujah.

God does not promise peace and freedom as the world spins towards Christ's Second Coming. *Quite the contrary*. The world shall grow increasingly corrupt until it has reached maximum corruption, which will trigger an hour of global catastrophes, directly followed by His Second Coming (these issues further discussed in Chapter 6).

If there is unprecedented "peace and freedom" on Earth, then why are there so many regional wars ongoing around the globe, and why are hundreds of millions of people suffering in ways unimaginable to most Americans? Is this unprecedented "peace and freedom?"

Crediting God for the brief, global coming-together of nations in celebration of the New Millennium, *adding that such a thing could never have happened years ago*, is nonsense. The reason why such a global mega-celebration did not happen years ago is because all of those year-end festivities were not celebrating the end of the millennium. The millennial "big show" celebrations around the globe were staged by man, not God.

■ ■ ◆ ■ ■

#37 - Schuller, Robert (October 10, 1999)

The cross is the world's great plus sign.

If we could only ask the masses of humanity brutalized and murdered by Christianity "in the name of God," I wonder if they would agree that "the cross is the world's great plus sign."

The cross is nothing more than an idolatrous, Pagan-based superstition like, *for example*, the fear of the number 13. Who was the Shepherd over the 12 "sheep" Apostles? Was He not of their group and yet separated from them at the same time? Was He not the 13th? Was He not the Redeemer, the Savior-Spirit that became the Open Door to Salvation for all devoted to the Good Spirit? *Was He "bad luck?"* And what of Apostle Paul's letters to his followers of The Way, writings that predate the Four Gospels and make-up over a third of the New Testament? Are they not the 13 Epistles? Why give life to some superstitious garbage about the number 13? *Why give life to any superstitions?*

Your Spirit Within has the power to disintegrate all fears and superstitions. Why empower fears and superstitions when you have a built-in Spirit that transcends all such things?

Chapter 5

CHURCH OF LAODICEA

Laodicea (lay-oh-dih-see-uh) is the last of seven churches that Jesus addressed in the Book of Revelation. His messages to the churches define seven stages of faith in God. The nature of each church is a message to you about Spirit versus anti-Spirit. The following overview of the seven churches is from my first book, *Revelation Earth*, a verse-by-verse study of the Book of Revelation.

THE "EPHESUS" NATURE

Jesus' message to the "church of Ephesus" (ef-feh-suss) is to those initially devoted to the Spirit with enthusiastic desire, but whose devotion has weakened over time (He condemns them for having lost their "first love"; Revelation 2:4). He commends them for rejecting the "deeds of the Nicolaitanes" (the deeds of religious idolatry; Revelation 2:6). Those who restore their initial devotion to the Spirit shall "eat of the tree of life" (Salvation; Revelation 2:7).

> The church era of Ephesus, founded by Apostle Paul, extended from about 40-170. [Paul, an Apostle who came after Jesus' crucifixion, had been Saul (Saul of Tarsus), who was widely feared for persecuting Jesus' followers, but a miracle involving Jesus led him to commit his life to the Gospel (Acts 9:1-20), after which he was renamed "Paul" (Acts 13:9).]
>
> Paul's testimony of Christ led many to convert. Their initial desire to eagerly embrace the Spirit eventually failed as the exceptionally brutal and murderous persecution by the Roman Empire increased, leading some to desert the faith altogether. [The persecution of the followers began in 64 under the reign of Nero (Roman Emperor from 54-68), the first of ten Roman Emperors infamous for persecuting Christ's followers.]
>
> In Greek, "Ephesus" means "desired." The members of the "church of Ephesus" fervently desired faithfulness to the Spirit initially, but their desire weakened when faced with persecution.

Ephesians are souls whose true and faithful devotion to the Spirit has, over time, grown dim due to fear (the Spirit knows no fear). Those who repent, restoring their initial devotion to the Spirit, shall come to Salvation.

THE "SMYRNA" NATURE

The "church in Smyrna" receives no condemnation from Jesus. His message is to those who suffer unto death for their commitment to the Spirit. To them shall go the Crown of Life (Salvation; Revelation 2:10).

> The church era of Smyrna extended from about 170-313. Persecution towards Christ's followers reached its greatest intensity near the end of Diocletian's reign (Roman Emperor, 284-305). Even after his abdication in 305, the Anti-Christian Movement he initiated continued until 313, when Emperor Constantine's Edict of Milan granted tolerance towards Christians, giving them religious freedom.
>
> The church in Smyrna, also known as the "martyr church," is about followers who, because of their devoted faith in the Spirit, were killed in unbelievably cruel ways. Jesus commends them without condemnation.
>
> "Smyrna" means "myrrh," a shrub that is crushed to bring forth its beautiful fragrance. The martyrs were also "crushed" (killed), bringing forth an everlasting remembrance of their Selfless Spirit.

THE "PERGAMOS" NATURE

Jesus' message to the "church in Pergamos" commends its strength in the Spirit during periods of affliction (Revelation 2:13), but condemns its idolatrous, false religion. The "church in Pergamos" represents the birth of the Roman Church, *the birth of corporate Christianity*. Those who overcome the false religion of the burgeoning, big-business of corporate Christianity shall know Salvation (shall "eat of the hidden manna," possess the "white stone," and have a "new name"; Revelation 2:17).

> The church era of Pergamos spanned from 313 to about 476 (the onset of the Dark Ages). In 313, Emperor Constantine, a brilliant and merciless leader, *merciless enough to have his wife and eldest son killed 13 years later*, gave Christians the freedom of worship, ending their persecution. Motivated by Imperialist politics, he united Christians and Pagans (non-Christians), strengthening his Empire and political power. He merged Church and State, making the Church an agency of his government. The corporate structure of the Roman Church was modeled after the hierarchical structure of Imperialism.

Before the birth of the Roman Church, the Empire saw ten Emperors who feverishly persecuted and killed Christ's followers. Finally, the slaughtering grew senseless to the Roman citizenry, who had come to respect the victims' brave and unyielding faith. This, coupled with the Empire's rapidly deteriorating strength, led Constantine to further empower himself as the Empire's religious leader by supporting and building the Christian faith. The Empire, which had failed to kill all the bodies of Christ's followers, would now work to kill their souls through false religion.

About fifty years later, Theodosius I (Emperor, 379-395) made Christianity the official State Religion. The newly-formed Roman Church was divided over many religious issues. One of the main issues was whether or not Jesus was actually God in the flesh. The many disagreements being argued opened the way for the early Roman Church to "relax" and manipulate Jesus' Message. Pagan-inspired beliefs and rituals were adopted, polluting the Church with idolatrous, false religion.

False religion is a gentler, less-offensive, but more effective way for the anti-Spirit to eliminate followers of The Way, as it works to mislead and corrupt, drawing them away from Salvation.

The Roman Empire "stole" the Gospel of The Way not to serve Christ's Selfless Spirit, but to serve their selfish wants for power and control over the minds of their masses. And what better way to do this than through corporate religion? Church Hierarchy wielded a "self-sanctified" right to bind a soul to hell or to Heaven, using that power to manipulate the people to their corporate will. *This was just the beginning!* The Roman Church ambitiously used Christ's Gospel for financial enrichment, self-aggrandizement, and domination over the souls of the masses through their man-made rituals, fears, and superstitions about Salvation and damnation.

The Roman Empire, once the ultra-cruel enemy of Christ's followers, was now an even mightier enemy to the Spirit in its role as the Roman Church. Like "leaven" that leavened the "loaf," the Church's idolatrous worship corrupted God's Message. The Empire's anti-Spirit would no longer work to destroy God's followers by killing their bodies, but by killing their souls through idolatrous, false religion. The Roman Imperialist "mindset" that had so hated Jesus' followers stole and "killed" His Message of the Spirit by honoring and teaching idolatry. Now, as "Master" over Jesus' Gospel, the Roman Church would turn against those not enslaved to ITS will.

The Roman Church grew rich and powerful. Some of the false religion indoctrinated [shown as the "doctrine of Balaam" (Pagan-inspired beliefs; Revelation 2:14) and the "doctrine of the Nicolaitanes" (the institution of idolatrous worship; Revelation 2:15)] include: Church Hierarchy; making the "sign of the cross";

prayers for the dead; mass; and worshiping saints, angels, and Mary (mother of Jesus).

False religion clouded the Light of Jesus' Gospel. This growing malignance within Christianity, followed by the fall of the Roman Empire, heralded the "Dark Ages" in 476, a spiritually unenlightened period lasting roughly 850 years until the Renaissance, the "Age of Enlightenment."

The Pergamos era allied Church and State, making an Imperialist-based, corporate, big-business of Jesus' Gospel. "Pergamos" means "marriage." Pergamos was a "marriage" of the world (idolatry; corporation-building) with the Spirit.

THE "THYATIRA" NATURE

Jesus' message to the "church in Thyatira" (thigh-yuh-tie-ruh) condemns the Roman Church for its increasing false religion, or denial of the Spirit (Revelation 2:19).

During the church era of Thyatira, the Roman Church became increasingly lost in false religion. The Papal system was in full swing, and some of the false rituals and beliefs indoctrinated during this period include: Holy water; icons set before the masses for idolatrous worship; celibacy for priests; the canonization of saints; fasting (during Lent and on Fridays); transubstantiation; purgatory; and Pagan-inspired festivals.

"Ishtar," a festival thought to have originated about 1,800 years before Jesus' birth, was named after the goddess who, every Spring, resurrected her brother (Tammuz). In 519, due to Pagan influences, the celebration of Jesus' Resurrection became the "Easter" celebration, a Christian-Pagan merge that served to attract more Pagans into the Church, increasing its membership, wealth, and power.

The greatest Pagan festival commemorated the birth of the Sun-god, celebrated on December 25th. This annual festival was indoctrinated into Christianity and renamed "Christmas" to celebrate the unrecorded birthday of the Son of God.

The two great Pagan-inspired, Christian festivals of Christmas and Easter both honor Jesus, but God instructs us not to enslave ourselves to the idolatrous worship of man-made, high-holy holidays (Galatians 4:8-11).

It was during the church era of Thyatira that the Roman Church's separatism against non-members intensified. In 1095, Pope Urban II "sanctified" religious terrorism when he ordered the First Crusade to free the Holy Land of "heretical" non-Christians, targeting Muslims and Jews in Christian-held territories (Spain, France, the Balkans, Greece, Asia Minor, Syria, Palestine, and Egypt). Those who refused to convert were persecuted, tortured, *often murdered*. The European campaign was successful, but Christianity lost its Middle East stronghold. The nightmarish Crusades ended in 1291, but the relationship between Christians, Muslims, and Jews remains divisive, even hostile to this day.

The Crusades intensified intolerance towards non-Christians (especially Jews), enabling a smooth transition into the Inquisition. Led by tribunals of the Roman Church, Inquisitors passed judgment upon sinners, particularly non-members, labeling them "heretics." Those found guilty were brutalized and/or murdered "in the name of God." The Inquisition served to convert/eliminate "heretics," strengthening the Church's grip on the masses.

An overview of the Inquisition:

1215 - Pope Innocent III created the Inquisition to prosecute "heretics."
1229 - Pope Gregory IX prohibited lay people from reading the Bible in Toulouse, France (the Roman Church's sole possession and control over the knowledge in the Bible was not to be compromised).
1231 - Pope Gregory IX sent Inquisitors (mostly Dominican monks) into Germany and France to find "heretics" and burn them at the stake.
1252 - Pope Innocent IV approved the use of torture upon "heretics."
1349 - Persecution against Jews began in Germany.
1380's - Spain's Jews were ordered to become Christians or leave.
1481 - Spanish Inquisition began upon Pope Sixtus IV's approval.
1492 - King Ferdinand ordered the expulsion of non-Christian Jews from Spain, giving them four months to either leave or convert (those who left lost their property to the King; those who stayed and converted were still persecuted).
1495 - Non-Christian Jews were banished from Portugal.
1499 - Muslims were forced to either convert or leave Spain.
1509 - Germany banned Jewish books.
1526 - Persecution against Jews began in Hungary.
1528 - Spanish Inquisition entered Mexico City, persecuting the New World's natives.
1532 - Portuguese Inquisition began, proving more cruel than the Spanish Inquisition.
1541 - The Society of Jesus (known as the Jesuits) is founded by Ignatius Loyola to support the Counter Reformation (Jesuits were militant devotees of the Catholic Church; the Counter Reformation served to suppress the growth of Protestantism).
1542 - Roman Inquisition began, run by Pope Paul III.
1562 - Spanish Inquisition began systematically burning Protestants at the stake, effectively ridding Spain of Protestants.
1566 - Netherlands abolished the Inquisition.
1772 - France abolished the Inquisition.
1773 - Portugal abolished the Inquisition.

1820 - Spanish Inquisition ended.
1942-1945 - The anti-Spirit of the Inquisition lived in the staggering extermination of Jews and other "defectives" by the Nazi Regime.
1965 - Roman Inquisition, begun in 1542, is never abolished, but reorganized by Pope Paul VI and renamed "The Congregation for the Doctrine of the Faith" to oversee issues within the Church itself.

England's Naturalization Act of 1753-1754 offered citizenship to Jews [as citizens, they gained freedom of worship (per England's Declaration of Rights of 1689)]. In 1790, Jews living in France were given civil liberties. In 1791, the freedom of worship provided in America's Bill of Rights encouraged many oppressed Europeans (mostly Protestants and Jews) to flee to America. The power of the Inquisition subsided as the freedom of worship gradually spread over Western Europe.

Hundreds of thousands (millions, by some reports) of "heretics" were tortured and murdered during the over-600-year-long Inquisition.

"Thyatira" means "continual sacrifice." This era saw the seemingly ceaseless killing ("continual sacrificing") of multitudes of non-Catholics, along with the indoctrination of sacrificial rites, like fasting (sacrificing food) and celibacy (sacrificing sexual nature).

Thyatirans (corporate religionists) who live and grow in the Spirit (who know not the "depths of satan"; Revelation 2:24) are commended by Jesus. He asks nothing more of them but to "hold fast" to the Spirit (Revelation 2:25). Those who do shall have Salvation (Revelation 2:28).

THE "SARDIS" NATURE

Jesus' Message to the "church in Sardis" is to the Protestant Churches. They are to be watchful, as their works are not "perfect before God" (Revelation 3:2).

Many in Renaissance Europe had grown outraged by the Roman Church, its false religion, and the terrorism of its Crusades and Inquisition. Fearing for their lives, they kept silent, but eventually organized and rebelled in 1517 after Martin Luther's famous protests. The "church of Sardis" is the era of the Protestant Reformation (1517 to the mid-1700's), which gave birth to Churches separate from the Roman Church. So divisive were the Protestants that hundreds of Protestant Churches were created.

Revelation 3:1 states, "thou hast a name that thou livest, and art dead," referring to the Protestant Churches, because they were truer to Jesus' Gospel than the Roman Church ("thou livest"), but failed to remove false religion ("and art dead"). Though the Reformation revived interest and faith in Jesus' Gospel, and though it was less idolatrous than the

Roman Church, it served the Letter of the Law over the Spirit of the Law.

The church era of Sardis is named after the remnant, empty city of Sardis that was ruined by earthquakes and abandoned. The Protestant Churches grew from the remnant believers (referring to those who were managing to survive the infamous Inquisition), and were empty (not full in the Spirit), having kept false religion. The Protestant Churches are warned to be watchful of false religion, and directed to "strengthen the things which remain" (they are to strengthen their faith by eliminating idolatrous, false religion; Revelation 3:2).

Jesus commends the "few" Protestants not defiled in false religion, and finds them worthy of Salvation (Revelation 3:4). Those who overcome false religion shall be "clothed in white raiment" and have the "book of life" (Salvation; Revelation 3:5).

Addressing the churches of Thyatira (the Roman Church) and Sardis (the Protestant Churches), Jesus commends Catholics and Protestants who have not exalted false religion (man-made rituals, superstitions, etc.) over The Way of the Good Spirit. Here, Jesus is revealing that it is not by our religious membership and rituals that we are saved, but by our devotion to His Spirit of Selfless, Good Works. In other words, *have your rituals*, but know that the One Way to God is through devotion to embodying His Good Spirit, no matter your religious dogma.

THE "PHILADELPHIA" NATURE

Born of the Protestant movement, the church era of Philadelphia ('brotherly love') began in the mid-1700's with missionary groups spreading Jesus' Gospel. The blessing of the missionaries was that they sowed Jesus' Gospel in a less idolatrous, more charitable way. The "Philadelphia" church revived the holy purpose of the *alive-but-dead* Sardis church, *the Protestant Churches*.

Philadelphians are missionaries of the Good Spirit, referring to all who devotedly plant His Spirit onto Earth through their Selfless, Good Works. He has set before them Himself, who is the Open Door to Salvation (Revelation 3:8).

The Philadelphian church is of "little strength," referring to its smallness in numbers upon Earth (Revelation 3:8). Like the Smyrnans, Jesus never condemns the Philadelphians, but does warn that there are those who "say they are Jews, and are not" (those who appear as holy "Philadelphians," but whose motivations are selfish; page 55). Philadelphians who "hold fast" (to the Spirit) shall possess the "new name" (Salvation; Revelation 3:12).

THE "LAODICEA" NATURE

The "church of the Laodiceans" (lay-oh-dih-see-ans) is the last and most corrupt of all.

> Only the church era of Laodicea is not commended at all. The Laodicean Church is given over to idolatry through its devotion to man-made superstitions, beliefs, and rituals. Laodiceans confess their love for Christ as Savior, but their outward confession is not wholehearted, having set their priorities upon "worldly gods" (money, power, politics, etc.).
>
> "Laodicea" means "common rights of the people." Its members are spiritually indifferent, having balanced their lives between corporate religion and <u>their</u> demands for <u>their</u> rights to live in a society wherein <u>they</u> can benefit from <u>their</u> worldly pursuits of money, power, and politics. They readily cast judgments and spout selected Biblical quotes to justify <u>their</u> agendas of intolerance, *even damning* those who do not follow <u>their</u> social and spiritual values. Though they shout belief in Christ, they are not aligned with His Spirit. Christ shows us that He stands outside "Laodicean" churches and will not enter, defining them as "Christless" churches.
>
> The Laodiceans are "lukewarm," their indifference so offensive that Jesus rejects them (Revelation 3:16). Lukewarm water is a mixture of hot and cold, but is neither hot nor cold. Indifferent Christians ('Laodiceans') are "lukewarm," being neither very faithful ('hot'), nor given completely over to worldly desires ('cold'). They have a middle-of-the-road faith, an offensive mixture of Spirit and selfishness. When the faithful are raptured, the "Laodiceans" will not be among them, as Christ will reject them ('I will spue thee out of my mouth'; Revelation 3:16).

"Laodiceans" see themselves spiritually "rich" and with "need of nothing," but they are self-deceived, being "blind" (to the Spirit) and "naked" (not "clothed" in the Spirit; Revelation 3:17). Jesus advises them to *open their eyes* and repent (Revelation 3:20). Those who do, overcoming the indifferent, idolatrous religion of the "last church" (the church of the "end times"), shall sit with Him on His Throne (Salvation; Revelation 3:21).

Jesus prophesied the birth, rise, and development of corporate Christianity in His Messages to the seven churches.

The global, institutionalized business of Christ's Gospel has worked much idolatry in its bid for money, power, and control over the masses *through the catechizing and brainwashing of generations upon generations of children in their Spiritless interpretations of Christ's Spiritful Gospel.*

Take a child, *any child*, and teach it that its physical body houses an invisible soul that will live on after its body dies. Fill its childhood with daily religious rituals. Threaten the child with the ultimatum: *Either you comply with this religion and be saved, or you deny this religion and be damned.* Teach the child that evil lives in everything that questions the religion. Twist and bend the child's mind to such religious mindsets, and what do you have? You have one of billions of souls enslaved to fears and superstitions created by and for exclusionary corporate religions.

One-third of the world's Christians will follow the coming anti-Christ (Revelation 12:4), *idolatrously worshiping the anti-Christ*, their minds so colored by idolatrous Christianity that they will not "see" the anti-Christ's deceptions.

It would be fair to say that most of today's Christians, *like most people*, are basically good-hearted, hard-working, peaceful humans, but it seems that many have been unwittingly misled from The Way by "marrying" their souls to corporate, groupist mentalities that embrace idolatry.

Corporate religions protect their businesses by molding children into the next generation of Catholics, Mormons, Baptists, Muslims, etc. From infancy, human minds are subjected to all sorts of selfish programming regarding family, race, religion, sex, sexuality, politics... *you name it*. Though children absorb and naturally reflect such programming, God does not hold them responsible for the selfish programming drilled into their weak, "innocent" mentalities. But as their "innocence" of ignorance dies to knowledge, wisdom, and life's experiences, they shall hopefully come to recognize their learned selfishness and replace it with the Selfless Spirit.

■ ■ ◆ ■ ■

#14 - Hagee, John (May, 2000)

Laodicea, the disgusting church. God says, "because you're not hot or cold, I will spew you out of my mouth." You're disgusting. The Laodicean church is the perfect portrait of the church in America. It's moderate. It takes no bold stands on the tough issues. The Laodicean church admits there is sin, but it never preaches about sin. It is politically correct and spiritually corrupt.

Yes, the Laodicean church *is* the "perfect portrait of the church in America." Though it might be called the "disgusting church," it is better described as the "spiritually indifferent" church. It *does* take bold stands on the tough issues and *does* preach about sin. It is not that Laodiceans are politically correct, but that they are political [so political are the Laodiceans that they have spawned such politically-focused Christian groups as, for example, the Moral Majority and the Christian Coalition (self-described as an "organization dedicated to mobilizing and training Christians for effective political action")].

This ministry correctly teaches that "Laodiceans" are "spiritually corrupt," but does not realize its own Laodicean nature.

■ ■ ◆ ■ ■

#28 - Parsley, Rod (December 27, 1998)

I wanna hear somebody say, "It's my time, it's my time. it's my time. I've waited long enough. I've fasted long enough. I've prayed long enough. I've believed long enough. I've shouted long enough. It's my time.

Selfish Laodiceans: *It's all about me. Me, me, me. What rewards do I get?*

■ ■ ◆ ■ ■

#32 - Paulk, Earl (May 9, 1999)

It's time for politicians to know that the authority on Earth is the Church to start with. It's the Church that has the power of God. It's the Church that has the anointing of God. It's the Church that has the answer today. They will just come by long enough to show their faces, and so we vote for 'em. Then they run off and do their little things. It's time for them to say, "Hey, you elected me, you're the ones who elected me, and I want to come in and be a part of what you're doing in the house of God."

Politics and big-business religion are both massive power-and-money-driven entities fraught with selfishness. Corporate churches are not the Authority on Earth, nor the Power of God, nor the Anointing of God, nor the Answer. *God gives you only One Authority, Power, Anointing, and Answer: the Selfless, Good Mind and Spirit Within you.*

■ ■ ◆ ■ ■

#16 - Huch, Larry (July, 1999)

Folks, listen to this, what the Scripture says, "God gives you the desire of your heart." We've kind of misunderstood this, and it's more powerful than just "God will give you the desires of your heart." It says, as you're serving God, you're born again, you love Jesus, [and] as you begin to desire things, understand that God is the one that put those desires in your heart. Now, why is that important to understand that as I begin to desire? Let's say, let's say you begin to desire to do something for God or you begin to desire to live in a better home or you begin to desire that you drive a nicer car or you begin to desire, this desire starts welling up, that your husband comes to Christ or your children get set free or that you get this new job or that you get this raise that's about to take place. The thing you need to understand is that you're a

Christian, you're born again, you're a child of the living God, and those things that you desire, God has put those desires in your heart. Now, why is that important? The Bible says that we're to come boldly before the Throne of Grace. That word "boldly" means "with confidence and with assurance," that, when we come before that Throne of Grace, that He not only hears our prayers, but He answers those prayers. So, when you come before God, and you're praying for a blessing in your life, you're praying for something very spiritual or something pertaining to this life, you're praying for a new house, a new car, and you're serving God, you can come with confidence and boldness before the Throne of Grace, knowing that it's God that put those desires in your heart.

God doesn't make Christians or anyone desire for worldly rewards (new houses, new cars, etc.). His One Desire, which He does not force upon us, is that we grow devoted to His Spirit, doing so because we love His Spirit. His followers shall be as He, and shall live for Selfless Love and Good Works.

Matthew 6:19-21 (spoken by Jesus; authored by Apostle Matthew)

19. Lay not up for yourselves treasure upon earth, where moth and rust doth corrupt, and where thieves break through and steal:

20. But lay up for yourselves treasures in heaven [here is an instruction to reap of the Good Spirit, accomplished only by sowing to the Good Spirit]**, where neither moth nor rust doth corrupt, and where thieves do not break through nor steal:**

21. For where your treasure is, there will your heart be also.

(moments later)

We say this wherever we go, and it's amazing, because people who watch the program and who have been to our church, they'll repeat it too. We say, "Somebody is gonna win, it might as well be me." Listen to me. Somebody's dream is gonna get answered, somebody's vision is gonna be fulfilled, and it might as well be you.

Evidently, only so much is given by God, so you better act now or it'll go to someone else. *Me, me, me.*

■ ■ ◆ ■ ■

#28 - Parsley, Rod (September 26, 1999)

The time is now, and the place is here. You can let our senators, congressmen, and our president know, make a demand through a Constitutional Amendment, that our legislators put prayer where it belongs, back in our schools.

(26 seconds later)

We're in a spiritual battle, and I'm calling for Christians across this nation to join me in raising a covering, a protective covering of prayer over our children, because it's our turn, now.

(15 minutes, 52 seconds later)

Satan has had dominion in our schools long enough. It's our turn now. My friends, this country was founded on Biblical values, and on the principles of a deep-rooted faith, and it's time to return to them. It's time to get prayer back in our homes, back in our lives, and back in our schools. Today, from Littleton, Colorado, I'm declaring a spiritual war on the war in our schools, and I'm putting into motion a massive counteroffensive against the powers of darkness. The Bible declares, in Isaiah 54:17, that "no weapon formed against them shall prosper." Before there's another "Littleton, Colorado" (referring to the April, 1999 massacre), I'm here to serve notice on the devil that he will not and can not have our kids.

On June 25, 1962, the Supreme Court ruled that it was unconstitutional to pray in school. When we took prayer out of the school, we gave our children over to liberal politicians, godless educators, and an atheistic force from hell.

Would you like to know what has happened to our kids since we took prayer away from them. Since 1962, when prayer was struck down, sexual activity among 15-year-olds has increased almost 1,000 percent. Venereal disease among 10 to 14-year-olds has increased over 400 percent. We're talking about 10-year-old babies. Between 1962 and 1993, the number of violent crimes has increased 669 percent. This is the heritage we've given our children when we took prayer away from them. We gave them a legacy of immorality, of violence, and of fear. We've stripped them of their trust and faith in Almighty God and replaced it with pandemonium and darkness.

Isaiah 54:17, which states that "no weapon that is formed against thee shall prosper," means, *when literally interpreted*, that no weapon can conquer over Christians. Clearly, this is not true, as human weapons can easily kill Christians. *When Spiritually interpreted*, this verse reveals that no anti-Spirit (idolatry; selfishness) shall conquer those devoted to the Spirit. Guns and bombs can kill your body, but they cannot "kill" your Spiritful soul. Only you can do that by loving selfishness over God's Selfless Spirit.

This ministry accuses the removal of prayer in 1964 as being the root of all of the problems in America's school system at present. *Blame, blame, blame*. What about the parents? Prayer or no prayer, don't the parents hold ultimate authority and responsibility for teaching and guiding their children to love and respect others? Regardless of the many laws that governments rule over their citizens, and regardless of the multitude of other external factors (technology, motion pictures, peer groups, etc.), isn't a child's immediate family its greatest nurturer? And what about corporate

Christianity's widespread rejection of Jesus' Selfless Way of the Good Spirit in Christian-dominated America? They teach their Christian masses to honor the Letter of the Law over the Spirit of the Law, then blame everyone else for America's increasingly troubled school system and schoolchildren when, in fact, they are the ones who keep teaching the majority of Americans to honor idolatry (Letter of the Law) over the Spirit! Maybe if Christian parents and children were taught non-separatist, non-fearful, non-superstitious religion that honored only God's Selfless Spirit, this commentary wouldn't exist.

Blaming is of the anti-Spirit, and yet one event, namely the removal of prayer from schools in 1964, is held responsible for selfish, *even violent* children. Look to the parents first.

Could it be that some parents solve problems with their children by throwing loving discipline out the window in favor of bargaining? The lack of attentive, loving discipline breeds insecurity, *naturally*, and certainly does not strengthen bonds of love between children and parents. What about parents who are too self-involved to spend more time raising their child, thrilled to pieces that the kid is glued to computer games and/or television? Though these technological wonders can be excellent learning tools, they can desensitize growing brains to drugs, sex, violence, etc. Such obsessive interests are often isolating. It is not uncommon for troubled children to find solace in isolation. Some seek companionship and a sense of love from their peers. And what if their peers are misguided? Do they sometimes follow their wayward friends? *You bet.*

What about America's schools? Is it not true that one of the cornerstones of America is religious freedom unto all? Our schools are filled with children of every religion from every corner of the globe. Why should non-Christians be forced to pray Christian prayers? Isn't it possible to teach the Spirit of Selfless, Good Works without turning to idolatrous religion?

Laodiceans are blind to the truth that they must change <u>within</u> to change their own "worlds." Until then, they will surely continue to blame others for the worldly conditions that "afflict" them and their children.

Jesus tells us that before His Second Coming, the world will grow more corrupt, and His followers, *particularly*, will suffer greatly. *Knowing this, wouldn't the removal of prayer from schools be something for Christians to rejoice about, being a possible indication that His Second Coming is nearing?* The Good Spirit reveals that the problem is not with taking "God" out of America's schools, but the lack of Spirit in families, churches, schools, and governments.

■ ■ ◆ ■ ■

#18 - Jakes, T. D. (October, 1999)

But I guarantee you that the reason our homes are messed up today is because of television. I guarantee you the stuff you didn't want your children to learn, you didn't want 'em to learn it as teenagers, and they learned it at five and six years old because of television. Television does not build your faith in God. When you get through watching all of the filth and all of the stuff that pours out of that television, you've got to really have something going on for God on the inside of you to keep faith alive. This world system is designed to totally destroy your faith in God.

Ohmygod... now it's television's fault. Are parents not ultimately responsible for leaving their kids unchecked in front of the television for hours on end?

We are told that television is full of "filth" and "does not build your faith in God," and is a "world system" designed to destroy faith in God. If this is so, then aren't televangelists responsible for this destruction in some measure? If television is so evil, *then why do so many preachers use it to their financial advantage?* Christ's Message of the Spirit reveals that there is nothing that can make you accept or reject the Good Spirit but, *ultimately,* yourself.

Like television, the world is filled with Spiritful and Spiritless influences. The "life" you give to any positive or negative influence is ultimately your responsibility. As far as all that "filth" on television, this book proves that much of that "filth" is coming from Christian pulpits.

Why all the fear-mongering about TV? *Because the cult mentality wants to control your mind, to deny your mind any and all knowledge that is not fed into your brain without its holier-than-thou permission.* Television is a most-excellent learning tool, filled with wonderful talk shows, awesome documentaries, joyous comedies, indispensable news, and thought-provoking dramas. There is so much Goodness in the knowledge and wisdom gained through television, yet we are instructed to be ignorant. Why? *Because Knowledge is power, and you might just get smart enough to realize that life is about freedom in the Spirit, not enslavement to idolatrous religion.*

■ ■ ◆ ■ ■

#37 - Schuller, Robert (November 14, 1999)

For the first time in history, it's almost impossible for any group, religious or political, to indoctrinate people. Why? Because almost everybody has access to television, and the opposite viewpoints are going to be proclaimed on television. And now the Internet is coming along. Trash and treasure is at your fingertips.

Not until after the Gutenberg printing press was created in the 1450's did the Bible become available to the masses. For nearly 1,100 years, from the 4th to 15th centuries, the Bible was banned from the general public and written in Latin, a dying language that most Europeans did not speak or read. Why didn't the powerful Roman Church want its members to read the Bible? *Fear.* They feared that the masses would come to learn The Way of God for themselves. The Church's control over its member's lives, children, politics, and pocketbooks was absolutely not to be compromised. The Bible was not to be read by the masses, but spoon-fed only.

Now, almost 1,700 years after the birth of the Roman Church and 500 years after the birth of Protestantism, we learn that "it is impossible for any group, religious or political, to indoctrinate people." Why? *Television.* And yet, this ministry's exceptional wealth would not exist without TV.

Could it be that people are not wanting to join Christian groups *not because of opposite viewpoints given on television,* but because more and more are awakening to the Spirit that makes evident the Spiritlessness of man-made religion?

(45 seconds later)

And in all of these ghettos (not referring to the impoverished neighborhoods of today, but to the ethnic 'territorial' neighborhoods that had dominated city-life) there were religious institutions, and these religious institutions indoctrinated their children from childhood up. And you grew up thinking, "This was it." You had the answers. Your answers were right. If anybody else had a different answer, they were wrong. <u>There's something kind of peaceful about that</u>. <u>Very peaceful</u>. Then came technology, mass media, television.

Here are reflections upon times past, a time when families, *brain-washed for centuries,* carried on their religious torches, judging others with differing beliefs as "wrong." Nevermind the fact that those times saw much division, fighting, and bloodshed. *Yep, those were the good ol' days... "There's something kind of peaceful about that. Very peaceful."*

Here's a solution: Recapture those "good ol' days" by tuning in to the news. Accusing, fighting, and killing over religion has not stopped, and never will, but will only get worse as we spin towards the day of Christ's Second Coming. Why? Because the self-serving, separatist, corporate religions of Judaism, Christianity, and Islam will not, *will not* quit their idolatry and exalt the One thing God wants from them... *Selfless Love and Good Works.*

■ ■ ◆ ■ ■

#21 - Kennedy, D. James (November 28, 1999)

Daniel Webster, one of the greatest statesman America ever produced, was a vocal Christian who memorized whole chapters of Scriptures. Samuel Adams, the father of the American Revolution, an evangelical Christian statesman. George Washington, the father of our country who said that "unless we learn to live as Christ lived, we would not be a happy nation."

Dear friend, these are not the words and actions of secular men or deists. These are the words of undeniable Christians. How is it that we have fallen so far from the ideals of these Godly founders? Today, a judge's ruling is overturned if he dares to quote one verse of Scripture. A child is told she cannot bring her Bible to school or pray at graduation. It's a complete reversal of everything our founders taught. They believed the Christian faith was absolutely essential to a free society. Yet, today, very few people know this vital information or understand the true identity of the nation given to us by our godly forefathers. That's why if we are to call America back to godliness, we must get this information out. I'm determined to do just that, at least all that I can do to bring that all about, but I truly need your help and support. Would you take a moment today to write or call with a generous gift?

If the forefathers "believed that Christian faith was absolutely essential to a free society," then they would have written a "Christians only" policy, requiring all citizens and immigrants to be Christians. *Who was it that wrote, "All men are created equal?"*

Stating that Samuel Adams was "the father of the American Revolution" and an evangelical Christian statesman serves to link this "evangelical Christian" with heroism. There is no doubt that Adams was an American hero. But God's truest "evangelists" live to personify Selfless Love, *Christian or not.* Maybe Adams was following his Good Spirit, maybe not. Nevertheless, when did Jesus involve Himself in war and killing? Didn't He tell us not to fear the death of our bodies, but the death of our souls?

Matthew 10:28 (spoken by Jesus; authored by Apostle Matthew)

28. And fear not them which kill the body, but are not able to kill the soul: but rather fear him [satan (anti-Spirit; selfishness; idolatry)] **which is able to destroy both soul and body in hell.**

If our nation's forefathers were such "Godly" Christians, then why did so many of them own slaves? Why did this enslavement continue for so long thereafter? Why were countless American natives mercilessly slaughtered?

George Washington had it right: "Unless we learn to live as Christ lived, we will not be a happy nation." And how did Christ live? In Selfless, Good Works. *"Faithful and True" is His name* (Revelation 19:11).

This ministry blames America's troubles upon the Bible's removal from public schools, calling it a "reversal of everything our founding fathers taught." *But didn't our founding fathers want freedom for all?* Presently, with so many schoolchildren of so many different nationalities and religions, imposing Christianity upon them would be contrary to America's "Freedom of Religion." Can't schools teach about the Good Spirit *without involving idolatrous religion?*

And what about the girl who can't bring her Bible to school or say a prayer at graduation? *Boohoo.* Why doesn't she know that God lives Within? Why can't she show herself an expression of His Spirit without man-made religiosity? If she is given the legal right to bring her idolatrous religion into school, what's to stop all religious books and prayers from entering in? And what about the religious rights of Witches and Satanists? Where does it end?

Why must Christian families fear the lack of religion in public schools? If these families are strong in the Spirit, then why fear? Simple solution: Take your kids out of public school and pay for private Christian schooling. Either that, or start teaching your children how to walk The Way in this world of sins, joys, sufferings, life, and death. You cannot protect your children from worldly selfishness completely, but you can teach them how to recognize and overcome it. Greatest stability lives in families who openly, respectfully, compassionately communicate about the sensitive issues of life without fear.

Shouldn't public school, to be most effective, be as much of a "level playing field" as possible? What is the one thing about school that parents agree on? Education. The Oneness agreement about school is Good: *Education.* Wouldn't it be logical to eliminate factors that separate children, distracting them from education? Maybe tattered togs and designer clothes should be replaced with uniforms? Maybe kids do not need multi-colored, freakish haircuts? Maybe kids don't need jewelry and make-up in public schools? Don't kids have easily-distracted minds that are easily tempted by social selfishness? Why not keep school as directly simple as possible for highly-impressionable, young minds, that they might best receive a stable, *reasonably painless,* good education?

The nature of America's schools, *by the insistence of selfish parents, lawyers, politicians, and voters,* has become quite the social institution. By legislating certain social rights for their children *in the name of freedom,* today's schools have little to no uniformity, and have grown into operations where a good education often takes a back seat. God forbid a parent's child is not allowed to express its "self" with raggedy jeans, pink hair, black lipstick, heavy cologne, propagandist Tee-shirts, colored scarves, nose rings, tongue-buttons, eyebrow piercings, stiletto heels, mini-skirts, midriffs, pants hanging down to the crotch, etc. Such freedoms of adult social appearance heaped upon the minds and lives of children seriously tempts greater selfishness. Children just do not have the mental sharpness it takes to seriously consider tattoos, ear piercings, mini-skirts or any other adult selfishness.

Childhood must be a time of uniformity in the Spirit so as to best produce Spiritful results. Children can be fine-tuned to the Spirit by not allowing them to "eat" of adult selfishness. Show them, *by your example,* devotion to Selfless, Good Works. When they wonder about certain issues of adult selfishness, as they will, don't patronize them or give them some half-ass answer. Speak to them appropriately at their lesser-developed "brain speed" and tell them the Truth. You are talking to an individual mind that needs your Selfless Love and guidance in Truth. Why lie? Children not disciplined in Selfless Love naturally grow in fears, like self-worthlessness, cowardice, internalized anger, vengeance, destructivity, intolerance, separation, isolation, etc. *The Truth will make you free.*

School is not the time and place for social division through personal social statements, but is the time and place for a uniform, disciplined environment to best serve a good education. How these children dress and act outside of school is the responsibility of their parents but, in school, the business at hand is a good education. If parent's truly care about having their children receive the best education as possible, then they must no longer care about insisting their children have adult freedoms in school.

Parents should want to give their full support to their schools by seeing to it that teachers are paid well, and by seeing to it that their children know to show their teachers and classmates kindness and respect. Why should unkempt, unruly, and undisciplined children be tolerated, for such are selfish children raised by selfish parents. *Needless to say, selfish parents, upon hearing this, will reject it and continue in their love for blaming everybody and everything else, blaming the Supreme Court, television, satan, rap music, and never accepting that they themselves are ultimately to blame.*

It is not the absence of Jesus or God or the Ten Commandments in our schools, but the absence of the Spirit of Jesus and God and the Ten Commandments.

■ ■ ◆ ■ ■

#5 - Paul Crouch and **#15 - Hill, E. V.** and **#30 - Paul, K. A.** (on *Praise The Lord;* December 19, 1999)

Paul Crouch (*speaking to K. A. Paul*)*:* Let me tell you what got my curiosity. Pastor Hill whispered in my ear before the program and said, "You may have a door opening for Christian television" (referring to an opportunity for Mr. Crouch's television network, TBN, to be aired in Asia).

K. A. Paul (a Minister from India, now residing in Texas): Absolutely. As a matter of fact, right now I am on Christian television every week (in India), preaching only Christ crucified, every Saturday from 4:00 to 4:30, every Saturday, this has been the third week...

Paul Crouch (interrupting): Does this go nationwide?

K. A. Paul: All over India, plus 21 other countries right now. See, that's the reason why I flew in to talk to you, Paul. I talked to you two years ago right here when Oral Roberts was on the program the same day he had heart surgery, or heart problems. I came to walk out to you. Really, couldn't walk out. Somehow I had to just jump on, and came to talk to you, and we prayed, and I kept on sending letters, and...

Paul Crouch (interrupting): But can we build TV stations in India?

K. A. Paul: Absolutely. The speaker of the house (in India) who got saved in my meetings, the head of 545 senators, he promised me three months ago when he was sick, I was there, and he said, "In three more months we'll have a privilege to open up this whole country." That could reach China, 1.2 billion. India, a billion. 200 million, Indonesia. Pakistan and Bangladesh, 225 million. Nepal, 25 million. We're doing crusade conferences in these places. We could build the station, we already have the land, 1,500 acres of the land.

Paul Crouch: But it would have to be on a satellite to cover that much territory.

K. A. Paul: Absolutely. Absolutely. But see, those six countries have half of the world's population, Paul.

Paul Crouch: Yes, I know. I know.

K. A. Paul: Just six of them. 2.8 billion.

E. V. Hill: <u>Half of the lost people of the world are in these little countries</u>. Over two-point-some-billion people, and a billion-and-a-half of those have never heard the name "Jesus."

This ministry definitely wants to expand ("But can we build TV stations?"). But why is the Asian market of such interest? *To teach Jesus' Message of the Spirit or to enslave more souls to false religion for immense financial profit?*

Here, we are taught that the "two-point-some-billion" Asian non-Christians are "the lost people of the world":

Yep... aaaaalllllll going to hell.

All going to hell because they've not been "born again" in an unsanctified, self-serving, money-hungry, globally-titanic, man-made, soul-less, religious "system" that absolutely refuses to teach that the One and Only Way to Salvation is by Glorifying the Good Spirit Within. The Spirit transcends race, sex, sexuality, religion, politics, and all worldly things because It does not care about such things. All the Good Spirit cares about is your devotion to the Good Spirit, as that is The Way by which your soul grows bonded with God. *That's it!*

All of your sins and blasphemies, *even if you speak against Jesus,* will be forgiven if you do not deny the Good Spirit (Matthew 12:31-33). In other words, Heaven waits for those who stay true to their Good Conscience as they grow through life's lessons. All are growing at different levels, and the best any of us can do for others, *ultimately,* is show them our Good Spirit through example, the best we know. What more can God want from us? *Nothing.* Per His Great Commandment, all He wants is our devotion to His Good Spirit. *That's it.* If the great Bible-based religions of Judaism, Christianity, and Islam were ever to exemplify and teach the Good Spirit as being the Way, the Truth, and the Life, they would stop all their "sanctified" separatism, hatred, idolatry, violence, and killing, *naturally.*

Chapter 6

REVELATION

First Thessalonians 5:14-22 (authored by Apostle Paul)

14. Now we exhort you, brethren, warn them that are unruly, comfort the feebleminded, support the weak, be patient toward all men.
15. See that none render evil for evil unto any man; but ever follow that which is good, both among yourselves, and to all men.
16. Rejoice evermore.
17. Pray without ceasing.
18. In every thing give thanks: for this is the will of God in Christ Jesus concerning you.
19. Quench not the Spirit.
20. Despise not prophesyings.
21. Prove all things; hold fast that which is good.
22. Abstain from all appearance of evil.

"Despise not prophesyings," and yet the phenomenal prophecies of Edgar Cayce (the world-famous, most-studied clairvoyant in history) are generally rejected by corporate Christianity which, *by the way*, has no problem referring to its own as: anointed; saints; prophets; angels; guardians of your soul; and mediums of God (all of these descriptions taken from Chapter 2).

Born in Hopkinsville, Kentucky on March 18th, 1877, Edgar Cayce was a quiet, gentlemanly, Sunday school teacher and photographer who left a legacy of over 14,000 clairvoyant "readings," the most ever recorded, all of which were spoken during an unconscious, trancelike state, during which his body did not register feeling [Cayce once agreed to be examined by doctors while unconscious, but they jabbed him with needles and tore off a fingernail, the pain felt only after awakening; Cayce never allowed any such examination again]. Only after regaining consciousness would he learn of the questions asked of him and of the answers given. Cayce died on January 3rd, 1945.

"Prove all things" was the driving force behind my five-year creation, *Revelation Earth*, a unique and thorough examination of the Bible's last and most feared book, the Book of Revelation. The work decodes all

404 verses of the Book of Revelation individually, providing two perfectly parallel interpretations: the "General Interpretation," about the end times, the Tribulation Period, Third World War, the anti-Christ, the Rapture, the Second Coming, Heaven, hell, etc.; and the "Spirit Interpretation," *based upon Cayce's extraordinary prophecies*, unveiling the detailed story of the workings of the evolutionary nature of the human soul. [Note: *Revelation Earth* is being restructured for re-release.]

"Pray without ceasing" does not mean to lock yourself away in ritualistic prayer for a lifetime, but about keeping the Good Spirit at the forefront of your consciousness in everything you think, say, and do.

■ ■ ◆ ■ ■

#14 - Hagee, John (August 22, 1999)

The dispensation of grace will end with something called the Rapture, in which the Church is taken out of the world. For those of you who are teaching there will not be a Rapture, you are simply teaching something the word of God does not say. You may wish that it doesn't happen but, I assure you on the authority of God, it's going to happen. We're going to the marriage supper of the Lamb to receive crowns of light, robes of glory. We're going to sit around with the Son of the Living God and have the communion. After seven years, we're coming back to Earth, in which the anti-Christ is going to rule.

Here, we see the all-too-common misconception that the Rapture (the sudden removal of all of God's true and faithful followers from Earth, body and soul) is going to happen on the first day of the seven-year Tribulation Period ("after seven years, we're coming back to Earth"). This theory is called the "Pre-Tribulation Rapture." But the Bible reveals that the Rapture occurs on the last day of the Tribulation Period, one-hour before Christ's Second Coming, proven in the following excerpt from *Revelation Earth*.

> The many interpretations of the Book of Revelation comment upon the same basic story involving the end times, the Tribulation Period, the Third World War, the anti-Christ, the translation of the believers, the Second Coming of Christ, the Millennial Kingdom, and the New Kingdom.
>
> There will always be arguments over interpretation, but the Rapture (the "translation" of the believers) is among the most argued. The Rapture is when the world's true and faithful believers are suddenly, miraculously lifted into Heaven, rescued from the "Great Tribulation" that begins immediately thereafter.
>
> The rescue of the believers by way of the Rapture is compared with the rescue stories of Noah and Lot. Just as Noah and his group of believers were lifted from the Earth (in an ark) and saved from the flood,

and just as Lot and his group were Divinely guided out of Sodom just before its destruction, so too will the end-time believers be saved from the Great Tribulation.

The Rapture will occur at the onset of the Great Tribulation, but which "Great Tribulation?" Some define it as the seven-year Tribulation Period. Incorrect. The Great Tribulation is the climactic, last hour of the Tribulation Period, *called the "Fall of Babylon,"* which directly precedes the Second Coming of Christ.

Was Noah's group lifted from danger seven years before the Great Tribulation (the flood) that drowned God's enemies? Did Lot's group leave Sodom seven years before the Great Tribulation (the fire and brimstone) that obliterated this city of unbelievers? No. Both groups were saved just before the destruction began. So shall God's end-time followers be raptured just before the Great Tribulation on the last day of the seven-year Tribulation Period.

In Matthew 24:5-9, Jesus tells us that there will come a time when the world will suffer wars, famines, pestilences, and earthquakes, during which His followers will be hated and killed. In Matthew 24:29, He calls this period the "tribulation of those days," referring to the Tribulation Period. But if His followers are raptured <u>before</u> the Tribulation Period, *then why does He reveal that they will suffer the Tribulation Period, being hated and killed?*

After describing the "tribulation of those days" (Matthew 24:10-20), Jesus remarks, "...then shall be great tribulation" (Matthew 24:21), referring to the day of His Second Coming on the last day of the Tribulation Period [the Great Tribulation begins with the Rapture (the Salvation of the "elect"; Matthew 24:22) and ends with His Second Coming].

Furthermore, Matthew 24:37-44 tells us that on the day Noah and his followers entered the ark, the flood came and they were saved, *as it shall be with the coming of the Son of man*, indicating that the Rapture will occur on the <u>day</u> of Jesus' return.

In the parable of Matthew 20:1-16, Jesus reveals that Salvation is His to give when He tells us that the householder (symbolic of Himself) can give unto those chosen at the "eleventh hour." Those chosen at the "eleventh hour" refers to the raptured souls, or those who join Christ one-hour before ("eleventh hour") His Second Coming [the Rapture happens one-hour before the Second Coming of Christ, during which the Great Tribulation, *or Fall of Babylon*, brings worldwide destructions upon the unsaved (Revelation 18:17)].

■ ■ ◆ ■ ■

#28 - Parsley, Rod (October 10, 1999)

As the year 2000 and the new millennium approaches, my spirit is stirred up because I believe we're in the final moments of human drama. Soon, and very soon the Trumpet of God is going to sound and Jesus Christ is going to triumphantly return to this Earth for his bride. But just before the great "gettin' up" morning, like Israel as they set out for the Promised Land, I believe the New Testament bears out the fact that God is about to restore all the devil has stolen. Acts, Chapter 3, declares, "And He shall send Jesus Christ, which before was preached unto you: Whom the heaven must receive until," listen now, "the times of restitution of all things" (quoting Acts 3:20-21). What the word of God is clearly saying is that restitution, or restoration, precedes the return of Jesus Christ, and since, spiritually, we know Jesus is coming soon, how much closer the restoration of all things must be. My friend, we are about to see the supernatural blessings of God poured out upon His Church without measure. What a glorious thing to see your health restored, your finances restored, your freedom restored, and every form of demonic attack destroyed through the anointing.

Every generation since Jesus' death has found signs pointing towards His "imminent" Second Coming. His Second Coming will happen at the end of the seven-year Tribulation Period, a time span that begins with the signing of a treaty binding Israel and nine other groups together in peace, *an event yet to happen.*

Here, we are taught that Acts 3:19-21 means that the health, finances, and freedoms of Christians will be restored prior to Christ's Second Coming. Incorrect. On the contrary, followers of The Way, *Christian or not,* shall know greater suffering as His Second Coming approaches (Matthew 24:5-9). In Acts 3:19-21, *when Apostle Peter instructs non-followers to repent and follow The Way, so that their sins be forgiven in the "times of refreshing" and the "times of restitution of all things,"* he is referring to the "times" of Christ's Second Coming and His Millennial Kingdom (His Second Coming initiates His thousand-year reign upon Earth, a period for the Redemption of unsaved souls).

(17 minutes, 24 seconds later)

On May 15, 1945, that white flag with the blue Star of David was recognized on the floor of the United Nations, and God in Heaven let his judgment gavel come down, and His clock began to wind down, and He said "This is the generation that will see the coming of the great and terrible day of the Lord."

Israel's Statehood happened in 1948. The generation who witnessed this event is getting old and dying out. Earlier in this sermon, *in a portion I did not transcribe,* Matthew 24:32-33 was cited to prove that Israel's Statehood means that His Second Coming is near. Incorrect, as follows.

Matthew 24:32-33 (spoken by Jesus; authored by Apostle Matthew)
32. **Now learn a parable of the fig tree; When his branch is yet tender, and putting forth leaves, ye know that summer is nigh:** [The "fig tree" symbolizes Israel, and its "putting forth leaves" refers to its rebirth.]
33. **So likewise ye, when ye shall see all these things, know that it is near** [referring to the Second Coming], **even at the doors.**

The "fig tree" that "putteth forth leaves" does refer to the rebirth of Israel, but not to its becoming a geopolitical nation. The rebirth of Israel refers to its inevitable Spiritual rebirth, its Jews suddenly awakened to the Spirit of the Law. The mass conversion of Israel's Jews will occur sometime shortly after the midpoint of the seven-year Tribulation Period.

The Tribulation Period begins with the binding of ten nations in "peace." The man most credited for this alliance shall be lauded and much-beloved worldwide, especially among the citizens of the ten "peaceful" nations. He shall have unrivaled power and influence over their ten leaders. They do not *see* that he is double-minded. He appears, *outwardly*, as good, righteous, and peaceful, but is, *inwardly*, motivated by the mega-selfish desire to control the world his "Utopian" way.

Shortly after the "peaceful" alliance is created, he shall convince its ten leaders to cut off all economic ties with several neighboring nations, nations heavily dependent upon these economic relations. This pivotal act shows the world that the "alliance of peace" among the ten nations applies only to itself. The economic stranglehold upon the cut-off nations shall cause them to ally and wage war, triggering the Third World War. But the ten nations, *prepared*, shall fight back with unthinkable violence, causing unprecedented destruction and death in this greatest-of-all-wars that dominates the first quarter (twenty-one months) of the Tribulation Period (Revelation 6:1-8; 13:1-7).

Halfway through the Tribulation Period, the man most responsible for creating the alliance will rise as King over the ten nations, requiring from all citizens their lifelong allegiance to him by accepting *a form of registration* that the Bible calls the "mark of the beast" (Revelation 13:16-18, 16:2, 19:20). It will probably not be a "666" branded upon their hands and heads, *as Bible literalists will have you believe*. Regardless, the "666" is most-certainly the mark branded upon the "heads" (thoughts) and "hands" (works) of those separated ("6" symbolizes separation; pages viii-ix) from the Good Spirit in body (6), mind (6), and soul (6).

However the binding allegiance of "666" is effected, Israel's Letter-of-the-Law Jews will know that their new King is the anti-Christ and that the Book of Revelation is true and being fulfilled. These "awakened" Israelites shall speak against the King and be labeled traitors. The King's armies will be sent to capture them, but they will flee into the "wilderness" (probably into the Sinai, the same "wilderness" where Moses led the newly-saved Jews after their exodus from Egypt; Revelation 12:6, 14-16).

(19 seconds later)

You're (referring to the Christian audience) God's last great hope, and the great thing is: He saved the best for last.

Christians are "God's last great hope" and the "best" under God in history ("He saved the best for last"). *No.* God's "best" are those devoted to His Spirit, *Christian or not.*

(25 seconds later)

Your Bible says it (Christ's Second Coming) will not happen until the Jews are gathered together back into their homeland. Even in nineteen-hundred-and-forty-eight that hadn't happened. There was still a divided Jerusalem. Jerusalem was still being trodden under foot by the Gentiles. Jesus said that Jerusalem will be trodden under foot by the Gentiles, Luke 21, until the time, until the fullness of the Gentiles has come. The fullness of the Gentiles symbolizes the last Gentile generation that will exist on this planet before God takes the Church in the Rapture and begins seven years of determined healing with the nation of Israel.

No, Christ's Second Coming is not contingent upon the world's Jews returning to Israel. Jerusalem will be overrun by unbelievers in the last-half of the Tribulation Period (Revelation 11:2).

The "fulness of the Gentiles" (the maximum corruption of the unbelievers) is an event that occurs on the last day of the Tribulation Period. The very moment when the "fulness of the Gentiles" has been reached, the Rapture occurs, which begins the one-hour Fall of Babylon (the Great Tribulation), followed by Christ's Second Coming, followed by the short-lived battle at Armageddon.

(8 minutes, 10 seconds later)

Listen to me. Here's what Zachariah said. He said there's gonna be a hundred-million of 'em, and in one-millionth of a second their eyes are going to disappear and vaporize in their sockets (referring to the destruction of Satan's armies at Armageddon). Their tongues are going to vaporize and weld to their skulls. Their flesh is going to consume off their bodies before they can fall to the ground. Now, let me ask you a question? Does that happen when you stick a man with a bayonet? Does it happen when you shoot him with a machine gun? Does it happen when he gets hit with a bomb full of shrapnel? No, no, no.

(19 seconds later)

What on Earth, in one-millionth of a second, can vaporize a hundred-million men? I can tell you what. You might want to ask the residents of

Hiroshima, if you could find any, or Nagasaki, if you could find any. An atom bomb, which is about one-million times weaker than a hydrogen bomb, which we have now in our arsenals. An atomic bomb produces Fahrenheit degrees of 150 million degrees in one-millionth of a second. Now, let me ask you, did Paul (Apostle Paul) have a weapon like that? Was it possible? No, but today it's possible.

Satan's armies at Armageddon will be killed by Christ's Spoken Word, after which their flesh shall be consumed by "birds of the air" (Revelation 19:15-21). Human weapons will play no part in the mass elimination of satan and his worshipers. *What does God need with hydrogen bombs?*

Those of satan's followers not destroyed during the Fall of Babylon and not present at Armageddon shall be targeted for death by great hailstones, each weighing a talent (82-95 pounds; Revelation 16:21). In Israel, the melting hail will mix with fields of blood, creating a river of blood-water that will rise to the height of horses' bridles and flow over 200 miles within the Holy Land (Revelation 14:20), and the corrupt Holy Land shall be cleansed by the Spirit, the blood, and the water (First John 5:6-8).

■ ■ ◆ ■ ■

#14 - Hagee, John (May, 2000)

And then He (Christ) says four things very quickly, four compliments to the church of Philadelphia. "You have little strength." That almost sounds like an insult. "You have little strength." But in the mind of God, God's not looking for great strength or great ability, He's looking for great dependability. Samson had great ability, but poor dependability. Many of you have the idea, "Oh, I'm so wonderful, God is so lucky to have such a magnificent person in the kingdom. How great I am. How great I am." And God looks from Heaven and goes (this sentence ends here with the following visual aid: the pastor puts his forefinger into his mouth, as if he is trying to induce vomiting). You see, He can't use you.

The "church in Philadelphia" (Revelation 3:7-13) is the sixth of the seven church eras of Christianity prophesied by Christ in the Book of Revelation. Philadelphians represent those who tread The Way, sowing the Good Spirit, not idolatry. They are not the "church of little strength" due to issues of dependability, but because the number of Philadelphians are few upon this planet full of false religionists (Chapter 5).

(21 seconds later)

So don't come to God with your great ability, come to Him with complete dependability. God says, "You have kept my word, you have not denied my name, you have kept the word of my patience." And then He said [regarding] the reward of the righteous, "I shall also keep you from the hour of temptation which shall come upon all of the world to try them that dwell upon the Earth." What is the "hour of temptation" that shall come upon all the Earth? He's talking about the Great Tribulation. He's talking about the seven seals. He's talking about the seven trumpets. He's talking about the seven bowls. He's talking about when He turns the anti-Christ loose on the Earth to bathe this world in blood. He's talking about the four horsemen of the apocalypse. He's talking about when the sun refuses to shine and every man, his body is filled with festering sores, and the great and the mighty men crawl in the caves, and they beg Almighty God to take their life, but He refuses to. He's talking about this literal hell on Earth called the Tribulation Period of time. There are some people teaching in America right now that the Church is going to go through this tribulation. Read my lips: No way. It's not going to happen, and here's why: In the 4th chapter of the Book of Revelation, John says, "Come up higher," and the next time you hear of the Church is when we're coming back right here, in the 19th chapter of the Book of Revelation, but not only in this chapter (here, the 4th chapter of Revelation is cited as "proof" of the Pre-Tribulation Rapture). In Acts 1:11, and listen to this, the angel says, "Ye men of Galilee, why stand ye hear gazing into Heaven, this same Jesus shall come in like manner." What does that mean? He shall come literally, He shall come physically, He shall come visibly as ye have seen Him go. I have had people in the last thirty days ask me, "Are we literally going up in the air?" Yes. Literally. In a moment. In the twinkling of an eye. Shazaam. We're out of here, in Jesus name. And let me give you another verse, in First Thessalonians 4:16, "for the Lord Himself shall descend from Heaven with a shout, descend from Heaven with a shout, and with the voice of the archangel and with the trump of God, and the dead shall rise first, and then we which are alive and remain shall be caught up together with Him in the clouds of glory to meet the Lord in the air, and so shall we ever be with the Lord." It happens right here, and it can happen before I finish preaching this sermon. Jesus Christ, the Prince of Glory, is getting ready to come to Earth. Are you ready, in Jesus name?

Revelation 4:1 does not prove the Pre-Tribulation Rapture, *that the Rapture happens before the onset of the Tribulation Period,* but is an invitation to Apostle John (writer of the Book of Revelation; Revelation 19:10) to be led to witness the nature of Heaven, *the nature of which mirrors the Heaven Within himself.* John is invited to "Come up hither" (not "Come up higher"), which does not signal the Rapture, as it is directed to John and *no one else.* Later on in Revelation, the Rapture is announced by these phrases: "they heard a great voice from heaven saying unto them, Come up hither" (Revelation 11:12); and "Come out of her, my people" (Revelation 18:4).

Acts 1:11 also does not prove the Pre-Tribulation Rapture, but reveals that Jesus will return to Earth in like manner as to how He left. He left with a cloud ("and a cloud received Him out of their sight," Acts 1:9), and will return in like manner ("He cometh with clouds," Revelation 1:7).

This preacher defines the Great Tribulation as being both the Hour of Temptation and the seven-year Tribulation Period. Incorrect. Only the Hour of Temptation is the "Great Tribulation" that happens in the span of one hour on the last day of the seven-year Tribulation Period upon the "fulness of the Gentiles" (which is the coming, inevitable point in our Universe when the anti-Spirit has reached its maximum "life," when every possible characteristic of evil has known "life" on Earth). These events mark the endpoint of evil's growth in the Universe and the beginning-point of the coming of the Eternal New Kingdom.

When evil is fully defined ("fullness of the Gentiles"), then Good is fully defined, *naturally*, which is the moment when the Rapture (the Salvation of the Good) will occur. Here is the beginning of the end of evil. What follows is an hour of global destructions that start the process of cleansing Earth of satan's followers (those devoted to selfishness). The hour ends with Christ's Second Coming, followed by Armageddon (the elimination of satan, the anti-Christ and the rest of their devoted followers), followed by Christ's Millennial Kingdom (the thousand-year opportunity for unsaved-but-redeemable souls to find Redemption), followed by Judgment Day (the eternal removal of all evil from the Universe), followed by the Eternal New Universe (the "New Jerusalem," inhabited by all who are One with God's Spirit).

Let's now examine Revelation 3:10, First Thessalonians 4:16, and First Corinthians 15:51-52. These Biblical verses, excerpted from *Revelation Earth*, clarify issues surrounding the Hour of Temptation and the Rapture.

Revelation 3:10 (spoken by Jesus; authored by Apostle John)

10. Because thou hast kept the word of my patience, I also will keep thee from the hour of temptation, which shall come upon all the world, to try them that dwell upon the earth. [Those true and faithful to The Way of the Spirit shall not suffer the Hour of Temptation (Great Tribulation) that shall come upon the rest of the world's population (all of whom are less than true and faithful to The Way).]

Only the true and faithful (those who "keep the word of my patience") shall be raptured unto Jesus' Presence, kept from the climactic, hour-long, Great Tribulation, during which the remaining souls (the unsaved souls) are given the opportunity to repent and embrace the Spirit.

Because the Hour of Temptation begins with the Rapture, all the souls remaining on Earth are divided into two groups: the unsaved believers, or those who were not true and faithful enough to The Way to have been raptured; and the unsaved unbelievers, or those who were not irreversibly devoted to the anti-Spirit, *or unregenerately selfish.*

The unsaved believers and unsaved unbelievers shall suffer the Hour of Temptation, which serves to "weed out" the unrepentant. Those who repent and choose the Spirit shall be afforded further opportunities for Redemption during Christ's Millennial Kingdom. The rest shall come to know the "second death," *or eternal separation from God*, which will be effected on Judgment Day.

First Corinthians 15:51-52 (authored by Apostle Paul)

51. **Behold, I shew you a mystery; We shall not all sleep, but we shall all be changed.** [Here, it is revealed that those who are true and faithful to The Way shall not all die, but shall be Raptured.]
52. **In a moment, in the twinkling of an eye, at the last trump: for the trumpet shall sound, and the dead shall be raised incorruptible, and we shall be changed.** [Some scholars define the "last trump" as the trumpet in Revelation 4:1, claiming that this proves the Pre-Tribulation Rapture theory. They are incorrect, because the "last trump" is the trumpet sounded on the last day of the seven-year Tribulation Period, signifying the Rapture. When this Trumpet of God sounds, the "dead in Christ," *referring to the dead believers* (the true and faithful souls in the realm of death; First Thessalonians 4:16), will be raptured first, followed by "we," the true and faithful believers upon Earth, *the entire process taking but a moment*.]

First Thessalonians 4:16-17 (authored by Apostle Paul)

16. **For the Lord himself shall descend from heaven with a shout, with the voice of the archangel, and with the trump of God: and the dead in Christ shall rise first:** [Christ's descent into the clouds above Earth is announced with the "trump of God" (this is the 'last trump' in First Corinthians 15:52; Christ is in the clouds to receive the raptured souls, where all shall witness the one-hour 'Fall of Babylon'). The Trump of God initiates the Rapture, and the "dead in Christ shall rise first" (the true and faithful souls in the realm of death shall be raptured first).]
17. **Then we which are alive and remain shall be caught up together with them in the clouds, to meet the Lord in the air: and so shall we ever be with the Lord.** [Then the true and faithful upon Earth shall be raptured, joining the "dead in Christ" in the clouds to meet with Christ in the air (Revelation 1:7; Revelation 18:4): and the raptured shall know Salvation.]

(7 minutes, 24 seconds later)

You're going to bow before Jesus Christ right now or you're going to bow before Him on the Day of Judgment. But I assure you, you're going to bow before the Son of God. If you bow today, He can cleanse you of all of your sin, and you can step into Heaven. But if you don't today, this is your future home right here (pointing to a graphics-board depicting Heaven and hell), the lake of fire (hell). You know the difference between here (pointing to Heaven) and there (pointing to hell)? One prayer. One prayer. And some of you are gonna pray it right now.

We are invited to either bow down before Christ today or bow before Him on Judgment Day. And what if you don't bow today? *You go to hell.* And what is the difference between Heaven and hell: "one prayer." *When will Christianity dump its idolatrous teachings and teach The Way of the Spirit?*

■ ■ ◆ ■ ■

#14 - Hagee, John (October 24, 1999)

Do you want to know the most earthshaking thing that's <u>just about to happen</u>, that will totally restructure society and all of the Earth? It's simply this, in the moment, in the twinkling of an eye, the trump of God is going to sound and the dead in Christ shall rise, and we which are alive and remain shall be caught up to be with the Lord in the air, and so shall we ever be with Him. We're getting ready for the meeting in the air. We're going to a city where roses never fade (referring to the Eternal City, the New Jerusalem). We're going to a city where Abraham, Isaac, and Jacob are, where Jesus Christ, the Living Word, is. Hallelujah for the word of God.

More Rapture r-r-r-rapping. The Rapture is not "just about to happen," but when it does happen, a thousand years must follow before Christ and His raptured souls enter into the Holy City, the New Jerusalem (Revelation 20:2-5, 21:2).

■ ■ ◆ ■ ■

#28 - Parsley, Rod (December 26, 1999)

The necessity of the Church being removed (raptured) is because the anti-Christ is birthed from the prince of darkness. He can't even get birthed into the world scene until the Light of the world, which Jesus Christ of Nazareth happens to call "the Church of Jesus Christ," is taken out of the way, making way for darkness to ensue.

The great, global system of corporate Christianity is not "the Church of Jesus Christ." His Church is the Spirit Within, and its members are those devoted to Glorifying His Good Spirit.

Here, the Pre-Tribulation Rapture is taught when we are told that Christians ("Light") must be raptured *before* the Tribulation Period in order for "darkness to ensue," or for the anti-Christ ("prince of darkness") to appear. Incorrect, otherwise it would have been necessary for darkness to have been removed before Jesus (Prince of Light) could have appeared on Earth, *which was not the case.*

There is no Pre-Tribulation Rapture. The Rapture happens on the last day of the Tribulation Period.

(17 minutes, 52 seconds later)

How can you recognize them (false teachers)? They walk after their own lusts. They have no self-control. They live and speak as they wish. They follow their own carnal affection and heart's desire. I was gonna preach all these, but I'll just give 'em to you. They will not allow that any revelation of God, even through His word, should dictate to them what they should believe. They shall try to unsettle the believers. Do you know that your Bible said God will shorten the last days, because if He did not shorten them, even the very elect of God would be deceived by these scoffers, these ones. These ones, they deny His promise. This they do because they wish He would not come, because they love darkness rather than Light, because their deeds are evil.

Firstly, I totally agree that false teachers "walk after their own lusts," lusts for such as money, power, control, and status. How many of the preachers excerpted in this book are powerful, high-profile merchants who operate businesses of sizable, *even immense* wealth, over which there is substantial, *even absolute* control?

Secondly, I disagree that false teachers have "no self-control." Surely they lack self-control in some areas and have great self-control in other areas. Some have the self-control to deliver their idolatrous interpretations of Jesus' Gospel with gentility, but many more, *less gentle*, reveal their Spiritlessness through sermons filled with judging, demanding and

INTENSE SCREAMING.

Thirdly, we are told that false teachers "follow their own carnal affection and heart's desires." *We only know about those whose sexual tastes have been publicized, some involved with adultery, prostitutes, and pedophilia.* Surely many, many more are wrestling with sexual lusts. Don't we all follow our own "carnal affection and heart's desires" to some degree? Isn't it possible that many who struggle with these things manage to remain true to their Good Conscience. *You bet.* The Spirit reveals that false teachers are those whose teachings deny the Spirit, propagating separatism, fears, superstitions, and all manner of idolatrous religion.

Lastly, false teachers will "not allow for any revelation of God, even through His word, to dictate to them what they should believe," meaning that false teachers believe what they want, regardless of the Bible. *So what about all the Bible-thumpers who interpret Scriptures to support the selfish agendas of their idolatrous religions?*

(3 minutes, 16 seconds later)

Rod Parsley: "The Lord is not slack," Verse 9 (referring to Second Peter 3:9), "concerning His promise as some men count slackness but is longsuffering toward us, not willing that any should perish, but" what? "That all should come to"... what?

Audience: Repentance.

Rod Parsley: And how are they gonna come to it if we don't preach it?

Yes, the New Testament reveals the value of true and faithful preachers, and makes apparent that such teachers of the Spirit are not necessarily planted in pulpits, but are those who produce Good "fruits." Christ's disciples are those who tread His Way, most of whom are not pulpit-people.

We are effectively asked: *How are people going to awaken to God without Christian preachers?* In countless ways that have nothing to do with Christian preachers. The Spirit is alive and growing Within everyone who seeks the Spirit, Christian or not. *I was not ritually baptized or raised in any religion. I am a self-motivated, self-taught scholar of the Bible which, I believe, led me to experience wonders that moved me to devote myself to proving and lifting the Bible's much-denied and much-ignored Message of the Spirit.*

For those who seek, life is full of the knowledge and wisdom of the Spirit for the taking. Enlightenment can spark through any number of experiences, and often when least expected. Seek, and ye shall find (Luke 11:9).

■ ■ ◆ ■ ■

#9 - Finley, Mark (January 16, 2000)

Revelation, Chapter 20, also presents a scene of judgment after Christ comes (Judgment Day). The books of Heaven are open and the final judgment takes place of the wicked. Those not saved, their very lives are revealed before the whole Universe, and God shows why He couldn't possibly bring them to Heaven, they would have started the rebellion over again. But those that have placed their faith in Christ, they're accepted as children of God, their names are written in the book of life. Jesus has been there to plead their case. His perfect life stands in place of their imperfect life. His sacrifice on the cross covers and blots out their sins. All this happens simply because they accepted Christ as their Savior.

As far as God not allowing unregenerate souls into Heaven because "they would have started the rebellion over again"... well, *this makes no sense.* They are not allowed in Heaven because they chose to deny the Spirit, and so too shall the Spirit deny them.

Judgment Day, which happens 1,000 years after Christ's Second Coming, is the day when Earth is destroyed by fire and our Universe is changed into the New Universe of Eternal Light (Revelation 20:9-11, 21:1). Jesus shall not need to "plead" for the Salvation of the Spiritful, as they have already justified themselves to The Way. Their names are written in the Book of Life (Revelation 20:12), having been judged by the Spirit of the

Law. Judgment Day is for those "dead" to The Way (Revelation 20:13), whose evils shall be exposed and judged by the Letter of the Law. *And the dead shall have eternal death.*

■ ■ ◆ ■ ■

#19 - Jones III, Bob (on *Larry King Live* with Larry King; March, 2000)

Larry King: Why can't black kids date white kids (at Bob Jones University)?

Bob Jones III: Well, being a Bible-believing institution Larry, we try to base things on Bible principle. The problem we have today is that our principle is so greatly misunderstood. People think we don't let 'em date because we are racist. In order to be racist you have to treat people differently. We don't. We don't let 'em date because we were trying, as an example, to enforce something, a principle, that is much greater than this. We stand against the one-world government, against the coming world of the anti-Christ, which is a one-world system, a blending of all differences, a blending of national differences, economic differences, church differences into a big, one-ecumenical world. Okay, the Bible is very clear about this. We said, you know, way back years ago when we first had a problem, which was, by the way, we started this principle back in the mid-fifties. I was a college student at BJU (Bob Jones University) at the time, and it was with the Asian and Caucasian, we didn't even have black students for another fifteen years, so it was not put there as a black thing.

Larry King: So, the fear of one-world relates back to two people dating?

Bob Jones III: We realize that interracial marriage is not going to bring in the world of the anti-Christ by any means, but if we, as Christians, stand for Christ and not anti-Christ, and we see we're against the one-world church, we're against one economy, one political system, and we see what the Bible says about this. So, we say, "Okay, if they're going to blend this world," and interracial marriage is a genetic blending, which is a very definite sort of blending, we said, "let's put this policy in here," 'cause we're against the one-world church. And way-back, seventeen years ago when I was on your program, I was saying on programs all across America: We're not going to the Supreme Court and fighting for our rule and our policy, we fighting for our right to it. There's a religious freedom issue. That's all we are at fault for.

(6 seconds later)
Larry King: I'm trying to find out why you have the rule (regarding interracial dating).

Bob Jones III: Yes. We have the rule, because it was part of a bigger, it wasn't a, it wasn't the rule itself. We can't point to a verse in the Bible that says you shouldn't date or marry interracially.

Larry King: You can't back it up.

Bob Jones III: No, we can't back it up with a verse in the Bible. We never have tried to. We never have tried to do that. But we've said there is a principle here, an overriding principle of the one-world government.

Note: Mr. Jones did go on to say that the University had just decided to remove their "no interracial dating" policy.

The reason why this private University had a "no interracial dating" policy is because its governing committee feared "blending," a "one-world government," and a "one-ecumenical church," and believed their fears were based on Bible principle. Their fears of an increasingly corrupt world denies Jesus' revelation that greater sufferings lie ahead, and that His Second Coming happens after the "fulness of the Gentiles" (the maximum corruption of the unbelievers). The Spirit knows no fear, yet they fear "blending," exposing their want for separatism, *their denial of Oneness in the Spirit*.

Corporate Christians who fear a Totalitarian Society want for themselves *their own Totalitarian Society* where they rule over the masses, where all beckon to their "way" of life. They fear individual thought apart from theirs, and want to "blend" minds to their "way" of separatism, *of us-versus-them*. The corporate mentality denies the Spirit when it teaches that you must have membership somewhere in the global system of corporate Christianity to get to Heaven. But Christ's Spirit of the Law reveals that we are saved through our devotion to God's Selfless, Good Spirit, regardless of religious membership.

Chapter 7

AS YOU SOW. . .

If it is happening to you, it is your responsibility in some measure, maybe not legally, *but always spiritually, otherwise it would not be an experience happening to your soul.* And so, now that it is happening to you, how will you deal with it?

Galatians 6:3-8 (authored by Apostle Paul)

3. **For if a man think himself to be something, when he is nothing, he deceiveth himself.**
4. **But let every man prove his own work, and then shall he have rejoicing in himself alone, and not in another.**
5. **For every man shall bear his own burden.**
6. **Let him that is taught in the word communicate unto him that teacheth in all good things.**
7. **Be not deceived; God is not mocked: for whatsoever a man soweth, that shall he also reap.**
8. **For he that soweth to his flesh shall of the flesh reap corruption; but he that soweth to the Spirit shall of the Spirit reap life everlasting.**

The Universe operates on cause and effect. Why should this be any different for the souls of humankind? The Bible tells us that God's Righteous Justice is "whatsoever a man soweth, that shall he also reap." In other words, the sufferings and blessings that we experience ultimately result from, *respectively*, the darkness (selfishness) and Light (Spirit) we have built into our own souls.

The difficult lessons life presents to us are lessons we need to experience and, hopefully, overcome. Maybe we do not understand why they happen, but know that we *own* our lessons, and that they come by way of God's Righteous Justice as opportunities to cleanse our soul's impurities. The soul is cleansed only by living and growing in the Spirit, especially in times of troubles. We are instructed to shed our selfishness and *put on the armor of God*, aligning body, mind, and soul with His Selfless Spirit.

Count your blessings and know that, *though your troubles are horrible, there are others suffering in ways even more horrible.* A Spiritful mind knows that everyone suffers, and counts its blessings with thankfulness in its pursuit to find the Light amidst the passing darkness. A Spiritful mind knows that the flesh shall die, but the soul is eternal, and that the One Way to overcome darkness is by devotion to the Light.

Our lives are ruled by karma ("as you sow, so shall you reap"), not fate. To view life's ups and downs as fate means that the destiny of your soul is sealed and unchangeable regardless of your behavior. But karma dictates that the destiny of your soul is relative to its balance of Light (Spirit) versus darkness (anti-Spirit), the balance of which changes according to the Spirit/anti-Spirit of your works, the "fruits" you bear.

Selfless, Good Works immediately or eventually result in positive consequences (blessings), even if not consciously recognized. Likewise, selfish works immediately or eventually result in negative consequences (trials and tribulations). Whether positive or negative, these consequences may manifest mentally, emotionally, and/or physically in this or subsequent lifetimes (reincarnation and karma are inexorably linked; Jesus spoke of reincarnation, examined in the next chapter).

The following is excerpted from *Revelation Earth.*

> Ranging from trivial to deadly, trials and tribulations are situations that arise from karmic debt. Karmic debt (darkness), *also known as bad karma*, is what fuels suffering, destruction, and death. [Jesus confirmed this in Matthew 9:1-6 when He demonstrated that healing comes through the forgiveness of sin, revealing that sin (darkness) is the source of dis-ease. He is telling you that strengthening the Spirit Within redeems your soul's sins. As your soul's Light grows stronger, its darkness grows weaker, *naturally.*]
>
> Trials and tribulations are situations that ignite strugglings with your Good Conscience, tempting you to deny the Spirit. Trials and tribulations can arise from making ordinary decisions that lead you to the "wrong place at the wrong time," to situations that are often called "accidents." In the world of karma, there are no accidents. There is a reason for everything. Just as all movement in the Universe is influenced by the forces of physical attraction and repulsion, all movement within a soul is influenced by its karma, its spiritual attraction and repulsion, its own condition of Spirit versus anti-Spirit.
>
> **Proverbs 26:2** (likely authored by King Solomon)
>
> 2. **As the bird by wandering, as the swallow by flying, so the curse causeless shall not come.** [Trials and tribulations are not without cause, but come for a reason.]
>
> For example, you make the ordinary decision to drive to work, but on this particular day you find yourself at the "wrong place at the wrong

time," where your car is involved in a multiple car collision. Legally, you may or may not be at fault but, *spiritually*, all the drivers involved are responsible. They are each responsible for simply being there, as each was led to that moment-in-time by way of his/her negative karma (we all have bad karma to some degree, as we are all impure to some degree, which is why any manner of troubles can come upon any of us at any time, often unexpectedly).

Ordinary decisions may become ill-fated choices that lead you to the "wrong place at the wrong time." Ill-fated choices arise from the darkness within your soul, leading to negative, *sometimes destructive* consequences. The suffering we meet upon Earth is a reflection of the suffering alive within our own souls. Even if it seems that someone else "caused" your suffering, that may be so, legally, but *spiritually*, the measure of suffering (darkness) you are reaping was born of a measure of darkness within your impure soul. By choosing to overcome that darkness with the Spirit, you cleanse your soul of that darkness, your soul becoming bonded that much more towards Oneness with the Spirit.

When you suffer trials and tribulations, how do you choose to react? Do you fume over certain troubles, giving them power for hours, days, even longer? If so, you have chosen to surrender to them. Fighting darkness with darkness (vengeance, jealousy, hatred, etc.) only empowers and builds more darkness within you. But overcoming darkness with the Spirit (love, peace, forgiveness, etc.) empowers and builds the Spirit Within your soul, *reconciling and redeeming the measure of anti-Spirit that was fueling the "inner war" you had just overcome.* This is the process of soul evolution. Give freely of the Good Spirit, and so shall God's Spirit Within be increased. This is how God instructs us to purify our souls and bond with Him eternally.

Romans 12:21 (authored by Apostle Paul)
21. Be not overcome of evil, but overcome evil with good.

Proverbs 3:5 (likely authored by King Solomon)
5. Trust in the LORD [the Good Spirit Within] **with all thine heart; and lean not unto thine own understanding** [selfish reasoning]**.**

The word "tribulation" comes from the Greek word, "thlipsis," which refers to the process of pressing grapes to bring forth its life-giving juice. Similarly, tribulations "press" upon your soul to bring forth your Life-giving spiritual "juice": the Good Spirit.

"Satan" means "the accuser." Though your bad karma is your responsibility, it can be easy to accuse others for your troubles. You may want to blame your troubles upon someone else, but do not be so deceived, thinking that blaming is of God's Spirit. The reason your soul is alive on Earth is to overcome the fruits of its darkness with the Spirit. The fruits of darkness are sufferings (trials and tribulations). When sufferings come to you, no matter how they come to you, they are yours to overcome. If you do not overcome your sufferings, you build more darkness (bad karma) within your soul, which shall lead to even more sufferings, *naturally*.

Mark 7:20-23 (spoken by Jesus; likely authored by disciple Mark)

20. That which cometh out of the man, that defileth the man.

21. For from within, out of the heart of men, proceed evil thoughts, adulteries, fornications, murders,

22. Thefts, covetousness, wickedness, deceit, lasciviousness, an evil eye, blasphemy, pride, foolishness:

23. All of these evil things come from within, and defile the man.

The destructive forces of bad karma eventually bring death, but if you work to redeem your sins, overcoming your soul's darkness as best you know, your soul will not become completely corrupted. Upon death, if your soul is not pure enough to enter Heaven, it will enter the realm of death, or Sheol [Hebrew for "grave"; the place of the dead; the unconscious realm of death (Genesis 37:35; First Samuel 2:6; Psalms 30:3; Proverbs 30:16)].

If your soul is not completely corrupted, it is still a viable candidate for Heaven, and God will grant your worthy soul another opportunity to live on Earth, that it may further purify itself. But if it is unregenerate, or spiritually dead (no longer a viable candidate for Heaven), it will remain in Sheol until Judgment Day (Revelation 20:13), when it shall be judged by the Letter of the Law it so idolatrously worshiped.

"God is not the God of the dead, but of the living" (Matthew 22:32; Luke 20:38), meaning that He offers no Mercy to those "dead" in the Spirit, because He is the God of the Living (He is the God of those who are alive in the Spirit, who are still viable candidates for Salvation).

■ ■ ◆ ■ ■

Though the following excerpt shows how false religion can be cruel, these preachers are simply teaching the only religion they've ever known, and there is no reason to believe that their innermost intentions were not true to what they believed to be God's Truth.

#14 - Hagee, John (January 9, 2000)

A father in my dad's church, on one particular Sunday night when my dad went back and asked him to come to the Lord, looked at my dad and said, "I don't need God, my life is my own business." My father asked his twelve-year-old son if he would like to come to know the Lord, and the boy said, "I'm following my dad." That night we went home and, as we were getting in bed, we could hear the sobbing of a woman coming across the front lawn, and she knocked on the front door, and my dad went to the door, and she said, "Pastor Hagee, my husband and son have just been killed in a head-on collision on the San Jacinto bridge. Could you pray for my husband?" My dad looked her right in the eye and said, "Its too late, they stepped into eternity without God." A father's sin had dragged a son into hell.

No one else's "sins" can drag you into hell, for as *you* sow, so shall *you* reap.

We are to have the faith of little children, like the son who faithfully followed his father in the above story. God also tells us to suffer the little children, for they know not the world like adults, being weak in free will and "innocent" of worldly, adult knowledge, wisdom, and manipulations. Who among us would so readily judge the eternal destiny of that father and child as burning in hell? Are any of us God?

In this story of the now-in-hell father and son, why is the father taking his son to church if he is not in some way accepting of God or at least seeking? Maybe he took his son to church because his wife insisted, which, *if true*, tells us that his statement about his life being his "own business" was not completely true. His wife had influence. *Don't all wives, to a degree?* He was obviously a tolerant-enough father to attend church with his son for whatever reason. If he had wanted, being the head of the household, he could have demanded that his wife not go to church and tithe their hard-earned money every week. But we know that she went to church, which affirms some degree of acceptance on her husband's part.

Though this father was distant from the church, for whatever reason, isn't it possible that he was a man of Good Spirit and Conscience? Take comfort, because God is no respecter of persons, and loves all who live and grow in His Spirit, even if they speak against Jesus (Matthew 12:31-33). *And yet, the woman was told by her beloved preacher that her husband and son just went to hell.*

■ ■ ◆ ■ ■

#39 - Swaggart, Jimmy (January 22, 1999)

If the thinkers, the intellectuals, who would dain to give a thought to the word of God, if they would speak, they would say, "Well, that being the case, it is not fair, right. It's not honest for God to condemn a soul to hell and burn that soul there forever and forever when that soul had no choice over the way it was born. It couldn't help it that it was born in original sin."

You had no choice over the circumstances of your birth, whether its state, status, or this spiritual, horrible spiritual problem we're talkin' about. "I didn't know anybody with the name Adam and Eve," many would say. "Not even sure they existed," most of the world would say. "You mean to say I've got to be lost in something, some darkness, some hellfire because of something somebody did (referring to Adam's sin) that I don't even know?

Romans 5:12, 14 (authored by Apostle Paul)

12. Wherefore, as by one man sin entered into the world, and death by sin; and so death passed upon all men, for that all have sinned:
14. Nevertheless death reigned from Adam to Moses, even over them that had not sinned after the similitude of Adam's transgression, who is the figure of him that was to come.

It was through Adam that sin entered into the world. Sin and its "fruits" (suffering and death) entered our "worlds" when our souls chose to follow in the likeness of Adam's sin. And though death reigned upon the Earth, there were some who did not sin (Revelation 14:1-4 reveals that 144,000 souls, *called the "harpers,"* remained Sinless, and will walk the Earth during the Tribulation Period).

It is incorrect to blame Adam for my sins or yours, as such blame denies "as ye sow, so shall ye reap." All of our souls, in the beginning, *like Adam*, chose selfishness over the Spirit of our own free will.

First Corinthians 15:21-22 (authored by Apostle Paul)

21. For since by man came death, by man came also the resurrection of the dead.
22. For as in Adam all die, even so in Christ shall all be made alive. [Our souls know death because we followed in the likeness of Adam's sin. Even so, we shall know Salvation if we follow in the likeness of Jesus' Sinlessness. We who live in the Good Spirit are "in Christ" and shall know His Resurrection of Life (we shall be "made alive"; Salvation).]

■ ■ ◆ ■ ■

#28 - Parsley, Rod (May 23, 1999)

God has come in here tonight to touch you. And you're not gonna have to worry about being quiet, 'cause He already knows where you are. He's already zeroed-in on you. You think you're hid in the crowd, but He already knows you by name. You think you came here tonight by choice, when the fact of the matter is you didn't have no choice.

If we are nothing more than God's marionettes, our lives predestined, then why did He give us free will, repeatedly revealing that we shall all reap what we sow?

■ ■ ◆ ■ ■

#18 - Jakes, T. D. (May 30, 1999)

I wish that Joseph's brothers and those that were jealous and intimidated of him had read the Book of Ephesians. They would have understood that God, from the Old Testament all the way through the New [Testament], has always had a plan. Whenever He raises one of us up, He is going to raise all of us up. In fact, the Book of Ephesians teaches us that God is going to raise us up together and make us sit in heavenly places in Christ Jesus. Don't be frustrated when you see somebody go first, because you're next in line for the blessing. it's gonna be for your whole house. You may go in one at a time, but before it's all over, every one of you, and everything connected to you, and everything related to you is gonna be, well, enough talking about this. I want to take you into the word of God, and I want you to get this message, and I want to you get your children, sons and daughters, mom and pop by the hand, because God is going to raise us up together.

Your devotion to the Spirit cannot be credited to another soul just because that other soul is a family member. We are each responsible for our own souls through our life's works. It is quite possible that Klara Poelz lived in the Spirit, maybe she didn't. But if she did, does that mean that her son, Adolph Hitler, gets a "Free Admission Pass" into Heaven? Are we to believe that Salvation is guaranteed for all the blood-relatives of ancestors devoted to the Spirit? C'mon! Each soul shall reap what it sows, not what another soul sows ["every man shall receive his own reward according to his own labour" (First Corinthians 3:8); "they that plow iniquity and sow wickedness, reap the same" (Job 4:8)].

■ ■ ◆ ■ ■

#21 - Kennedy, D. James (June 6, 1999)

Well, what's so amazing about grace? Let me try to name the ways. First of all, <u>it's amazing because it is so rare</u>. This world doesn't operate by grace. Grace is virtually alien to it. We operate on the basis, at best, of equity. Unfortunately, in many cases on inequity, crime, theft, deceit, but, at best, on the basis of equity, that is, a quid pro quo, a tit for tat, this for that, you pay so much and you get so much in return. That is the basic operative principle of this world. <u>It is the antithesis of grace</u>. And therefore we don't see it.

Equity is not the antithesis of grace. The antithesis of grace is unforgiveness. If you live in the Spirit your whole life, spotless before God excepting one sinful incident and, in the end, God does not give you Salvation due to your one trespass, then <u>that</u> is the antithesis of His Grace. But God tells us that if we live in His Spirit, *though we have sinned*, our sins will be forgiven through His Grace, which is His Righteous Justice (sow to the Spirit, and so shall the Spirit be Magnified Within, purifying your soul).

Grace is not rare. If it were not for God's Grace and merciful humans, evil would have destroyed us long ago. Even so, human grace is lessening and its selfishness growing. It will be on the last day of the seven-year Tribulation Period when evil shall reach its maximum "life." This event, known as the "fulness of the Gentiles" (Romans 11:25), will trigger the Rapture, beginning the hour-long Fall of Babylon (the Great Tribulation), followed by Christ's Second Coming.

(3 minutes, 2 seconds later)

Secondly, it's amazing because it's so undeserved. That, I think, is probably the first thing that hits people. And when I ask a number of people why grace was amazing, that was the only reason that anybody gave, "because it is so undeserved." And that's what grace is. It is undeserved favor. Well, not exactly. Grace isn't undeserved favor: that's the definition of mercy, not grace. And mercy is lower than grace, as love is lower than grace. We may mercifully give a beggar five dollars when we pass him in the street. That's an act of mercy, of undeserved favor. He didn't do anything for that. He didn't work for you. You had compassion and you gave him five dollars. Ah, but had that beggar, the previous week, climbed through a window of your home when you were away, raped and killed your wife and two daughters, and you found him and gave him five million dollars, <u>that would have been grace</u>. <u>Undeserved favor to people who deserve absolute disfavor is the meaning of grace</u>.

God's Grace <u>is</u> deserved, per God Himself, for "as you sow, so shall you reap," which is His Merciful, Righteous Justice. Human grace, on the other hand, may be deserved or undeserved, and can be born of Selfless or selfish intentions. Giving a undeserving beggar five dollars may be born of the Good Spirit (Selfless Charity), maybe not. There are all sorts of people who do not give their charity quietly, in secret, but give to gain such worldly rewards as publicity, social status, medals, applause, tax write-offs, etc. All charity given with the intention of receiving world rewards has had its reward and shall know no heavenly reward (Matthew 6:1-4).

Now, if a beggar committed heinous crimes against your family and, a week later, you gave him five million dollars, that may or may not be an act of Selfless Charity, depending upon your innermost intentions. But if you eventually come to truly forgive him... *that's the Grace of God.* And your Grace unto Him <u>is</u> deserved. *Why?* Because you too are a sinner, and God's Righteous Justice commands that as you sow forgiveness unto others for their sins, so shall you reap forgiveness for yours. *And why not eventually forgive?* Why carry that unforgiveness within your soul when you know how God's Righteous Justice works upon you, *and how it will work upon him.* No matter how he is punished on Earth, know that his crime shall be reconciled unto the Spirit through God's Righteous Justice.

God's Grace dictates that we are judged of ourselves, reaping what we have sown. By God's Grace, there shall be no "undeserved favor to people who deserve absolute disfavor," meaning that those of devoted selfishness ("absolute disfavor") shall be denied the Savior-Spirit they so carelessly denied.

All of us already possess God's Grace, and it is up to us, *individually*, to use it to Glorify or crucify His Spirit Within.

■ ■ ◆ ■ ■

#18 - Jakes, T. D. (October, 1999)

Some of you are facing challenges that you never faced before, just because God wants to show you a different facet of His glory. You never needed Him in the way you need Him right now, and God created the problem so that He could show you His Presence in the midst of the problem, because if He didn't create the problem in your life, you would never see His Presence in the way that you are seeing it now.

God does not create our problems. We have all sinned. It is the darkness within us, *sown into our souls by our own selfishness,* that brings (reaps) trials and tribulations. Our sufferings are not without cause (Proverbs 26.2), but come so that we may know Salvation (Second Corinthians 1:6).

■ ■ ◆ ■ ■

#20 - Jones, Noel (November 28, 1999)

<u>Everything that God is going to give you, He has already given it to you</u>. <u>It's already yours before the foundation of the world</u>. So why don't I have it? Because it's not my season yet. Are you all with me? <u>He decides the gift, and He decides when to give it</u>. And He put you together first. So, that's why the text says, "He marks out beforehand, He sets limits, He predestinates and He holds it together" (Romans 8:29?). And so, now He brings us in when He gets ready, because no man comes except the Father draw. He's got to draw you in. He draws you out of cocaine, draws you out of the wrong thing, draws you out of the mental institute, draws you out of yourself, and sets a time when you have to come to Him.

Predestination is a denial of "as ye sow, so shall ye reap." If fate (predestination) is truth, then why bother trying to live in the Spirit? After all, no matter what you do, your fate was decided the moment God created your soul. To what purpose would this serve God? If He already knew who was going to be saved, then why would He bother having us suffer on Earth? *Is this "Earth thing" all some sort of cruel joke?*

If God is Love and All-Goodness, then why would He create some souls to purposefully send them to hell for no reason? His Selfless Spirit has revealed that He is "not willing that <u>any</u> should perish, but that all should come to repentance" (Second Peter 3:9).

Obviously, there is a problem here with predestination. Before we examine the two times predestination is mentioned in the Bible, let's first understand Matthew 22:14.

Matthew 22:14 (spoken by Jesus; authored by Apostle Matthew)

14. **For many are called, but few are chosen.** [Many are sought ('called') by the Spirit, because many have sought the Spirit (those who are called are those who have called). Though many have sought, few have chosen devotion to the Good Spirit. Those who have chosen the Spirit shall be chosen by the Spirit, and shall know Salvation (those who are chosen are those who have chosen).]

Ephesians 1:3-14 (authored by Apostle Paul)

3. **Blessed be the God and Father of our Lord Jesus Christ, who hath blessed us with all spiritual blessings in heavenly places in Christ:** [Blessed be to God who has blessed us with all spiritual blessing by His Spirit Within ('heavenly places in Christ'; the Kingdom of Heaven is Within).]
4. **According as he hath chosen us in him before the foundation of the world, that we should be holy and without blame before him in love:** [According as He created our Pure souls before the Physical Universe was created, that we should be Sinless before Him in Love (here is confirmation that God knew our souls before He created the Physical Universe).]
5. **Having predestinated us unto the adoption of children by Jesus Christ to himself, according to the good pleasure of his will,** [Knowing that our Pure souls would sin, God pre-planned for sinful souls to be chosen by Christ in agreement with His Good Will (God's Will is that we overcome evil with Good, for those who choose His Spirit shall be "adopted" by Christ).]
6. **To the praise of the glory of his grace, wherein he hath made us accepted in the beloved.** [To the praise of the Glory of His Grace (His Righteous Justice), wherein we are chosen by Christ.]
7. **In whom we have redemption through his blood, the forgiveness of sins, according to the riches of his grace;** [In whom we have Redemption through His Blood (His Spirit Within), the forgiveness of sins, according to the fortunes of His Grace.]
8. **Wherein he hath abounded toward us in all wisdom and prudence;** [Wherein is abundantly supplied to us All Wisdom and Good Judgment.]
9. **Having made known unto us the mystery of his will, according to his good pleasure which he hath purposed in himself:** [Having Enlightened us to the nature of His Grace, according to His Good Will which He had planned in Himself.]
10. **That in the dispensation of the fulness of times he might gather together in one all things in Christ, both which are in heaven, and which are on earth; even in him:** [That on the day of the Second Coming ('fulness of times'), He might gather together in one group all things in Christ, those which are in Heaven (those souls already saved, including the Saints), and on Earth (referring to the raptured souls), and

His Angels (referring to those 'even in Him'). Here, it is revealed that the Great Day of Christ's Second Coming will see the gathering of all the Saved Souls of Humankind and His Angels "in the clouds" above the Earth to witness Him descend upon Earth for His Second Coming (Revelation 19:1-6, 14).]

11. **In whom also we have obtained an inheritance, being predestinated according to the purpose of him who worketh all things after the counsel of his own will:** [In whom also we have gained Salvation, as pre-planned according to God's Grace.]

12. **That we should be to the praise of his glory, who first trusted in Christ.**

13. **In whom ye also trusted, after that ye heard the word of truth, the gospel of your Salvation: in whom also after that ye believed, ye were sealed with that holy Spirit of promise,** [In whose Mind and Spirit you trusted, sealing you with His Savior-Spirit, His Promise of Salvation.]

14. **Which is the earnest of our inheritance until the redemption of the purchased possession, unto the praise of his glory.** [His Promise of Salvation is our determined Inheritance until it is received ('until the redemption of the purchased possession') unto the praise of His Resurrection (it was by His Resurrection that He became the Open Door to Salvation).]

Romans 8:28-30 (authored by Apostle Paul)

28. **And we know that all things work together for good to them who love God, to them who are the called according to his purpose.** [All things work together for Good unto souls who live in the Spirit, to those who seek the Spirit according to "his purpose" (God's Plan is that we join Him of our own free will, coming to Him because of our love for His Good Spirit).]

29. **For whom he did foreknow, he also did predestinate to be conformed to the image of his Son, that he might be the firstborn among many brethren.** [God pre-planned, through His Righteous Justice, for our souls ('of whom he did foreknow') to reap what we sow, that of this process we might grow to become One with His Mind and Spirit ('conformed to the image of his Son'), and might be among the first to come to Salvation from among many.]

30. **Moreover whom he did predestinate, them he also called: and whom he called, them he also justified: and whom he justified, them he also glorified.** [Those who find the Spirit have sought the Spirit, and of their devotion to the Spirit shall be justified by the Spirit, and be Glorified, receiving Salvation.]

God knew that our souls would grow away from Him by following in the likeness of Adam's sin, and so He pre-planned The Way back to Him. The Way back is through His Grace, or Righteous Justice, by which we, *each of us*, have the power to return to Him of our own free will by sowing to His Spirit. The Spiritful are the "Children of Promise," fulfilling God's Promise that Salvation comes to those who sow His Good Spirit.

Corporate Christianity, *intentionally or not*, misinterprets the above Biblical passages to teach predestination, meaning that God preselected, from the very beginning, those souls that would be saved and those that would be damned. To believe this would be, *of course*, a denial of God's free-will Spirit and merciful, Righteous Justice.

■ ■ ◆ ■ ■

#38 - Schuller, Robert A. (son of #37; September 19, 1999)

Any religion that requires us to earn our way into Heaven is a toxic religion, because there is no way possible for you to earn your way into Heaven.

The Bible makes it clear that Salvation is a gift from God, a gift that comes to those who have earned (magnified; built) the Spirit through their faith (devotion) in the Spirit. You are saved by God's Grace through your faith, *and your faith is justified by your Selfless, Good Works.* If you cannot rightfully earn Salvation, then fate rules. And what if you deny fate? Well, then, you're associated with a "toxic religion." Bummer! *Hey Jesus, did you know that your Gospel was a toxic religion?*

Romans 4:4-5 (authored by Apostle Paul)

4. **Now to him that worketh is the reward not reckoned of grace, but of debt.** [Those who force themselves ('worketh') to do Good Works, believing they *have* to, should not have bothered, for such works are not counted of God's Grace.]
5. **But to him that worketh not, but believeth on him that justifieth the ungodly, his faith is counted for righteousness.** [But to those whose Good Works come freely and naturally ('worketh not'), believing on Him that absolves sins (the Spirit Within; the Christ Within), their faith shall be counted for Righteousness.]

Chapter 8

REINCARNATION

God does not care if you accept reincarnation or not, as it has no bearing upon the eternal destiny of your soul. All that matters is your growing devotion to the Spirit. So, why bring up reincarnation? Because it is an important issue, important enough for the Roman Church to have crushed groups of Judeo-Christians, silencing any mention of it.

Reincarnation, *a central theme in most religions*, was openly accepted until the birth of the Roman Church in 325, when the Council of Nicaea (a council of 312 Christian Bishops) began the process of annihilating the notion of reincarnation understood by such early Judeo-Christian groups as the Gnostics, Nazarenes, and Origenists. It took nearly 250 years to extinguish openly-public belief in reincarnation through persecution and mass murder.

Why was the "one lifetime" agenda so important to the Church? *Because it needed individual minds to believe that life was a one-shot chance at Heaven, a destination reserved for only those who obeyed the Church.* This further enslaved the masses to the Church, which "sanctified" itself as God's Mediator, denying the One Mediator (the "man Christ Jesus," or Mind and Spirit of God alive in the flesh, *alive in your flesh*; First Timothy 2:5).

Eventually, by the thirteenth century, there was a notable resurgence in the belief of reincarnation in several groups, predominantly the openly rebellious Cathars. In 1244, the Roman Catholic Church again used violence to "fix" their problem: they burned 210 Cathars at the stake, a most-merciless method of killing "in the name of God."

Why would the Catholic Church resort to horrifying public executions? *To effect silence!* And also because its control over the masses would be compromised if reincarnation was endorsed. The masses submitted to the Church's control, *naturally*, having seen how public dissension was handled.

The cyclic processes of karma and reincarnation are of God's Righteous Justice and central to the evolution of the human soul. But corporate Christianity denies soul evolution, teaching that no matter your good or evil, you are "saved" by its idolatrous "ways" to God. This denies Jesus' One Way, and denies that you own ultimate responsibility for your acceptance/rejection of His Selfless Spirit. Christianity also refuses God's Righteous Justice, except when it can be used to serve the Church, like, *for example*, teaching that only those who tithe ("sow") fully to the Church shall receive ("reap") God's bounty of wealth, health, etc.

Why deny Righteous Justice? Because not only does it go hand-in-hand with karma and reincarnation, but it teaches that you are ultimately responsible for your own Spiritful and Spiritless works and, *consequently*, ultimately responsible for your life's blessings and curses (trials and tribulations) and, *consequently*, ultimately responsible for your soul's eternal destiny. Religions that thrive upon enslaving souls to their idolatrous "ways" to Salvation deny such personal responsibilities.

If we are all impure souls who get one chance at life to prove our eternal souls for all Eternity, then why would God, *who is All-Goodness and Righteous Justice*, show Himself so TOTALLY UNFAIR by allowing some souls to be born into wealth and others into poverty? Why is it that one soul gets to indwell a body that has good heath and another gets a body that suffers with physical impairments from the onset? How is it that a soul is planted into one culture versus another?

The Bible tells you that your soul was originally created One with God, and that it fell from Oneness by following in the likeness of Adam's sin. This event, known as the "Fall" of souls, is how your soul initially became impure (Romans 3:23), an event during which 144,000 remained Sinless (Revelation 14:4). The reason your soul indwells an impure body, subject to dis-ease and death, is because your soul is impure. Your body and its surrounding environment presents your impure soul with blessings and sufferings to "meet" its unique lessons, so that it may best overcome its darkness (unreconciled sins) with the Spirit.

Every day, the Spirit of Life prepares and births new human bodies to be indwelt by the evolving souls of God's Children. The unique nature of a soul's Spirit and anti-Spirit is its karma, which is why we are all relatively blessed and afflicted from the onset in various manners and differing measures. Your soul, of its karma, was led to your human body, which was prepared by God's Spirit as a vehicle of flesh within which your soul *might come to learn its lessons well.*

The one-lifetime belief raises important questions. *After my pure soul sinned, why would God keep my soul in some state of limbo for eons just to eventually let me live upon Earth for a few measly years as the one chance to prove myself for Eternity?* Why would God give us, His beloved Children, *created of His Good Spirit*, LESS than a micro-fraction of a split-second of Eternity to forever prove our souls?

James 4:14 (likely authored by James, Jesus' brother)

14. **For what is your life? It is even a vapour, that appeareth for a little time, and then vanisheth away.** [In the scope of Eternity, our lives appear and vanish, lasting "a little time."]

If we adhere to the belief of having one lifetime to become a Christian religionist in order to receive Salvation, then most human souls have perished. God is "not willing that *any should perish*, but that all should come to repentance."

The one-lifetime belief is supported by the phrase in Hebrews 9:27, stating, "...it is appointed unto men once to die." Note that it does not state, "...it is appointed unto souls once to die" (for souls to experience earthly death only once). A human body dies only once in the sense that death is permanent upon the body, but a human soul dies more than once (the soul experiences the realm of death more than once through reincarnation and near-death experiences).

Jesus' Apostles knew the famous prophecy that Elijah would come before "the day of the Lord" (Malachi 4:5), and when they asked Jesus about this prophecy, He told them that Elijah had already come: *"Then the disciples understood that He spake unto them of John the baptist"* (Matthew 17:13). Without using the word "reincarnation," Jesus had just told His Apostles that John the baptist was Elijah reincarnated (Matthew 17:10-13). Even so, some reject this notion, though Jesus flat-out says that John the baptist is Elijah (Matthew 11:12-14; Mark 9:13).

Those looking to disprove that John was Elijah cite John 1:21, where John the baptist, *when asked if he is Elijah*, says "No." But, *reading further*, John tells us that there is One who is coming who is greater than he, referring to Jesus. So then, are we not to believe Jesus' revelation that John is Elijah? When John denies being Elijah, is it not possible that he has no remembrance of being Elijah? Absolutely, *as follows*.

Ecclesiastes 1:3-11 (likely authored by King Solomon)

3. **What profit hath a man of all his labour which he taketh under the sun?** [What profits have our fallen souls gained through their labors on Earth? Do we sow Spirit and profit Salvation or do we sow anti-Spirit and profit damnation (as shall be further proven, those who continue in selfishness shall remain locked in the cycle of reincarnation until their souls have earned either Oneness or unregenerate separation; the process of soul evolution towards God has a time limit, ending on the last day of Christ's Millennial Kingdom: Judgment Day).]
4. **One generation passeth away, and another generation cometh: but the earth abideth for ever.** [One generation of souls dies from conscious life (the harvesting of human souls), and as these souls are "born" into the unconscious realm of death (Sheol), a generation of souls "dies" from Sheol and are born into conscious life (the planting of humans souls). And all the while the Earth

continues on, a habitation for the conscious souls of humankind ('the earth abideth for ever' is true, but know that the Earth shall be destroyed and made anew after the evolutionary process of the souls of humankind is finished, an event that will occur on Judgment Day; Revelation 20:9-15, 21:1).]

5. **The sun also ariseth, and the sun goeth down, and hasteth to his place where he arose.** [The cyclic nature of the sun is that it is reborn, and dies to the day, and hastens to be reborn again.]
6. **The wind goeth toward the south, and turneth about unto the north; it whirleth about continually, and the wind returneth again according to his circuits.** [The cyclic nature of wind currents is that they come from where they go, and return to their source.]
7. **All the rivers run into the sea; yet the sea is not full; unto the place from whence the rivers come, thither they return again.** [The cyclic nature of the waters is of evaporation and precipitation.]
8. **All things are full of labour; man cannot utter it: the eye is not satisfied with seeing, nor the ear filled with hearing.** [All things labor ceaselessly. So immense and Universal are these processes that the human mind cannot capture, see, or hear their Totality.]
9. **The thing that hath been, it is that which shall be; and that which is done is that which shall be done: and there is no new thing under the sun.** [The cyclic processes of the Physical Realm (the sun, wind, waters, etc.) are of atoms assembling and disassembling. It is not new atomic matter, but matter recycled. The cyclic processes of the Physical Realm are governed by like forces attracted to unlike forces. The cyclic processes of the Spirit Realm are governed by like forces attracted to like forces. Our impure souls are caught in the cycle of cause and effect, sowing and reaping. Our souls' experiences are not of new Spirit-matter and new anti-Spirit-matter, but of Spirit-matter and anti-Spirit-matter recycled. Our troubles and blessings are relative to our souls' karma. The lessons that come before us are not without cause (Proverbs 26.2), coming unto us according to our karma (according or our soul's evolving nature of Spirit and anti-Spirit).]
10. **Is there any thing whereof it may be said, See, this is new? it hath been already of old time, which was before us.**
11. **There is no remembrance of former things; neither shall there be any remembrance of things that are to come with those that shall come after.** [Those who reincarnate ('those that shall come after') shall have no memory of former things, nor of future things.]

Though our souls have no conscious memory of our past lives or lives to come, we all receive impressions about past and future, most-usually through levels of unconsciousness (dreams, hypnosis, meditation, deja vu, etc.).

In Matthew 16:13-14, Jesus asks His disciples who they think He is, and they answer, saying: "Some say that thou art John the baptist: some

Elias (Elijah); and others, Jeremias (Jeremiah), or one of the prophets." *Had His disciples' minds not understood reincarnation, then why did they think Jesus was the soul of a long-dead prophet?* Jesus never corrects or mentions their references to reincarnation. If reincarnation was not of God's Plan, Jesus would have told us. He certainly would not have revealed that John the baptist was Elijah, nor would He have repeatedly spoken of resurrection.

Both Resurrection and reincarnation involve a soul's reappearance on Earth.

- A reincarnated soul indwells a newborn human [most reincarnated souls are impure, being "born again" on Earth to continue their spiritual evolution, but some reincarnated souls are Pure and Saved, being reborn into the flesh to fulfill a specific purpose for God (like, for example, Elijah's reincarnation as John the baptist; Elijah was a Saved soul, per Second Kings 2:11)].
- A Resurrected soul is translated from Heaven, appearing upon Earth not in human flesh, but in the incorruptible Resurrected Flesh, or "strange flesh" of the Spirit [Jude 7; Luke 24:39-43; John 20:17-27].

Romans 1:20 (authored by Apostle Paul)

20. For the invisible things of him [God] from the creation of the world are clearly seen, being understood by the things that are made, even his eternal power and Godhead;

Romans 1:20 reveals that by looking at the nature of our Physical Universe, we can understand the "invisible things" of God. We know that the Universe operates via:

- <u>cycles</u> (seasons, tides, the movement of solar systems, galaxies, etc.);
- <u>evolution</u> (life and the Universe is constantly evolving via gravity, sunlight, wind, water, earthquakes, reproduction, disease, etc.); and
- <u>cause and effect</u> (where there is an action, there is an equal and opposite reaction; the basic operating system of our Universe).

Are we to believe that the human soul is the one thing that is free from the cyclic, evolutionary nature of cause and effect that applies to the rest of the Universe?

God's Righteous Justice is spiritual cause and effect, by which we are able to change our karma, further purifying or corrupting our souls. Reincarnation is God's Plan by which our souls cycle through consciousness (life) and unconsciousness (death), evolving towards or away from Salvation. Souls that grow ever-increasingly bonded with the Good Spirit shall eventually "go out no more," receiving Salvation.

Revelation 3:12 (spoken by Jesus; authored by Apostle John)

12. Him that overcometh will I make a pillar in the temple of my God, and he shall go no more out: and I will write upon him the name of my God, and the name

> **of the city of my God, which is new Jerusalem, which cometh down out of heaven from my God: and I will write upon him my new name.** [Souls that overcome their selfishness with the Spirit shall "go out no more," or no longer reincarnate, as they have no further need for Spiritual growth through cycles of sins, sufferings, and deaths upon Earth. They have earned God's gift of Salvation ('name of my God'; 'new Jerusalem'; 'new name').]

When Moses led the Israelites from Egypt to the Promised Land, their trek through the Sinai took forty years. *Why so long to travel only about 300 miles?* Because God would not let them enter the Promised Land until they had grown true and faithful to His Will (the Promised Land, symbolic of Heaven, is for only the true and faithful).

If you, *like the Israelites of the Exodus*, personally witnessed God in action, not just once, but many times, would you actually continue in your selfishness before God? And yet nearly all the Israelites who had been miraculously delivered from bondage in Egypt repeatedly denied God afterwards. It took them forty years of troublesome sojourns in the desert to finally grow purified through devotion to God's Will.

In the Sinai, the rebellious Israelites eventually died off along with their idolatrous ways. The group grew spiritually cleansed as their children and grandchildren (all of whom were born in the Sinai) learned obedience to God's Will (of the original mass of Israelites led out of Egypt and its idolatry, *all died before entering the Promised Land due to their idolatry*, excepting Joshua and Caleb).

Through the purification processes of death, birth, and faithfulness to God's Will, the Israelites evolved into *a living "body" of God's Will.* Now purified of their idolatry, God led them into the Promised Land.

Like the Israelites in the "wilderness" of the troublesome Sinai, it is through birth, death, and sojourns upon the troublesome "wilderness" of Earth that our impure souls will know Redemption by evolving into "bodies" of God's Spirit. Our many sojourns upon Earth come so that we might learn, through our trials and tribulations, to surrender our selfish ways for God's One Way, by which we shall eventually, naturally, be led into Salvation... the "Promised Land."

Reincarnation, the central theme of both Hinduism (one of the oldest known religions) and Buddhism, was also central to the religions of the ancient cultures of the American Indians, Incans, Mayans, Chinese, Japanese, Druids, Celts, Sumerians, Phoenicians, Egyptians, Grecians, Scandinavians, Germans, Romans, and Judeans (including the Essenes, thought to have been the writers of the Dead Sea Scrolls). It has been estimated that over 70% of the world's population accept reincarnation, including some of the world's most extraordinarily intelligent people.

Pythagoras (Philosopher and Scientist of Samos; -581 to -497)
Socrates (Athenian Philosopher; -470 to -399)
Plato (Athenian Philosopher; -427 to -347)

Aristotle (Athenian Philosopher; -384 to -322)
Voltaire (French Philosopher and Author; 1694-1788)
Johann Goethe (German Author; 1749-1832)
Ben Franklin (American Statesman, Inventor, and Author; 1706-1790)
Henry David Thoreau (American Author; 1817-1862)
Leo Tolstoi (Russian Author; 1828-1910)
Mark Twain (American Author and Humorist; 1835-1910)

The reason you live is to "learn your lessons well," overcoming evil with Good, so that you return to God forever. The lessons your soul fails to learn in the here and now remain unreconciled unto God's Spirit. As long as you continue sowing to the "world" (selfishness, idolatry), your soul will have worldly lessons to reap, and as long as your soul has worldly lessons to reap, it will continue to live in the world. Only by merging your soul with the Spirit shall your soul eventually become One with the Spirit and *go out no more*, your life-and-death cycles of reincarnation forever broken.

The Hindus believe that the human soul can indwell animals, even bugs, but such is not the case according to the Bible, which reveals the human body as having been prepared by God as the temple for the living soul. The wonderful stories in Hinduism about the soul reincarnating from lower forms of life to, finally, the highest form, *the human body*, is symbolic of the soul's evolutionary graduation from once living in a mindset of unenlightened consciousness (base, worldly, idolatrous desires) to living in the Enlightened, New Consciousness (the Mind of the Good Spirit, shown in this book as the Christ Within). Hinduism is correct in its revelation that it is only through *the human incarnation* that the soul can come to break its cycles of reincarnation.

Our souls cycle through life (Earth; consciousness) and death (Sheol; unconsciousness). While upon Earth, sowing to Spirit or anti-Spirit builds the same Within, evolving souls towards or away from God. While in Sheol, a soul is "sleeping" in an unconscious, *dreamlike* state, where it sojourns upon many "worlds" relative to the nature of its karma (the nature of its Spirit and anti-Spirit). In Sheol, a soul's "experiences" shall be a *Righteous and Just* reflection of its karma (as you sow in life, so shall you reap in death).

Though the mind is capable of learning while in the <u>unconscious</u> realm of death (Sheol), its learning is only relative to its karma, which changes through the sowing of Spirit and anti-Spirit in the <u>conscious</u> realm of life. Thoughts and desires, *conscious or unconscious*, whether aligned with either Spirit or anti-Spirit, are not justified until given "life." It is by our conscious free-will, *ruled by our hearts and motivations*, that we change our karma, ultimately defining the essence of our souls and, consequently, our eternal destinies.

While alive on Earth, our souls cycle through wakefulness (consciousness; "life") and sleep (unconsciousness; "death"). In sleep, our dreams are literal and/or symbolic reflections of our soul's karma, speaking to our soul's blessings and fears.

As the sun dies to the day and is reborn, and hastens to be reborn again (Ecclesiastes 1:5), souls sleep when the day is over, and hasten to awaken to a new day, so as to continue their spiritual lessons. Similarly, souls die from consciousness when their lives are over, and hasten to be reborn into consciousness to continue their spiritual lessons. If Nature and the Universe operates on cycles of life and death, don't our souls? *You bet.*

One of the reasons people refuse reincarnation is that they do not remember their past lives. Yes, you do not have total recall, but *listen* and *hear* the nature of your own soul through your fears, joys, passions, talents, dreams, etc. Karma and reincarnation explain why there are child geniuses and virtuosos, and why souls suffer from the onset, and why we all have various, strong, seemingly inexplicable interests, disinterests, loves, and lusts. Who we are is a reflection of our soul's karma. Who we become is of our own free will.

Job 24:19-20 (authorship unknown)

19. **Drought and heat consume the snow waters: so doth the grave those which have sinned.** ["Drought and heat" represent that which overcomes life-giving forces ('snow waters'; the Spirit Within). *Spiritually interpreted,* as Spiritlessness ('drought and heat') overcomes the Life-giving Spirit ('snow waters'), so too does death ('grave') conquer those who have sinned, *not referring to all who have sinned,* but referring specifically to those whose selfishness has depleted ('consumed') their Spirit Within ('snow waters'). This verse reveals that those who live to personify selfishness over God's Spirit shall, in the end, become void of Spirit and, consequently, separated from God.]

20. **The womb shall forget him; the worm shall feed sweetly on him; he shall be no more remembered; and wickedness shall be broken as a tree.** [It is only after a temple of flesh is "built" and birthed that a soul indwells the newborn via the process of reincarnation (more about this in the following chapter). Life shall forget all unregenerately selfish souls, *or those who have depleted their Spirit of Life* ('the womb shall forget' them), meaning that they shall not reincarnate. On Judgment Day, they shall be eliminated and forgotten forever (ultimately, they are eliminated of their own doing, and there shall be no remembrance of them in the New Universe of Eternal Life; Revelation 21:4).]

Psalms 90:3-6 (this Psalm's authorship attributed to Moses)

3. **Thou turnest man to destruction; and sayest, Return, ye children of men.** [God allowed our once-Pure souls to fall into the world of sin, suffering, and death of our own free will, and instructs us to return to Him of our own free will.]

4. **For a thousand years in thy sight are but as yesterday when it is past, and as a watch in the night.** [God's Spiritual Time is not that of man's physical time, for a thousand years to God is but a day, as if it was yesterday, as if it had already passed.]
5. **Thou carriest them away as with a flood; they are as a sleep: in the morning they are like grass which groweth up.** [Our souls are carried away into Sheol, and when our "sleep" is through, we live again "in the morning," in temples of flesh that, like grass, grow (Note that God does not personally kill us, but that our souls meet death and are "born again" through His Righteous Justice. Note also that this verse is not about the unregenerately selfish, as such souls never live again; Job 24:20).]
6. **In the morning it flourisheth, and groweth up; in the evening it is cut down, and withereth.** [In the "morning" of our lives, our temples of flesh grow. In the "evening," they die and decay. Like the cyclic nature of plants, *subject to seedtime and harvest,* so too are the fallen souls of humankind cyclically "planted" and "harvested" upon Earth through temples of human flesh.]

John 11:23-26 (authored by Apostle John)

23. **Jesus sayeth unto her, Thy brother shall rise again.** [Martha, *sister of the recently-deceased Lazarus,* is told that her brother shall live again.]
24. **Martha sayeth unto him, I know that he shall rise again in the resurrection at the last day.** [Martha told Jesus that she knows Lazarus will live again when the believers are resurrected on the last day (the believers shall be resurrected on the day of His Second Coming; John 6:39-40).]
25. **Jesus said unto her, I am the resurrection, and the life: he that believeth in me, though he were dead, yet he shall live:** [Jesus reveals to Martha that He is the Resurrection and the Life, and that those who follow His Way (those who personify God's Spirit; "believeth in me") shall have Life, though their impure souls naturally deserve death.]
26. **And whosoever liveth and believeth in me shall never die.** [And whosoever lives and believes in the Good Spirit shall have Life. *But if believers "never die," then why did He reveal in the previous verse that there are "dead believers" who shall live again? How did they become dead if believers never die?* Those who "shall never die" are those who will not know the "second death," or the eternal realm of soul-death (Revelation 20:14-15). The "dead" from Verse 25 refers to those souls "asleep" in the temporary realm of death called "Sheol," wherein they exist until ready to "wake up" to a "new day," or reincarnate. Only the unregenerately selfish, or completely corrupted souls, shall know the "second death." Jesus raised Lazarus from the dead so that we might know the Glory of God, *and know that the Spirit that raised Lazarus is the same Spirit that raised Him (Romans 8:11), the same Spirit that will raise those devoted to the Selfless, Good Spirit.*]

John 3:3-7 (authored by Apostle John)

3. **Jesus answered and said unto him, Verily, verily, I say unto thee, Except a man be born again, he cannot see the kingdom of God.**

4. **Nicodemus saith unto him, How can a man be born when he is old? can he enter the second time into his mother's womb, and be born?**
5. **Jesus answered, Verily, verily, I say unto thee, Except a man be born of water and of the Spirit, he cannot enter into the kingdom of God.** [Unless you are reborn of Repentance (the baptism of water; Matthew 3:11) and of the Spirit, you cannot know Salvation.]
6. **That which is born of the flesh is flesh; and that which is born of the Spirit is spirit.** [Jesus differentiates between that which is born of flesh and that which is born of Spirit. He tells us that sowing worldliness reaps worldliness ('That which is born of the flesh is flesh'), and that sowing Spirit reaps Spirit. There are two types of rebirth, rebirth in flesh and rebirth in Spirit. All souls reborn in the flesh have unreconciled sins still to be reconciled (all souls, excepting Saved souls, like Elijah; your 'new life' on Earth affords many opportunities to cleanse your soul's unreconciled sins). Those reborn in the Spirit are those awakened and devoted to The Way of the Good Spirit. You must be reborn in the Spirit to eventually "go out no more," *to stop being reborn in the flesh.* The ministry of Christ is the ministry of reconciliation (Second Corinthians 5:18-21). Our impure souls are reconciled unto God through our Spirit Within.]
7. **Marvel not that I said unto thee, Ye must be born again.**

John 9:1-3 (authored by Apostle John)

1. **And as Jesus passed by, he saw a man which was blind from his birth.**
2. **And his disciples asked him, saying, Master, who did sin, this man, or his parents, that he was born blind?**
3. **Jesus answered, Neither hath this man sinned, nor his parents: but that the works of God should be made manifest in him.**

Whose sin caused this blind man to be blind? Jesus tells us that it is not that the parents have sinned that a child is born blind, but that God's Righteous Justice ("works of God") be made manifest in the life of the soul inhabiting the blind body.

If it was not any sin that the mother, father, or blind man committed that caused him to be blind, then why was he suffering blindness? *Because of unreconciled sins within his soul.* It was by God's Righteous Justice that the fetus was prepared (built) with blindness that, after its birth, it would house a "spiritually blind" soul deserving of this lesson. The man's blindness is a lesson unto his soul, that his soul might overcome its "blindness" to the Spirit, seeing the Light. His lesson of physical blindness, *like all trials and tribulations*, has come for the Good of the Spirit, that Salvation might be realized.

God's Righteous Justice prepared and birthed the blind infant so that its incoming sinful soul might best learn its unique set of still-unlearned lessons. It was because of the impurity (sin) within the incoming soul that preparations were made for that soul to meet with the affliction of blindness, an affliction relevant and relative to its unreconciled sins.

Our souls experience what they need to experience, always. You are not to fear the death of your body, but the death of your soul. *In other words, be careful what you sow.*

■ ■ ◆ ■ ■

#32 - Paulk, Earl (May 9, 1999)

Honey, listen to me. Death is final. You're not gonna come back for another chance. It is appointed unto man once to die, once to die, once to die and, after that, the judgment.

Don't even think about reincarnation!

■ ■ ◆ ■ ■

#21 - Kennedy, D. James (June 20, 1999)

Ah, dear ones, open your eyes. Soon this life will be over faster than you think, and you will descend into that pit from whence no man returns. But Christ offers your Eternal Life freely, as a gift, if you will invite Him into your heart as Lord and Savior of your life.

To believe in the one-lifetime supposition along with the idolatrous worship of Christ is to believe that countless billions of souls have perished throughout history simply because God, *oops*, forgot to tell them that Salvation came by simply "inviting" Christ into their hearts. This is idolatry that, once again, wins out over The Way of the Good Spirit. By this selfish perception, only an exclusive, small percentage of souls will come to Salvation.

If most souls have perished because they did not "invite" Jesus Christ into their hearts, then how do you reconcile the Truth that God is "not willing that any should perish, but that all should come to repentance?" The Spirit of the Law reveals that those who live to deny God's Selfless, Good Mind and Spirit shall, by their own doing, be denied the Kingdom of His Mind and Spirit (Salvation; Heaven).

■ ■ ◆ ■ ■

#32 - Paulk, Earl (September 26, 1999)

I wonder how many in this house and in my television audience will know why children were given in the Garden of Eden? Have you ever read it carefully? God said to Adam and Eve, "I want you to be fruitful and multiply, because through this I will take dominion back on the Earth." Our success is when our successors succeed.

How many houses of glory have been built by great ministries, but nobody was raised up to carry it on, and people passed by and say, "That used to be a great ministry. That house use to be a house of praise." I honor men of God who raise up their children to follow them in their pulpits, raise them up and teach them how to receive the glory of God, whether it's an Oral Roberts or Robert Schuller, whoever it is.

Children were not born in the Garden of Eden. Shortly after Adam and Eve were confronted by God regarding their sin, God expelled them from the Garden, after which they had children. Furthermore, God's instruction to "be fruitful and multiply" was given to Adam and Eve *when they were Pure and Sinless in the Garden* (Genesis 1:28). God's instruction to "be fruitful and multiply" to Adam and Eve was a revelation about the Spirit, instructing them to Produce ("fruitful") and Magnify ("multiply") the Spirit [those who seek the Spirit in all wisdom are advised to be "fruitful in every good work, and increasing (multiplying) in the knowledge of God" (Colossians 1:10); "Grace and peace be multiplied unto you through the knowledge of God" (Second Peter 1:2)].

"Be fruitful and multiply" can be interpreted as being about reproduction, but that understanding is secondary, being literal, not Spiritual. God's instruction for us to "be fruitful and multiply" was first given to our Pure souls at a time when our individual minds had no conscious knowledge or wisdom of Good and evil, no understanding of such worldly things as sex and reproduction. The primary, most-relevant understanding of "be fruitful and multiply" is: *Sow to the Good Spirit Within and so shall you reap (build) the Good Spirit Within.*

"Our success is when our successors succeed" is not about parents and children. Why? Because it is evident that your "success" (whether professionally, financially, educationally, or any other form of success) does not necessarily mean that you had Spiritful parents and parenting, nor does it necessarily mean that you will produce "successful" children. There are all sorts of "successful" people who have risen above sufferings heaped upon them by parents/guardians.

And what if your child is a "failure"? Are you automatically labeled a "failure" too? Though parents can be remarkably Spiritful and Spiritless influences upon a child's mind, that child's soul shall ultimately be responsible for how it chooses to deal with its perceived sufferings and sins as its life enters adulthood and unfolds towards death.

"Our success is when our successors succeed" is about karma and reincarnation. Your "successors" are not about your children, but about your soul's future incarnations (the successive generations of your evolving soul). When your body dies, your soul "dies" to life and is "born" into the realm of death ("Sheol"). When your soul "dies" to death and is "born" into life, it carries with it the same spiritual purities and impurities (karma) that it had the moment it died from its previous incarnation [we cannot change the karmic nature of our souls in the unconscious "sleep" realm of death, but in life only, through the Spirit and anti-Spirit we sow].

Being reincarnated from death to continue your soul's evolution towards or away from God is like waking up from a long sleep. Before you died and went to "sleep," your soul still had lessons to learn (unreconciled darkness). Upon waking from your "big sleep," it takes years for your newly-born physical brain to develop fully for your soul's mind to get revved-up to full-speed consciousness for a life filled with learning.

A seed yields after its own kind (Genesis 1:11-12), meaning that the end-condition of your soul's karma from its previous incarnation is the beginning-condition of its karma in its next incarnation.

Your soul's successes in the Spirit in this incarnation shall have grown from your soul's successes in the Spirit in its previous incarnations. The success of your soul in this incarnation is when your "successor" (your next incarnation) succeeds. *See?* Sow Spiritual success in the here and now, and so shall your soul reap greater Spiritual success in its coming incarnations. Eventually, your soul will have the ultimate Spirit-success: *Salvation.*

Your success in the Spirit *in the here and now* is <u>justified</u> when *who you are in the future* is of greater success in the Spirit. Instead, the phrase, "our success is when our successors succeed," is taught to mean that we are to honor preachers who keep their "Holy" businesses alive through their children. But have they not heard that their worldly successes (power, financial enrichment, adulation, etc.) shall have no value towards their Salvation? Worldly successes account for nothing if you have not the One Way to Spiritual success, effected only by living and growing in the Selfless, Good Spirit.

Exodus 20:2-6 (authorship unknown, probably Joshua, maybe Moses)

2. **I am the Lord thy God, which have brought thee out of the land of Egypt, out of the house of bondage.** [It is the Lord God (the Spirit Within) that brings us out of our enslavement to spiritual corruption ('out of the land of Egypt,' the land of idolatry).]
3. **Thou shalt have no other gods before me.** [If gratifying any desire involves denying the Spirit, then do not gratify that desire, for all who do shall have committed idolatry.]
4. **Thou shalt not make unto thee any graven image, or any likeness of any thing that is in heaven above, or that is in the earth beneath, or that is in the water under the earth.** [No idolatry.]
5. **Thou shalt not bow down thyself to them, nor serve them: for I the Lord thy God am a jealous God, visiting the iniquity of the fathers upon the children unto the third and fourth generation of them that hate me;** [God tells us that idolatrous worship serves selfishness and is repulsive to His Selfless Spirit,

naturally. We then learn that a soul's selfishness shall be met (reaped) in subsequent incarnations, up to its third and fourth successive incarnations. The "iniquity of the fathers" refers to the selfishness of souls. Their "children unto the third and fourth generation" refer to their souls' 3-4 successive incarnations. Like a seed that yields after its own kind, (Genesis 1:11-12), the "child" (the soul's new incarnation; 'seed') succeeds the "father" (the soul's previous incarnation; 'its own kind'). *Literalists will deny this Spiritual Interpretation, insisting that the Bible is to be interpreted their way, though Jesus tells us differently* (Matthew 4:11-14). But, let's say that the literal interpretation is correct, that a father's sins shall be reaped by his offspring unto the third and fourth generations. How, then, is this verse to be reconciled with "as you sow, so shall you reap?" *The Bible does not say, "as the father sows, so shall the child reap."* God tells us that His "mysteries" are no mystery to those who have eyes to see, not referring to twenty-twenty vision, but to their realization of His Spirit. Didn't God know that the Bible would see itself through many language translations, and that corrupt humans would interpret Scriptures to suit themselves? *You bet*. How else better to keep His Message of the Spirit safe than to preserve it within parables, symbolism, and Spirit-of-the-Law Truths?]

6. **And shewing mercy unto thousands of them that love me, and keep my commandments.** [God's Mercy is His Righteous Justice. Those who choose His Spirit shall, by His Merciful Spirit, be quickened unto Eternal Salvation (Romans 8:11).]

■ ■ ◆ ■ ■

#14 - Hagee, John (July 4, 1999)

First, everything that God does on the face of the Earth comes from the principle of seedtime and harvest. Genesis 8:22, "while the Earth remains, seedtime and harvest shall not cease."

The ceaseless Earth and "seedtime and harvest" is about the cyclic nature of reincarnation, necessary for the evolution of our souls (Ecclesiastes 1:4).

(continuing)

Consider the spiritual realm. How did Jesus Christ get to Earth? The answer is: seedtime and harvest. Genesis 3:15, "and the seed of the woman..." Who was that? Jesus. "... Shall crush the head of the serpent." Who was that? Satan.

Jesus Christ came to this Earth when the Holy Spirit planted the seed in Mary's' womb, and the kingdom of satan was defeated at Calvary. And now, because of seedtime and harvest, demons tremble at the mention of His name. Because of seedtime and harvest, we have salvation, healing, and deliverance. We have love, joy, and peace, and power to walk in victory over the world, the flesh, and the devil, because of seedtime and harvest. If it works in a physical principle and a spiritual principle, it's a universal principle.

If the "kingdom of satan was defeated at Calvary," satan would have been bound *at that time* and none of us would be here on Earth working to overcome evil with Good. Yes, Jesus overcame satan, by which His Mind/Spirit became the Open Door to Salvation. Only by crowning your mind with His, *living His Way of the Spirit,* shall you, like Him, overcome satan (death and hell). Make no mistake, the forces of satan's realm are vigorously alive and well on planet Earth and in the minds of those who choose selfishness over the Selfless, Good Spirit.

"Seedtime and harvest" is about reincarnation. Jesus was the "Word of God" who came to plant the "Good Seed" of The Way of God's Spirit. It was through His Mind that He delivered God's Message. You are to "crown" your mind with His, giving life to the Spirit, *that the Good Seed Within you will grow into the Tree of Life (Salvation).* Those who plant the Good Seed into their lives shall harvest Salvation (souls who conquer their selfishness with Selfless Love shall no longer have reincarnation, but Resurrection after Christ's Second Coming). Those who plant the "worldly seed" shall be planted again in the world (selfish souls *who are not unregenerately selfish* shall reincarnate, that they might overcome their unreconciled selfishess with the Spirit).

Matthew 13:37 (spoken by Jesus; authored by Apostle Matthew)

37. He that soweth the good seed is the Son of man; [Jesus, who was the Spirit and Mind of God alive in the flesh, *and is the Spirit and Mind of God alive in your flesh,* is the Sower of the Good Seed that is the Way of the Spirit.]

Chapter 9

ABORTION

God knew us before He created the Physical Universe (Ephesians 1:4). He prepared for us temples of flesh into which our souls would dwell (Genesis 1:27). The first soul indwelt the human body on the sixth day of creation, when God breathed into the nostrils of an *already-birthed, living male*, making him a "living soul" (Genesis 2:7), changing the living human animal of body and brain into a living human being of body, mind, and soul.

The Physical Universe had to be birthed before biological life could take root on Earth. The Earth had to be birthed before the human soul could live upon it. The body (Temple) of Adam, the Tent (Temple) of the Congregation, and Solomon's Temple all had to be built and birthed before God's Glory dwelt Within. The same applies to our "Temples" (God's Glory is His Mind and Spirit that created *and is Within* our souls).

The Bible does not reveal that our souls indwell at the moment the sperm fertilizes the egg, nor does it indicate that our souls enter in the 1st, 2nd, or 3rd Trimesters. But the Bible does indicate in several places that our souls enter after the body is birthed. *The vehicle (Earth; Adam; the Tent; Solomon's Temple; the body) must be birthed before the Glory of God enters.*

God gave Moses specific Holy Measurements to build the Tent of the Congregation and all its features. It was a portable Temple that Moses and the Israelites carried with them during their forty-year trek in the wilderness of the Sinai before they reached the Promised Land. Only after the Tent was birthed did God's Glory enter (Exodus 40:33-34). After settling in the Promised Land, the Israelites built Solomon's Temple and, like Moses' Tent, God's Glory did not enter Solomon's Temple until after it was birthed onto Earth (pages xvii-xix, xxii; First Kings 7:51-8:11).

The flesh (body; temple) of a fetus has the Spirit, because the Spirit is Life [where there is no Spirit, there is no life (James 2:26)]. It also has life because the mother (nurturer) lives. But the temple does not have God's Glory (the Mind and Spirit of a soul) until after it is built and birthed.

Abortion is the destruction of an unfinished (unborn) temple of flesh (resulting in the loss of the potential habitation for a human soul), not the murder of an already-birthed, living soul. The soul does not indwell the body until after the body is born. Instances of abortion that are not natural, not accidental, not medically necessary, and *not of Good Conscience* are acts of selfishness which, *like all sin,* is a denial of the Spirit.

The deliberate, medically unnecessary destruction of an unborn body is, *matter-of-factly,* a denial of the Spirit of life (in general), and the denial of the Spirit of life nurturing the fetus. But a woman's decision to have an abortion may or may not be a denial of her Good Conscience.

Sin is relative (page xvii). If you, *by your Good Conscience,* know that having an abortion is wrong, then do not have one as, by doing so, you would be willfully denying the Good (God) Mind and Spirit Within you, forsaking that which gave *your soul* its life (existence) in the first place. But if having an abortion is not a denial of your Good Conscience, then know that God knows your heart and motivations. Know also that your soul shall not suffer the greater sufferings that shall come upon those who abort against their Good Conscience. *No two souls have the exact same lessons in life.* Your Good Conscience is relative to your growth in the knowledge and wisdom of the Spirit. God shall forgive all the sins of those who do not deny their Good Conscience (Matthew 12:31-33).

The abortion of an unborn human temple is tantamount to, *metaphorically speaking,* Solomon's Temple being destroyed before completion. <u>In terms of the evolutionary process of incoming, impure souls</u>, *the destruction of a human body before its birth is of no consequence in the sense that each incoming soul shall, by God's Righteous Justice, have its fair opportunities to live and grow upon Earth.*

While fetuses are destroyed every day naturally, accidentally, and deliberately, others are being birthed to house souls. The choice to abort is not the killing of an already-birthed, living human soul, but the killing of the Spirit of Life in the flesh of the fetus *and in the soul of the woman to some degree, relative to her heart and motivations.*

Corporate Christianity often teaches that fetuses and children who die or are murdered go directly to Heaven. *If this is so, then why not rejoice at every abortion? Why not rejoice over the death of every child? Why not kill your own children?* It is because of this idolatrous mindset, in part, that children have been murdered by a Christian parent.

The infamous cases of John List and Andrea Yates reveal how this idolatrous reasoning was part of their decision-making process. They were comforted in the false religion that their soon-to-be-dead children would go directly to Heaven. This horrible lie helped "sanctify" the murdering of their children, making these killers out to be, *in their twisted minds*, as sort of "saviors" of their children, having "saved" them from sinful lives that might have led them to hell.

Romans 9:11 (authored by Apostle Paul)

11. **(For the children being not yet born, neither having done any good or evil, that the purpose of God according to election might stand, not of works, but of him that calleth;)** [Apostle Paul is referring to the births of the souls that would be known as Ishmael, Isaac, Jacob, and Esau, and tells us that their souls were "elected" to live on Earth, not because of their soul's Good Works, but because of their soul's Spirit Within (of 'him that calleth'). Paul tells us that the unborn have done no Good or evil. This is true. *But why?* Because the fetus has not yet been indwelt by a soul. Until the <u>soul</u> indwells an already-birthed body, it is unable to consciously effect Good and evil through the flesh. The soul is "elected" to incarnate by God's Righteous Justice. If the physical temple (fetus) is destroyed before it is birthed, the soul for which it was prepared shall indwell another physical temple. *When a temple of flesh is destroyed before its birth, this does not mean that the soul being prepared to enter that temple shall not have further opportunities for life on Earth.* Quite the contrary. It will, being worthy in the Spirit, have life on Earth to continue its spiritual evolution.]

Christianity points to the story of Mary's cousin, Elisabeth, as proof that the fetus is a living soul. In Luke 1:41-68, it is upon Elisabeth's hearing (awareness) of Mary's arrival that her fetus (which would become John the baptist) leaped in her womb "for joy," filling her with the Holy Spirit. This is not proof that her fetus had a conscious, "living" soul, but rather illustrates the interconnectedness of the Holy Spirit.

The angel Gabriel told Elisabeth and Mary, separately, that each would bear a son. But Gabriel only told Mary of Elisabeth's pregnancy, and so Mary went to see Elisabeth, an unexpected visit. When Mary arrived, pregnant with Jesus, the *Spirit Within* Elisabeth "registered" the Presence of the Coming of the Lord, accompanied by her unborn babe's *leap for joy,* a significant event that illustrates the inseparable and Divine relationship between Elisabeth, Mary and their soon-to-be-birthed sons. Mary's "unheralded" arrival was heralded by the babe's *leap for joy,* born of the *Spirit Within* Elisabeth (the babe's adult life, as John the Baptist, would serve to herald Jesus' Coming).

Elisabeth's fetus was being prepared to house the soul of Elijah [per Jesus, John the baptist was Elijah reincarnated, sent to prepare The Way of the Lord, fulfilling Malachi's famous prophecy (Chapter 8)]. It was John the baptist who, born first, would "prepare" the people for Jesus' and His Gospel of the Spirit (Matthew 3:3).

Corporate Christianity's *literal interpretation* teaches that Elisabeth's unborn babe was the <u>living soul</u> of John the baptist, having consciousness and cognizance when he chose to "leap for joy" upon realizing that Mary and the unborn Jesus had unexpectedly arrived.

Don't pregnant women, to this day, experience moments of sublime joy, *even Spiritual Enlightenment* when sensing their growing fetuses? In Elisabeth's case, it may seem that her soul's Enlightenment and her babe's "leap for joy" were coincidental. There are no coincidences, as all the Universe was built via the Spirit and therefore interconnected with the Spirit. Our conscious, living souls are active conductors of Spirit and anti-Spirit, *sowing and reaping*. Nothing is causeless, or coincidental, though it may seem to be that way at times (Proverbs 26:2).

Perception, however imperceptible, comes first, *then action*. Elisabeth's awareness of Mary's unexpected arrival came first, then her *Spirit Within* "felt" the Presence of the Coming of the Lord, manifested physically in her babe's *leap for joy*, illustrating the interconnectedness of God's Spirit and how it communicates between and through us.

Consider this tale: Every Sunday in church you, *a zealous pro-lifer*, meet with a kindly old lady. You love your weekly visit with her, sharing photographs and talking about your children and grandchildren. She is quite the wonderful lady, but did you know she once had an abortion forty years ago? On one hand, you shun those who have had abortions, judging them hellbound, yet show great respect for this little old lady. What's the difference? *The difference is that you are ignorant of the fact that the ol' gal once had an abortion.*

What if, after years of knowing this lady, you find out she had an abortion? She tells you that she kept this painful secret "inside" for forty years, and cries on your shoulders, explaining that she aborted, fearing retribution from her family and church for being pregnant and unwed. What then? Do you instantly shun her like all the others? Do you judge her differently? *How many pro-lifers are aware of the hidden secrets of their relatives and friends? How many know the hearts and motivations of those who have aborted?*

If Christians were truly "Christian," being God's "Jews" (Chapter 4), the issue of abortion would, *before all else*, consider the living soul of the mother. Instead, corporate Christianity seeks power and control over the mother's mind and life when, come Judgment Day, only the soul of the mother shall ultimately have to answer for her decision... *no one else*. Only she and God know her heart, knowledge, wisdom, Spirit, motivations, fears, and all aspects of her decision. Christians who persecute abortionists are "playing God," putting their idolatry before the Spirit. As they judge abortionists and their patients as hellbound, so too shall their "Life-killing" (Spiritless; hateful; selfish; intolerant) agendas be likewise judged.

Militant anti-abortionists teach that the "innocent blood" of fetuses is more valuable than the living souls of the mothers and abortionists.

Effectively, they are teaching that *taking a living soul's life* to protect the "innocent blood" of a soul-less fetus is commendable to God. *They are using a selfish vision of God's Word to "sanctify" the murdering of living souls.* Their minds, so polluted with idolatry, do not see that a fetus owns no living soul until after it is birthed, and that the Innocent Blood (the Spirit Within) being shed is their own, by their selfishness.

In the Parable of the Good Samaritan (Chapter 3), we are told of a *holy* priest and a Levite who ignore an injured man on the roadside, who is later aided through the Selfless Spirit of a "heretical" Samaritan. Jesus commends the Samaritan for his Good Spirit, *instructing us to do likewise,* confirming that religiosity means absolutely nothing to Him if you deny His Spirit. He does not care if you call yourself a Christian or Pagan, but knows you by your devotion to Selfless Goodness.

How have today's *holy* priests and religionists changed? Don't many still ignore the "wayside" injured. Souls seeking abortions are, like the rest of us, *spiritually injured,* struggling with life's sufferings. Yet many Bible-thumpers judge such women "hellbound," *forsaking the "born," or living soul of the mother for their love of the unborn.*

■ ■ ◆ ■ ■

#8 - Falwell, Jerry (on the *Neil Cavuto Show;* November 27, 2001)

On the subject of cloning for stem cell research.

> I believe, again, that life begins at conception and that is, to me, a cardinal truth. I, therefore, cannot, in my own heart, sanction the taking of human life for any purpose.

This preacher truly believes that abortion is the killing of a living soul, but somehow forgets that corporate Christianity conquered Earth not through Jesus' Selfless Love and Good Works, but through its "sanctified" persecution and slaughtering of countless living souls judged "heretic." It enslaved masses of souls to its idolatrous "ways" to Salvation through fear and force. All that bloodshed and cruelty thrust upon humanity by the Spiritless leaders of corporate Christianity, and yet this leader of corporate Christianity is offended by stem cell research that might bring medical breakthroughs and greater wellness to many?

Who gave the separatist, intolerant, judgmental, murderous, global system of corporate Christianity, *which is soaked in more blood and brutality than can ever be measured,* the permission to act as Judge upon the souls of others? *It gave itself the permission to be Judge,* as it always has, thinking itself the "Kingdom of God" on Earth.

Are we to understand that corporate Christianity, *birthed of unparalleled violence,* has a "problem" with a few soul-less human cells being cloned for the purpose of stem cell research? When will they stop climbing the slopes of Mt. Hypocrisy and tread The Way to Mt. Zion (Heaven; Revelation 14:1)?

■ ■ ◆ ■ ■

#1 - Mother Angelica (November, 2001)

I think everything that has happened so far, the abortions in the world, some of the Russian women have had as much as eight abortions. When you think of all the millions of people that might have been. Now, I cannot help but think of the weight of the spilt blood of all these children, and the consequences of those women who were heartsick, disturbed, mentally disturbed, because they had one. I think that weight is upon the world at this point, and encourages more and more evil, and I have asked the president, not privately, to get rid of the terrorists of abortion. To me, a doctor who is given the talent to heal, and he kills innocent and helpless little babies, to me he is a monster who is creating such a, putting such a weight on society, on the world, on the Earth. At this point, God only knows how many millions and millions of children have gone. I think that's part of the problem we have today. There's no reason for any of this to have happened.

This, coming from a Catholic nun, a woman who has, *knowingly or unknowingly,* given her life to one of Earth's most idolatrous doomsday cults, a cult that has committed untold crimes against humanity. *Whether or not you like it, that's the matter-of-fact truth regarding the birth and rise of Catholicism. After witnessing September 11th and the murder of nearly 3,000 souls, no one is rushing to join Bin Laden's cult, and yet the Catholic Church has "sanctified" countless crimes against peoples and nations since its inception and currently has around a billion followers.*

Had the Catholic Church taught the Oneness-Spirit of Christ, the Protestant Reformation would not have occurred, nor the Inquisition, nor the Crusades, nor all the other religious terrorism and persecution heaped upon non-Catholics in the name of their idolatrously-worshiped "God."

Here, this Catholic "mindset" speaks of the "weight of the spilt blood" of unborn children, but considers not the monstrously-gross weight of blood spilled by the Catholic Church throughout history.

How does corporate Christianity claim moral authority over others' souls when, in fact, its very existence was built upon slavery, deceit, idolatry, murder, persecution, etc.?

■ ■ ◆ ■ ■

#21 - Kennedy, D. James (January 19, 2002)

And, by the way, a number of geneticists had a meeting some years ago to consider the question, "When does a person, a human being, become a human being?" And, after spending a number of days studying that, they released their conclusion which said [that] there is no point in the development of the fetus where we can say yesterday this was not a human being and today it is. There is no point that it is a human being. And the excuse that was given for 30 years to people who talked about that was that "this is just a P.O.C., a product of conception. It (the fetus) is just like a wart or a growth, and it is not a human being." In fact, from what I've heard, it probably was rarely ever that a young woman was told that that was a human being that she carried within her. And they got by with that for years, but with the advent of partial-birth abortion, something has happened. That entire argument, used successfully for over 30 years, has fallen kaput on the floor, like an egg, breaking. There's no way that you can say that this baby, that has been brought three-fourths of the way out of the womb, whose fingers, and arms, and hands, and toes are moving like this, is not a baby. In fact, the baby would be screaming were it not for the fact that his head, or her head is still inside the birth canal. And then, when a pair of scissors are jammed into the back of the neck, a tube is inserted and the brain is pulled out, sucked out, the skull is crushed and the rest of the baby is brought out. There's no way anybody can say that was not a human being. It is a big lie that was foisted-off on people for 30 years. They have given the lie themselves by this new and even more ghastly procedure. Well, I said, I said to my friends at the front door of the church, I said, "Do you believe in abortion?" [They replied] "Yes." And I said, "Do you believe in capitol punishment?" They said, "Absolutely not." I said, it seems to me that the difference between the two of us is very simple. I believe in sparing the life of the innocent and taking the life of the guilty, whereas you believe in taking the life, killing the innocent, and sparing the guilty. But the Bible says, "Woe unto him that takes the life of the innocent ("Cursed be he that taketh reward to slay an innocent person," Deuteronomy 27:25). Woe unto him that calls evil good and good evil" (Isaiah 5:20). And that's exactly what we've been doing in this country. We have been condemning the innocent and sparing the guilty. And that, God is most-definitely not pleased with.

Here, the issue of abortion is reconciled through God's 6th Commandment of "Thou shalt not kill." Yet at no time are we taught Jesus' Spiritual Message regarding killing, sin-relativity, or judging others.

None of the evolving souls of humankind are innocent, not even those entering newborns, and all are impure in some measure (small children are "innocent" in the sense that their souls are relatively powerless in the world, their vulnerability magnified by their not-fully developed brains and bodies, making them targets for selfish adults who seek to oppress and afflict; others, like the infirmed, are also "innocent" in the sense that they too are relatively powerless and targets for those who seek to oppress and afflict).

The Bible repeatedly references the shedding of "innocent blood." The Innocent Blood is Jesus Christ. The shedding of Innocent Blood refers to the death of Jesus. The shedding of your "Innocent Blood" is your denial of His Spirit Within. Deny God's Spirit and you "crucify" a measure of your Christ Within ("Innocent Blood"; Spirit Within), weakening Its Power, further corrupting your soul.

Jesus tells us that those who kill, or are angered without cause, or judge others as "fools" shall be in danger of hell (Matthew 5:21-23). He does not say that our sins will <u>commit</u> our souls to hell, but that they <u>endanger</u> our souls to hell. Killing, like all sin, is relative to the sinner's growth in the Spirit. God knows the Truth of the matter, and regardless of human justice, His Justice will be met.

A stirring controversy is that of partial-birth abortion [the medically correct term is Intact Dilation and Extraction, a procedure rarely used when the fetus is in its second trimester, but most-often used when the fetus is in its third trimester (over 20-21 weeks of gestation)]. This preacher provides a lurid description to horrify and shock, *to instill fear*. The scissor-stabbing story is surely from the famous article titled, *What The Nurse Saw*, published in July, 1995, by the *National Right to Life News*. No opposing viewpoint is given.

The book, *Abortion: Opposing Viewpoints*, refers to partial-birth abortion as a procedure "described with inflammatory inaccuracy as the scissor-stabbing murder of a conscious baby," and as a "malicious attack aimed at families wanting babies, but whose pregnancies went terribly awry."

Groups of women, *many Christian women*, have testified before our government to keep legal the Intact Dilation and Extraction procedure. Forty-nine percent of the pregnancies in America are unplanned. Less than one-half of one percent of all abortions use the IDE procedure. Drugs are often administered to stop the fetal heartbeat before the procedure begins, depending upon the situation. Pregnancies aborted in the third trimester are usually due to complications threatening the mother's life or to serious health problems with the fetus. *But... on the other hand*, pro-life sources report that sometimes healthy fetus' are destroyed via the IDE procedure, and that upwards to two percent of all abortions are by IDE. Who are we to believe?

Why would a woman carry her fetus to near full-term and then casually decide, *as if choosing between beef and chicken*, to abort? If her life is not threatened and the fetus is healthy, why should she be allowed to abort? After all, is she not ultimately responsible for having carried that fetus for so long? But if safe medical procedures are not available, such women will find other means (called "'back-alley abortions"), which may result in serious damage to her, even death.

If 82% of America is Christian, then most women aborting are Christian. *Does Christianity not know that the majority of American women having abortions are Christians?*

Those who believe the fetus has a living soul upon conception would have you believe that a zygote (a fertilized egg) in a petrie dish is a living human soul, *a human being*. And what if that zygote dies due to its caretaker's negligence? Do we press murder charges? Do we hold a funeral? *Will there be an open casket?* Then there are those who are not sure if the zygote has a living soul, but believes it has life. Well, yes it does have life. Everything that exists has life. Even a cadaver has life in the sense that the atoms disassembling within its decaying flesh are alive, having movement. The Spirit of Life is present in all the physicality of the Universe.

The Bible reveals that the Glory of God does not enter until after the physical temple is birthed, making the living soul of the mother of greatest value in the abortion debate. I would not wish to take responsibility for legislating a woman's choice to abort, seeing as how God has provided us with the free will to make our own choices in life. I do not know a woman's heart and motivations, nor am I to judge her as hellbound for her decision to abort. Who knows? Maybe her decision will be the "right" decision for her soul, *leading her and others to greater growth in the Spirit through the ordeal.*

I can only ultimately answer to myself for my decisions and, as I am not a woman, shall never abort. If you believe that abortion is an unforgivable sin, then see to it that you do not have one, *and be reminded that Jesus revealed that all sins shall be forgiven those who do not deny their Good Spirit, and that we are judged of our own hearts and motivations, and that all of us are at different levels of growth in the knowledge and wisdom of the Spirit.*

Aren't there abortion doctors who truly believe that their services are their duties as caregivers and healers? Maybe, for some, it's nothing more than a nine-to-five grind that pays the bills. *Let them be judged of themselves*. Some shall reach the Heaven-goal, some shall not.

Though I hope no woman is faced with the decision to abort, and though I might disagree with her decision, I would not hate, judge, persecute, or discard her. I would respect her decision and love her nonetheless. After all, what more can I do as one who believes in the Good Spirit? Should I, *instead*, be a political influence that might refuse her medical care? Would I rather know that she had a "back-alley abortion" and died? In this world where, *per varying statistics*, somewhere around 35,000 to 40,000 children die every single day due to starvation and disease (per the 2005 statistics from www.starvation.net), would I take comfort in knowing that I influenced the birth of an unwanted child? And what of that unwanted soul? Will I be there to make sure that the little one is properly cared for, nurtured, and loved?

(2 minutes, 10 seconds later)

And then there is the case of, "What about war?" Well, I think war is a terrible, horrible thing. And I think many wars have been without any kind of justification. But the Christian Church has always held through 2,000 years that there is something called, "a just war." Now, it's the same principle as the principle of defending your own life when someone attempts to kill you or your family, comes into your home with the attempt to kill you or your family. Now, that's what the state has been established for, to prevent that kind of wanton criminality and murder and, therefore, the fact that defending your life or the life of your family against an intruder has always been justified by law.

Now we are taught that killing can be justified! *Aah... so now sin is relative! I guess sin is only relative when it suits one's own agendas.* This preacher justifies killing in one situation, but not in another, yet is not personally responsible for the killing in either matter that he should judge one type of killing as "justified" and another as "unjustified."

It is understandable that a man might kill to protect his own life or the life of others because that man's "world" of understanding is such that he truly believes he is doing the "right thing" according to his Good Conscience. We all live in our own respective "worlds." If you know, by your Good Conscience, that something is a sin, and yet you willfully deny your Good Conscience, then you have sinned indeed.

Romans 14:14 (authored by Apostle Paul)

14. I know, and am persuaded by the Lord Jesus, that there is nothing unclean of itself: but to him that esteemeth any thing to be unclean, to him it is unclean.

(2 minutes, 1 seconds later)

In the Old Testament, what sacrifice did you bring if you were guilty of murder? There was none. There was no forgiveness for the murderer. He could flee to one of the cities of refuge, but there was no forgiveness. But in the New Testament, we are told that, in Christ, we can find forgiveness even for those things for which there was no forgiveness in the Old [Testament]. If you are guilty of killing someone, if you are guilty of killing your own child, there is mercy with the Lord. You can find forgiveness with the Lord, and that is the good news.

It is precisely this false religion about Jesus' Message that "sanctified" Christianity's crimes against humanity. Just confess your belief in Christ and you are "saved." America's prisons are full of violent Christians, *but none need be concerned that their souls may be hellbound, as all have been "saved" through the idolatrous worship of Jesus.*

Sowing idolatry tempts and breeds greater enslavement to idolatry, nurturing all sorts of Spiritlessness, even violence. Corporate Christianity teaches children not about the Good Spirit that transcends all religions, but indoctrinates their super-impressionable minds into the service of man-made fears and superstitions. Some have idolatry (6) so stamped upon the their bodies, minds, and souls ("666"; pages viii-ix, 96) that they can easily justify their violence "in the name of God."

The following is an excerpt from "Politically Incorrect," aired February 8, 2002. I thought it interesting, as it mentions partial-birth abortion. The host, Bill Maher, is discussing whether or not churches, *which do not pay taxes*, should be political, endorsing candidates. The guests involved in this discussion are Andrea Sheldon Lafferty (Executive Director of the Traditional Values Coalition) and Elayne Boosler (Comedienne).

Elayne Boosler: I just want them (churches) to pay taxes no matter if they endorse anyone or not. I think this is really what's wrong: they own property; they're for profit; they certainly effect...

Andrea Sheldon Lafferty (interrupting): They aren't for profit.

Bill Maher: Are you kidding. They own more property than Ken Lay (the notorious Enron executive).

Elayne Boosler: They are for profit. Please, if they sold one of those books in the Vatican, they could take care of everybody's teeth who's in the street, poor and dying. Are you kidding me?

Andrea Sheldon Lafferty: They do take care of people.

Elayne Boosler: Yeah, they sure do. Did you see the news today with the endorsing of Ohio's law on the most personal decision a woman can make? Churches should pay taxes...

Andrea Sheldon Lafferty (interrupting): Partial-birth abortion?

Elayne Boosler: That's what you call it, and...

Andrea Sheldon Lafferty (interrupting): When the baby is delivered, and you put the scissors in the head of the baby?

Elayne Boosler: The most anti-abortion Christian women...

Andrea Sheldon Lafferty (interrupting): Oh.

Elayne Boosler: Excuse me, let me finish. The most anti-abortion Christian women testified, and they're still anti-abortion, they testified to Congress begging them not to step-in here, because they had to have it done to save their lives in the most heinous circumstances, and you guys treat it like it's something we do because we got a date and we don't want to be pregnant now.

■ ■ ◆ ■ ■

#14 - Hagee, John (May, 2000)

What about abortion? Proverbs 6:16 says these six things the Lord hates: a proud look; a lying tongue; and hands that shed innocent blood. There is no blood more innocent than the blood of a baby in the mother's womb. I want to say this to every doctor and every nurse watching this telecast across the nation: God says these six things I hate, and when you participate in an abortion, you go in that book that God says, "I hate." When you commit an abortion, God says you're going to be convicted of murder in the first degree when you stand before Him on the Day of Judgment.

God has already "convicted" us through His Righteous Justice, by which we shall be convicted of our devotion *or lack of devotion* to the Good Spirit. There are some who have persecuted or killed in Good Conscience who are now in Heaven (for example, Apostle Paul, when he was Saul).

When will idolatrous religionists ever understand that God does not hate? God, *who is Love and All-Good,* naturally rejects that which denies His Spirit. His "hate" is not of human emotion, but of His natural, unemotional rejection of that which is not One with His Spirit. God loves all of us, even those who, *ultimately, by their own choices,* are growing eternally separated from Him. Is it any wonder that corporate "evangelical" Protestantism in America, *through its history-filled, often-incendiary rhetoric about Jews, abortion, homosexuality, women, slavery, Catholics, and Muslims,* has enabled the births of such hateful Protestant-based groups as the Army of God, Christian Identity, the Aryan Nation, the Universal Church of God, and the Ku Klux Klan?

(continuing)

Many of you say, "Well, it's just a ball of flesh, it's a fetus that has no life." That's an absolute lie. Even Moses, in the Book of Exodus, addressed this subject so clearly <u>that a fool cannot miss it</u>. He said, "if two men are fighting and there's a pregnant woman nearby, and the fruit of her womb, the baby, is injured so that it die, you shall give life for life." Moses covered that in the word of God. This is not something that's cropped-up lately as a politically-correct something. I want you to hear this: abortion today is wrong, tomorrow it's wrong, it will always be wrong, it is murder in the council of God.

Exodus 21:22-25 (authorship unknown, probably Joshua, maybe Moses)

22. **If men strive, and hurt a woman with child, so that her fruit depart from her, and yet no mischief follow: he shall be surely punished, according as the woman's husband will lay upon him; and he shall pay as the judges determine.**
23. **And if any mischief follow, then thou shalt give life for life,**
24. **Eye for eye, tooth for tooth, hand for hand, foot for foot,**
25. **Burning for burning, wound for wound, stripe for stripe.**

The scenario in Exodus 21:22-25 is not about abortion, but about a man who hurts a pregnant woman badly enough that she aborts her fetus. It is obviously not about a woman who *chooses* to abort her fetus, *or maybe that truth is so clear "that a fool cannot miss it."*

The Bible says absolutely nothing about abortion. The closest mention to abortion is about a woman who loses her fetus after having been physically hurt by another person.

When King David committed adultery with Bathsheba, impregnating her, and then had her husband killed to avoid scandal, God was so angered with David that He struck down the baby seven days after its birth. So, does that mean that every time a child is born of an adulterous affair that leads to the death of the woman's husband by her lover, that the newborn should be slain on its seventh day of life? *After all, it's right there in the Bible!*

Zealous abortionists pervert the meaning of a Biblical verse regarding the loss of a fetus in order to justify their Old Testament "punishment" upon today's abortionists. But the Old Testament's Letter of the Law is, per Jesus, superseded and fulfilled by His New Testament's Spirit of the Law regarding "an eye for an eye," as follows.

Matthew 5:38-46 (spoken by Jesus; authored by Apostle Matthew)

38. Ye have heard that it hath been said, An eye for an eye, and a tooth for a tooth:
39. But I say unto you, That ye resist not evil: but whosoever shall smite thee on thy right cheek, turn to him the other also.
40. And if any man will sue thee at the law, and take away thy coat, let him have thy cloke [your more-expensive overcoat] also.
41. And whosoever shall compel thee to go a mile, go with him twain.
42. Give to him that asketh thee, and from him that would borrow of thee turn not thou away.
43. Ye have heard that it hath been said, Thou shalt love thy neighbour, and hate thine enemy.
44. But I say unto you, Love your enemies, bless them that curse you, do good to them that hate you, and pray for them which despitefully use you, and persecute you;
45. That ye may be the children of your Father which is in heaven: for he maketh his sun to rise on the evil and on the good, and sendeth rain on the just and on the unjust.
46. For if ye love them which love you, what reward have ye?

Chapter 10

HOMOSEXUALITY

The Spiritful mind is of compassionate understanding in its discernment of others' life-situations. Having not lived in their shoes, *your Spiritful mind* can only try to fathom: the unique constructs of *their* minds; the experiences and lessons of *their* complex lives; the conflict between *their* Spirit and anti-Spirit; and the full nature of the fruits *they* bear. The "world" of one's reality is built upon one's physical, mental, emotional, and spiritual knowledge and wisdom of Good and evil. As every soul was born of God, we are all spiritual siblings, having life through the Spirit Within.

Your Spiritful mind knows that your spiritual siblings are evolving at their own pace, and that what is Good for them, *though maybe not Good for you*, is part of *their* evolution towards or away from God. Do not be so sure that their works, in the end, will not have been for the best, *not just for them, but for those whose lives were affected by them.*

All God cares about is that we live and grow in His Spirit of Selfless Love and Goodness more and more with every passing day, giving life to His Spirit willingly and joyfully as often as possible. It is difficult to believe that in this country of mostly Christians, so many homosexual children and adolescents kill themselves, three times more than heterosexual children and adolescents.

There comes a time in one's life when one's sexual nature is realized, beginning an acceleration of unfoldment into lessons regarding human sexuality, lessons that shall bring joys and sufferings. Where heterosexuality presents its problems, homosexuality presents an entirely different dimension of problems, as it is most-often rejected, *even feared and hated* by corporate religions, governments, and societies. A person awakened to his/her homosexual nature, *if having been subjected to homophobia by society, peers, and/or family,* may decide that it is best to keep it a "secret."

Souls raised in homophobia are naturally horrified when they, one day, discover their own homosexual nature. Homophobia often breeds homophobic homosexuals. On one extreme are the homophobic homosexuals who "turn the pain inward," who do not seek to blame or hurt other gays, but who become their own worse tormentors against their own homosexuality (self-loathing, self-worthlessness, etc.). On the other extreme are the homophobic heterosexuals who "turn the pain outward," who seek to blame, *even hurt and destroy* gays due to their own homosexual "issues." Homophobia, like all other fear-based selfishness, can be overcome, *building the Spirit Within*, or compounded, *further corrupting the soul.*

On one extreme, the fear of being a rejected, loathed homosexual is so overwhelming that adolescents, *even children* commit suicide. On the other extreme, homophobia teaches children and adolescents to openly hate homosexuals. So, on one end of the spectrum are the self-destructive, homophobic homosexuals, even suicidally so, and on the other end are the heterosexual homophobes who seek to destroy the homosexuality around them *in order to "defeat" the homosexual nature within themselves* [it stands to reason that such extreme homophobes wrestle with homosexual desires, *whether consciously realized or not*, otherwise homosexuality would not be such an all-consuming, unresolved, explosive issue in their lives.]

How is it that a "Christian" parent would hate, *even disown* a homosexual son or daughter simply because that person's soul has its own life's lessons to experience and learn? Where does the Bible instruct refusing Selfless Love to one's own child? Could it be that the powerful force of corporate Christianity has so perverted God's Message as to have made acceptable the blaming, rejecting, *even hating* of homosexuals?

Billions of households, Christian and non-Christian, invite the fear of homosexuality into their lives with regularity, some so much that their homophobia is a way of life. Many refuse to believe that homosexuals are their spiritual siblings. *Homophobia is the idolatrous "fear-worship" of homosexuality over and above the fearless, Selfless Love of the Spirit.*

Do you not know that you are going to die one day? Do you live to fear death or do you know that death is part of life, and live not for death, but for life? Have you not heard that homosexuality is a part of life? Do you live to fear homosexuals or do you choose live in the Spirit that knows no fear?

Homosexuality, like any issue, can be understood by the Letter of the Law or the Spirit of the Law. Christians who seek to fear, blame, and reject homosexuals find "support" in their literal interpretations of the Bible, the main one being that homosexuality is an "abomination." Many believe they have the right to judge and persecute homosexuals because the Bible calls homosexuality an "abomination." But God tells us that all of our selfish lusts are abominable to Him, *naturally*. Everything that is a denial of the Spirit is: "abomination"; "hated"; "wicked"; "unclean"; and "sin."

> Leviticus 20:13-14 proves "abomination" is wickedness.
> Deuteronomy 20:18 proves "abomination" is sin.
> Leviticus 5:3-5 proves sin is uncleanness.
> Romans 14:23 proves that sin is anything not of faith in God (sin is that which denies your Good Conscience, *the Good Mind and Spirit Within you*).

All sin is an abomination and, *naturally* (not emotionally), repulsive to God, as everything that is an abomination lacks Oneness with His Spirit. Judging others as "abominations" and hellbound for what you perceive as "sin" is to judge yourself likewise for your own abominations.

Homosexuality is no more an abomination than heterosexuality which, per the Bible, is an abomination in every way except between faithful partners in "marriage" [meaning that sex is always an "abomination" when lustful, but not when consensually bound in Selfless Love, as such are "marriages" aligned with the Spirit; marriages (in the Spirit) are "'honorable in all" (Hebrews 13:4)].

If about 10% of humanity is homosexual, then there are far more heterosexual abominations committed daily upon Earth. So why all the preaching that propagates fear and intolerance towards homosexuals when heterosexuality, daily, manifests far more abominable acts?

In the Old Testament book, *Leviticus*, a huge list is given of things "unclean" to eat, and how those who eat such things have committed abominations, causing themselves to be unclean for a time. In the New Testament, Jesus' Gospel of the Spirit of the Law supersedes the Levitical rules of the Letter of the Law when He preaches, *"Hear, and understand: Not that which goeth into the mouth defileth a man; but that which cometh out of the mouth, this defileth a man"* (Matthew 15:10-11). Later, He continues, *"Do not ye yet understand, that whatsoever entereth in at the mouth goeth into the belly, and is cast out into the draught? But those things which proceed out of the mouth come forth from the heart; and they defile the man. For out of the heart proceed evil thoughts, murders, adulteries, fornications, thefts, false witness, blasphemies: These are the things which defile a man"* (Matthew 15:17-20).

Here, Jesus reveals that selfish thoughts and desires precede the abominable (selfish) action. It is our selfish actions that *give "life" to and justify* our selfish thoughts and desires. It is not the selfish actions, but the anti-Spirit fueling them that further defiles our souls. The One Way to cleanse our souls of anti-Spirit (selfishness) is by not giving "life" to it (we are to overcome our selfish thoughts and desires with the Selfless Spirit).

Per Jesus, it is not the "sinful" act that is the end-all issue, but rather what is in our hearts and motivations. We are not saved or damned by our works, but by the Spirit or anti-Spirit *behind and within our works*. People surrender to sin (selfishness) for a myriad of complex reasons. We have all sinned, and are all unclean, and will remain so until our ascension to Salvation. Knowing this, that all are unclean due to various measures and types of sin, *including consensual, sexual "sin," whether homosexual or heterosexual,* what is it that God desires for our unclean souls? *That we grow in His Good Spirit.*

We are all spiritually impure, which puts every one of our souls a "level playing field," so to speak. Each of us are, *ultimately, by our own choices,* headed towards either the hell-goal or the Heaven-goal. Our movement on the "playing field" is our karma, which is the evolutionary nature of our soul's Spirit versus anti-Spirit, *an ever-changing, personal process.*

First Peter 2:11 (authored by Apostle Peter)

11. Dearly beloved, I beseech you as strangers and pilgrims, abstain from fleshly lusts, which war against the soul;

"Fleshly lusts" is not just about sex, but about worldly lusts (lusts for money, power, status, vengeance, food, etc.). All lusts rise from selfishness. Consensual sex, *heterosexual or homosexual,* can be born of lust or Selfless Love. Consensual sex born of lust *is among the least of all sins.*

First Corinthians 6:18 (authored by Apostle Paul)

18. Flee fornication. Every sin that a man doeth is without the body; but he that committeth fornication sinneth against his own body.

"Fornication" is sexual lust that is a sin against only your temple. In order for fornication to be a sin against only your being, it must be:

- between consenting adults (otherwise it is pedophilia or rape);
- private (otherwise it is an offense against the general public); and
- non-adulterous (otherwise it is an offense against your spouse).

First Corinthians 6:18 reveals that consensual sex born of lust, *heterosexual or homosexual,* is a sin against only your being, making this among the least of your sins, *naturally,* as you are not "sinning" against anyone else but, ultimately, yourself. And so, we understand that the greatest of all spiritual crimes are, *naturally,* when you deliberately hurt others (rape, adultery, theft, murder, deception, etc.).

Must we not keep sexuality in its correct perspective? The biological blast-off that sends every soul from childhood into adolescence brings all sorts of sexual awakenings. It is a deeply personal experience that hits all of us differently. Some spend the rest of their lives trying to get control over their sexual lusts. But whatever you do in your sexual self-discovery, *consensually, that is born of lust,* is a sin against only your temple, *and among the least of all sins.*

First Thessalonians 4:3-8 (authored by Apostle Paul)

3. For this is the will of God, even your sanctification, that ye should abstain from fornication [abstain from sexual lust]**:**

4. That every one of you should know how to possess his vessel in sanctification and honour;
5. Not in the lust of concupiscence [carnal, animalistic sex], even as the Gentiles which know not God:
6. That no man go beyond [the Spirit] and defraud his brother in any matter: because that the Lord is the avenger of all such, as we also have forewarned you and testified.
7. For God hath not called us unto uncleanness, but unto holiness.
8. He therefore that despiseth, despiseth not man, but God, who hath also given unto us his holy Spirit. [Those who reject other souls are not rejecting them, but rejecting God.]

God knows that our souls shall be faced with sexuality, as our bodies come with sexual organs and sexual hormones. We are instructed to overcome our sexual lusts ("uncleanness") through either abstinence or Selfless Love ("Holiness").

Romans 1:24-27 (authored by Apostle Paul)

24. Wherefore God also gave them up to uncleanness through the lusts of their own hearts, to dishonour their own bodies between themselves: [It is through the lusts (selfishness) of our own hearts that our fallen souls have dishonored themselves.]
25. Who changed the truth of God into a lie, and worshiped and served the creature more than the Creator, who is blessed for ever. Amen. [The Truth of God is to conduct His Spirit only, but when our fallen souls deny the Spirit through idolatrous worship, we serve "created things" over our Creator-Spirit.]
26. For this cause God gave them up unto vile affections: for even their women did change the natural use into that which is against nature: [It is because of a soul's idolatry (selfishness) that it suffers Spiritless affections, or lusts. The true "natural use" of the woman is for the giving of her sexual nature in the Spirit of Selfless Love, not lust. All who lust shall be given up to their lusts. Even women will give of their sexual vitality in lust, which is against the nature of God's Spirit.]
27. And likewise also the men, leaving the natural use of the woman, burned in their lust one toward another; men with men working that which is unseemly, and receiving in themselves that recompence of their error which was meet. [And likewise shall men lust one toward another, reaping ("recompence") the lust ("error") they have sown.]

The Letter-of-the-Law mindset misinterprets the above verses to justify their "in the name of God" disagreement with homosexuality, though the Spirit of the Law regarding the homosexuality issue reveals a greater problem that afflicts <u>all</u> of our fallen souls: Lust! All who lust, *whether their lusts be sexual or not*, shall suffer their lusts, *naturally*, as they are living in their lusts. Nonetheless, if your lusts, *whatever they be,* hurt no one, then they are sins against only your being, and among the least of your sins, *among the least of God's concerns regarding your soul's growth in His Spirit.* Your personal lusts are relatively insignificant as long as you do not hurt others. Stay true to the Spirit and, in time, your lusts shall lose steam.

A most-widely misused Scripture about homosexuality is Leviticus 20:13, which reveals that homosexuality is an "abomination" and that homosexuals shall be "put to death." *When literally interpreted,* it is a firm argument supporting intolerance towards homosexuals. Do not forget that other verses in the Bible, *when also literally interpreted,* state that those who curse their mother and father shall be "put to death" (Leviticus 20:9), and that adulterers shall be "put to death" (Leviticus 20:10), and that those who afflict widows or fatherless children shall be "put to death" (Exodus 22:23-24), and that all idolaters shall be "utterly destroyed" (Exodus 22:20).

Corporate Christianity, which has tempted and bred idolatry within millions of souls, conveniently ignores God's revelation about idolaters being "utterly destroyed," but rather holds itself up as "Holy and Righteous" in its Spiritless teachings about homosexuality.

God tells us that sin brings death. The fact that all of us die is proof-positive that our souls have sinned. The Bible is stuffed-full of information revealing that if you do this thing or that thing, you are going to die. Have you known anyone during your lifetime who has not sinned? Do you not know that a multitude of deaths happen daily? Are you not preceded by generations upon generations upon generations of dead ancestors? So, death of the physical body is not the issue. It is the Life, *the Spirit Within,* that is the issue, as that is what determines whether or not your soul will, in the end, of its own choices, have Life Eternal or not.

Another homophobic belief is that homosexual feelings are a choice. Homosexual "feelings" are no more a choice than heterosexual "feelings." *The choice is whether or not to act upon your sexual desires, making your sexual desires a reality aligned with selfishness or Selfless Love.* Homosexual desires are an inseparable truth to homosexuals just as heterosexual desires are an inseparable truth to heterosexuals.

Most will say they never made a conscious choice to be gay or straight, but that their sexual nature has always been a natural part of their being. Nonetheless, there are a few who say that their homosexuality was a conscious choice. *Fine. Who am I to question another's sexual self-identity?*

The United States sees twice as many suicides as homicides, an average of 3 suicides an hour. The biggest group of self-killers are teen homosexuals. Is this not a direct consequence of America's corporate churches that, *knowingly or unknowingly,* propagate hatred and intolerance by teaching that all homosexuals are going to hell? Are there not

Christians who will show their kindness and love to scoundrels, even murderers on death row, and yet shun and disown one of their own children for being gay? *God forbid they should show themselves examples of the Spirit unto their own children.* When the truth, wisdom, peace, kindness, and forgiveness of the Spirit is the foundation of a child/parent relationship, then every "trouble" shall be overcome.

Another issue regarding homosexuality is marriage. In the New Testament, Apostle Paul tells us that "it is good for a man not to touch a woman" (First Corinthians 7:1-2). *Does this not contradict the Old Testament's literal interpretation of "be fruitful and multiply?"* (actually, no it doesn't; page 130). Paul continues, "Nevertheless, to avoid fornication, let every man him have his own wife" (First Corinthians 7:1-2). Literalists interpret "wife" as proof that marriage, in God's eyes, must be between a man and woman. But how can that narrow definition of "wife" be so embraced when Christ refers to the Saved Souls of Humankind as His "bride" and His "wife" (Revelation 18:23, 19:2, 19:7)? Furthermore, souls do not have genitals and there is no sex or marriages between souls in Heaven (Matthew 22:30; Luke 20:34-36).

Spiritually interpreted, the term "wife" refers to anyone who is a companion of God, who lives to conduct the Good Spirit. *When interpreted literally,* "wife" is a legal term for the female partner of a man-made, contractual marriage. Like confession and baptism, a "marriage" before God is not simply by way of some "outward" ritual. Being legally married does not ensure being mutually "wed" in Spirit. Currently, around half of all marriages in America end up in divorce. Isn't this proof that these marriages were not One with the Spirit, not True marriages?

Marriage was first seen in the Garden of Eden between Adam and Eve... a marriage in Spirit, without a legal contract, *as marriage in Spirit was not intended to lead to divorce, and therefore without need of a worldly, man-made, legal contract.*

Truest marriage between humans is an everlasting bond in Spirit, the physical-mental-emotional-spiritual bond of shared Selfless Love. We are "married" to our parents, our siblings, our friends, and our jobs in some measure. Every experience "marries" us to that experience. We are to be married to the Spirit before all worldly "marriages."

The Bible never instructs us to utilize legally-binding, written, marriage contracts. In the days of Moses, it was the man who created the marriage to a woman through his spoken order and, as well, created the divorce through his spoken order. Ironically, the only written contract regarding marriage in the Bible is the "bill of divorcement" (Deuteronomy 24:1).

God permitted Moses to allow divorces via a Bill of Divorcement, which was to be used for divorce only if the wife was "unclean," having had sex outside the marriage. Though it sounds as if such a wife is solely guilty, Jesus tells us that this bill was created because of the cruelty, *or "hardness of heart,"* of some husbands (Mark 10:4-5). The Bill of Divorcement was initially created because of cruel husbands.

Because a man could, *by his spoken word*, divorce his unfaithful wife, such women lost everything... their children, their family unit, their means of support. The Bill of Divorcement was created to protect "unclean" wives from being abandoned without recompence by the verbal divorces of their hardhearted husbands.

Marriage is not "sanctified" unto God by way of legalism or ritual. With or without the ritualistic ceremony, a legally-binding marriage means nothing before God if it is not, before all else, a *Divine Companionship* in His Selfless Spirit of Love and Goodness.

Homosexuals who want a legally-binding marriage simply want the same legal benefits afforded to partners in heterosexual marriages. Though legal, contractual marriages afford certain benefits, a "marriage" is not a marriage before God unless it is bound to the Spirit of Selfless Love and Good Works.

Marriage requires no diamond rings and no expensive, over-the-top marriage rituals. If these worldly things are desired, that's fine, but that which proves a marriage is the inner, invisible, "Spirit contract" between partners, justified by a partnership of Selfless Love and Good Works.

There are two end-all marriages. Those *married* to the Spirit shall have the Marriage Supper of the Lamb (Salvation; Heaven; Revelation 19:9). The rest shall have the Supper of the Great God (damnation; hell; Revelation 19:17).

Romans 12:1-2 (authored by Apostle Paul)

1. **I beseech you therefore, brethren, by the mercies of God, that ye present your bodies a living sacrifice, holy, acceptable unto God, which is your reasonable service.**
2. **And be not conformed to this world: but be ye transformed by the renewing of your mind, that ye may prove what is that good, and acceptable, and perfect, will of God.** [Give not yourselves over to lusts, but be transformed through the New Consciousness of the Spirit-Mind ('renewing of your mind').]

■ ■ ◆ ■ ■

#26 - Mohler, R. Albert (October, 1998)

The Bible so clearly says that homosexuality is wrong. My conscience is bound to the word of God: homosexuality is a sin, an abomination before God.

Here is the all-too-common idolatry of the Letter of the Law over the Spirit of the Law. If your Good Conscience rejects homosexuality, *then do not have homosexual sex.*

When one's "conscience is bound to the word of God," then one's Good Conscience knows to live by the Spirit of the Law and to leave Judgment to God's Grace. Instead, groupist "mindsets" love us-versus-them, embracing separatism, as doing so exalts *their* group over non-groupies judged "unholy" and "hellbound." The Truth, *of course*, is that there are Spiritful and Spiritless souls of every kind in all walks of life.

Fear lives in the hearts of Christians who hurl the word "abomination" whenever the subject of homosexuality arises. How is it that they so readily ignore their own abominations? Are they not denying the Spirit in their idolatrous worship of the Letter of the Law? Have they not read that idolaters shall be "utterly destroyed" (Exodus 22:20).

■ ■ ◆ ■ ■

#19 - Jones III, Bob (on *Larry King Live* with Larry King; February, 2000)

Larry King: The hardest thing, I've discussed this with others in the clergy, I've never understood it because, do you know when you chose heterosexuality? I mean, if homosexuality is chosen, then heterosexuality must be chosen. Did you make a conscious decision one day to like women?

Bob Jones III: No. Heterosexuality, according to Genesis, when He created woman for the man and of the man, and said they too will be one flesh...

Larry King (interrupting): So, you think that's natural.

Bob Jones III: That is a God-given natural choice. God ordained that. God put that in me. Homosexuality is a perversity. It is a choice of sin.

Larry King: But God loves the sinner as much as He loves you. Right?

Bob Jones: Absolutely. Absolutely.

Larry King: So, He loves the gay. He loves the Pope. Right?

Bob Jones III: Yes. A homosexual can be saved. The Pope can be saved if he would embrace Jesus Christ and His finished work on the cross as the only means to Salvation. If he would say, "Grace is by Christ alone, Salvation is not of works but by grace through faith in Jesus Christ." If he would believe that he could be saved.

There are hundreds upon hundreds of mammal and bird species that naturally engage in same-sex behavior (this issue is discussed at greater length later in this chapter). Homosexuality is as natural as heterosexuality. What is not "natural" before God is when we choose selfishness over the Good Spirit.

Our sexual desires come as karmic lessons to our souls. Like all of life's lessons, we have the free will to empower selfishness or Selflessness. Just as heterosexuals have their sexual loves and lusts, so do homosexuals. We are not judged by the sexual act itself, but judged by our Selfless and/or selfish hearts and motivations regarding the act.

Here, this Protestant "mindset" instructs the Pope and homosexuals to Salvation by following its particular "way" to God. It readily labels homosexuality "perverse," but does not see the perversity of its own selfishness.

■ ■ ◆ ■ ■

#35 - Rogers, Adrian (August 22, 1999)

Sexual perversion. The perverts (homosexuals) are becoming bold, even arrogant, saying that America must approve this lifestyle, and unless you believe the word of God, you have no authority to stand against it, because you have no set standards for what is right and what is wrong.

Selfless Love ... that is "what is right." Name-calling and fear... that is "what is wrong."

■ ■ ◆ ■ ■

#21 - Kennedy, D. James (October, 1998)

Here is reference to Oscar Wilde (1854-1900), the famous British author who was jailed for homosexuality.

Wilde said, "I can stand anything but temptation." It's not hard to understand why Oscar Wilde, who was a total effete and an ungodly man, would have said that he could stand anything but temptation. There are millions who follow in his trade. They are like the dead, bloated corpses of fish, floating down the stream. They have no power whatsoever to swim against it. And yet we are called not to the broad way that leads to destruction, but to the narrow way we are called to fight through this life.

(later)

Faith is a plant that grows best in winter. Faith grows best in the midst of trials and tribulations and persecutions.

Mr. Wilde is judged an "ungodly man," but who among us knows the very joys, sufferings, and Spirit of his soul? When will high-holier-than-thou preachers stop readily judging others as ungodly and hell-bound? They pass themselves off as "Holy and Righteous," but deny Jesus' Spirit.

Mr. Wilde's wisecrack about being able to stand anything but temptation was surely just that... *a humorous wisecrack, born of a witty, highly-intelligent mind*. But Mr. Wilde is judged by this singular witticism, marking him as some guru for the "millions" who follow in his "trade" of powerlessness over temptation. We are then taught that these powerless millions are unable to "swim" against their powerlessness. How can this make sense? To believe such is to believe that some souls are caught in a vortex of powerlessness that, no matter their efforts, cannot be escaped. To believe such is to believe predestination, which denies free will. If change (repentance) is not an option for these souls, then how shall God hold them responsible for their powerless lives if they never had the power to change?

It is correct that faith grows best in the midst of trials and tribulations. Being so, why not speak to Wilde's spiritual growth amidst his sufferings instead of judging him "ungodly?" Wherever his soul is, it is quite possible that it is far-more evolved in the Spirit than the soul of this minister.

■ ■ ◆ ■ ■

#21 - Kennedy, D. James (June 6, 1999)

> There is nothing in the realm of human life which is as powerful as the grace of God. It is the most transforming power on this Earth. It transforms drunkards into sober men and women. It breaks the shackles of addicts. Cocaine, alcohol, cigarettes, or whatever other dope a person may be addicted to. It sets men free. It makes the homosexual straight, and thousands can attest to that. It makes the lascivious and the vile, the profane, the vulgar clean. It's the most powerful force in the world.

It is through sufferings that men and women choose to change their lives. If alcoholics and addicts did not suffer physical, emotional, spiritual, mental, financial and/or other sufferings due to their addictions, they would have no reason to change. *Their desire to overcome their sufferings* is the first step towards repentance, or change. They change because they know, *a knowing within*, that they must do so to return to wellness. This does not necessarily mean that they have had a "religious experience."

Once again, the incendiary word "abomination" is used regarding homosexuals, though there are more heterosexual abominations committed daily. The "cure" for homosexual lusts is not becoming "straight," as the cure for heterosexual lusts is not by simply getting married. *Consensual lust is about one's heart and motivations underlying the sexual act, and is the least of all sins, having harmed none but your own being, each person responsible for his/her own consensual actions.*

There are surely many homosexuals who are living conduits of Selfless Love and at peace with their homosexuality. So be it! "Sin" is relative, and what we deem to be unclean is unclean (Romans 14:14).

Why this ongoing and ever-increasing battle between the Church and homosexuals? Because of selfishness alive in the hearts and motivations of those Christians who deny homosexuals the love, acceptance, and humanity afforded to others. Also responsible is the selfishness alive in the hearts and motivations of those homosexuals who fear or despise their "enemies." None of this ill-will is aligned with the Spirit.

Every soul has its lessons to learn. Learn your own lessons well, and pour out your Spirit Within upon others as best you know, that they might see your Spirit and follow. If you have not the strength to pour out the Spirit, *then put the issue to rest*, but do not be tempted to pour out selfishness.

Who is to say that life's lessons, whatever they be, are not, *in the end*, for the best? Who among us, *all having sinned*, can point a finger and judge another's lessons as a "curse" or "blessing?" What you may deem a "blessing" for yourself may be a "curse" for another, *and vice versa*. All of our lives are met with different situations, blessings, and trials and tribulations so that we might awaken to the Spirit and follow.

If it wasn't for the darkness in our souls, we would not be on Earth with the capability of growing in the Light. The purpose of darkness is so that we might come to know the Light, for how can you know the value and definition of the Light without knowing the value and definition of that which is not the Light? How can you know the value of anything without having "experienced it" in some measure?

■ ■ ◆ ■ ■

#8 - Falwell, Jerry (on *CNN with Wolf Blitzer;* February, 2000)

Wolf Blitzer: First of all, explain to us what you have been doing on this issue of reaching out to homosexuals, and what do you think Governor Bush (governor of Texas) should be doing?

Jerry Falwell: Well, Wolf, first of all, as a Christian who believes the Bible as the inerrant word of God, I do believe that homosexuality is always sin, its always wrong. But hating sin and loving sinners is what Jesus and all of His followers have done for two thousand years.

Believing that the Bible is "the inerrant word of God" is meaningless if you know not the *Spirit* of the word of God. Teaching that "homosexuality is always sin" denies Jesus' revelation that sin is relative. Though it is true that Jesus hates sin and loves the sinner (Revelation 2:6), it is untrue that this is what "all of His followers have done for two thousand years." History shows how corporate Christianity has judged and labeled non-Christians as "heretics," often persecuting, terrorizing, and/or murdering them so as to convert regions and nations. The savage methods used to *cleanse* their Christian "realm" of non-Christians forced countless souls to convert, subsequently enslaving centuries of generations of souls to idolatrous, man-made, Letter-of-the-Law religion.

■ ■ ◆ ■ ■

#8 - Falwell, Jerry (on *Rivera Live* with Geraldo Rivera; with guest Larry Flynt, Publisher of Hustler Magazine; November 14, 1999)

Jerry Falwell (responding to Larry Flynt regarding obscene books and pornography): Larry, I'm coming at this not from a First Amendment perspective, but as a pastor for 44 years, nearly, at the same church, and with thousands of people that I've pastored, counseled, worked with. I have known so many lives wrecked, ruined, hurt, damaged because of pornography, soft core and hard core, and I realize, I fully understand that, now, you're a "Sunday school league" in that industry compared to what's on the Internet and many other places. But I think it's all bad, and think it's all hurtful, and no I'm not for censoring the printed word. That's not where I'm at.

Larry Flynt: Well, look, I wanted to make one quick point here with the reverend. You know, there's nothing wrong with having values, I am sure the reverend does, if they work for you and your family. Where I part company, now where I think you're wrong is when you try to impose them on other people.

(2 minutes, 32 seconds later)
Larry Flynt: Reverend Falwell, one thing that I think you need to take into your heart, and that is we pay a price for everything, and the price we pay to live in a free society is toleration. We have to tolerate things that we don't necessarily like, so we can be free. So, you may not like your neighbor's lifestyle, you might not like his reading material, you might not like what the bookstore down the street sells, but that's all part of living in a free society.

Jerry Falwell: But that doesn't keep me from saying that I don't like it, and I think it's bad, and doing all I can to keep everyone from patronizing it.

Geraldo Rivera: Well, let's see if John from Texas likes it. John from Texas, you're on the air, John.

Caller (John): Reverend Falwell, I'd like to ask a question for you sir. The question is that, in the New Testament, doesn't it say for the person to turn the other cheek?

Jerry Falwell: Yes, it does. It says seven times seventy, that's 490 times, by which time the Lord, I think, implied that you would have learned, habitually, to forgive, continue forgiving. That has nothing to do with the tolerance or acceptance of that which displeases the Lord.

That which displeases the Lord is that which denies His Spirit. Here, we are taught that forgiveness has nothing to do with the tolerance or acceptance of sin. *Oh, oh... yes it does. It has everything to do with tolerance and acceptance of what you perceive as others' "sins," at least the best you know.* All have sinned and fallen short of God's Glory. If someone's selfishness is so offensive to you, depart peacefully and do not take any of that person's "dirt" with you (Matthew 10:14).

If Jesus had no tolerance or acceptance of others' selfishness, we would all be in hell right now. He certainly would not have said, *while suffering on the cross,* "forgive them, for they know not what they do" (Luke 23:34). If forgiveness has nothing to do with the tolerance or acceptance of others' selfishness, then it has everything to do with the intolerance and rejection of others, or, in a word: *separatism.* The wellspring of corporate Christianity's every manner of hatred, violence, and wars is *separatism,* the rejection of Oneness with God's Selfless, Good Spirit.

■ ■ ◆ ■ ■

#14 - Hagee, John (January 9, 2000)

God judged Sodom and Gomorrah because of their homosexual lifestyle, and he buried it with fire and brimstone, and God will judge America for its endorsement of the homosexual lifestyle.

Sodom and Gomorrah... the great cornerstone of Christian homophobia. Let's see what Jesus, His brother Jude, and the prophet Ezekiel had to say on this subject.

Matthew 10:11-15 (spoken by Jesus; authored by Apostle Matthew)

11. **And into whatsoever city or town ye shall enter, inquire who in it is worthy; and there abide till ye go thence.**
12. **And when ye come into an house, salute it.**
13. **And if the house be worthy, let your peace come upon it: but if it be not worthy, let your peace return to you.**
14. **And whosoever shall not receive you, nor hear your words, when ye depart out of that house or city, shake off the dust of your feet.**
15. **Verily I say unto you, It shall be more tolerable for the land of Sodom and Gomorrha in the day of judgment, than for that city.**

Jesus' displeasure is towards those who reject His Spirit. *Why does Jesus tell us that Sodom and Gomorrah will suffer less on the "day of judgment" than a city that rejects the Spirit?* Because Sodom and Gomorrah, destroyed long before Jesus' birth, knew not His Gospel of the Spirit. As given in Luke 12:48, Jesus tells us, *"But he that knew not (like the people of Sodom and Gomorrah), and did commit things worthy of stripes, shall be beaten with few stripes. For unto whomsoever much is given* (*referring to the living souls of today who have the benefit of His Gospel*), *of him shall be much required."* In other words, today's living souls are presently in greater danger of hell than were the sinful souls of Sodom and Gomorrah who did not have the Gospel of the Good Spirit, as we have.

Matthew 11:20-24 (authored by Apostle Matthew)

20. **Then began he** [Jesus] **to upbraid the cities wherein most of his mighty works were done, because they repented not:**
21. **Woe unto thee, Chorazin! woe unto thee, Bethsaida! for if the mighty works, which were done in you, had been done in Tyre and Sidon, they would have repented long ago in sackcloth and ashes.**
22. **But I say unto you, It shall be more tolerable for Tyre and Sidon at the day of judgment, than for you.**
23. **And thou, Capernaum, which art exalted unto heaven, shalt be brought down to hell: for if the mighty works, which have been done in thee, had been done in Sodom, it would have remained until this day.** [Jesus reveals that had His Gospel been preached in Sodom, the Sodomites would have heard and repented.]
24. **But I say unto you, That it shall be more tolerable for the land of Sodom in the day of judgment, than for thee.**

Jude 7 (authored by Jude, Jesus' brother)

7. **Even as Sodom and Gomorrha, and the cities about them in like manner, giving themselves over to fornication, and going after strange flesh, are set forth for an example, suffering the vengeance of eternal fire.**

The phrase, "going after strange flesh," supports the erroneous belief that the sin of Sodom was homosexuality. Yes, the men of Sodom encompassed Lot's house wanting to force sex upon the two visitors inside that had recently arrived. These two visitors appeared as men, *but were actually Angels, Pure and Sinless.* Here is the meaning of "strange flesh," *for their flesh, unlike all the flesh in Sodom, was that of Angels, Pure and Sinless.*

If the sin of Sodom was homosexuality, then why hadn't the Sodomites ever forced sex upon Lot, his sons, and sons-in-law? Because Lot and all the members of his family, like all the other residents of Sodom, were not Pure and Sinless, *not uncorrupted like the two visitors of "strange flesh."*

The crime of the Sodomites was that they sought to corrupt the uncorrupted, *to corrupt the uncorrupted Mind and Spirit alive Within the flesh,* the same crime that satan successfully committed in Eden, the same crime that satan unsuccessfully attempted upon Jesus who, by having never sinned, overcame death and hell.

Ezekiel 16:49-50 (spoken by God; authored by the prophet Ezekiel)

49. Behold, this was the iniquity of thy sister Sodom, pride, fulness of bread, and abundance of idleness was in her and in her daughters, neither did she strengthen the hand of the poor and needy.

50. And they were haughty, and committed abomination before me: therefore I took them away as I saw good.

Per God to His prophet Ezekiel, Sodom rejected the Spirit through self-exaltation, idleness, self-satisfaction, lack of Charity (Selfless Love), and "abomination." But what abomination did they commit? Nothing is defined as an "abomination" in the story of Sodom and Gomorrah. Clearly, the "abomination" was the Sodomites' desire to corrupt the uncorrupted Spirit of God by seeking to rape the "strange flesh" of His two Angels.

The sins of Sodom and Gomorrah are not about homosexuality, but about the selfishness of pride, wealth, greed, inhospitality, inhumanity, and laziness. Their greatest sin was that the corrupted sought to corrupt the uncorrupted: *the Mind and Spirit of God Within the flesh.* Jesus reveals the sin of Sodom and Gomorrah not as homosexuality, but as their rejection of the Good Spirit (Matthew 10:11-15, 11:20-24).

■ ■ ◆ ■ ■

Crimes against homosexuals doubled between 1990 and 1998, per the FBI (reported on PBS' *Frontline: Assault on Gay America*).

In the early morning of February 20th, 1999, a well-respected, 39-year-old, churchgoing, Christian man in Alabama was murdered for being gay. He had been stabbed in the neck, savagely beaten with an ax handle until dead, then set on fire. His murderer cited the Bible as proof that homosexuality is an irredeemable, hellbound evil, and that Heaven is for people like him. His exact words: *"God forgives for everything. If you ask you shall receive, and I asked for forgiveness and that's what I got. I repented. He's in hell because he's a homosexual, and it tells you in the New Testament that that's wrong."* His only regret, tearfully given, was that he was in prison for the rest of his life. When asked where he was going to go after death, he confidently stated, *"Heaven,"* adding that his belief in Christ would see him to Heaven.

One of the two brothers who murdered a gay couple in Northern California stated, *"I had to obey God's law rather than man's law. My brother and I are in jail for our work in cleansing a sick society."*

Is it any surprise that corporate Christianity denies any responsibility for the ever-increasing crimes against gays committed by Christians? To this day, it insists it teaches God's Truth. How can this be when there is so much evident "Christian" blaming, hatred, and violence towards homosexuals?

■ ■ ◆ ■ ■

The King James Version of the Bible is one of the most, *if not the most* printed book in history. Countless souls have gained Enlightenments through this famous and widely-used translation of the Bible. King James I of England (son of Lord Darnley and Queen Mary of Scotland) commissioned the Bible to be translated from Latin into English in 1601, an intense effort consuming the better part of ten years, translated by the greatest linguists of the time, analyzed by Church officials and Privy Council, then made official by the King's authority. Interestingly, King James I, though married, is thought to have had homosexual tendencies, as did his father.

To some, the issue of King James' homosexuality is inflammatory propaganda spread by those who seek to discredit King James, his rulership, and his commissioned version of the Bible. Nonetheless, it is reported that James' first homosexual love affair began at the young age of thirteen, shortly after meeting his older French cousin, Esmé Stuart. Another relationship is said to have begun in 1607, when James was in his early forties. By this time, King James was married with children when his involvement with Robert Kerr began, a man in his twenties from a prominent Scottish family. Along with teaching him Latin, James elevated Kerr to a Viscount four years later, then to Earl of Somerset two years thereafter, making a relative "nobody" into a man of financial prosperity and social prominence in the King's Court.

King James' most notable homosexual relationship is said to have begun in 1614 with George Villiers, of whom James referred to in a letter as his "only sweet child" and his "sweet child and wife" (as revealed in *King James VI of Scotland, I of England,* written by the famed British historian, Antonia Fraser). Within a year, Villiers was knighted. Two years later, he was made Earl of Buckingham, then titled Marquess in 1619, and finally Duke of Buckingham in 1623.

The problem with the issue of King James' questionable homosexuality is that Protestant "mindsets" get very upset and defensive when asked to consider their famous Protestant king's homosexuality. Why get so offended, even angry? Who cares if James had homosexual relations? *Does that discredit his Goodness?* Do they fear that if word gets out about James' homosexuality it might compromise their position on homosexuality? *You bet.* If their great hero, King James, had homosexual relations, *then he is in hell and his commissioned version of the Bible owes its existence to a queer.*

History is full of homosexuals whose lives have had a positive impact on cultures and civilizations. Just because they were homosexual, are we to believe that none of them lived in the Spirit, that all of them are now in hell? *God forbid.* Corporate Christianity might be relieved if all of them were stricken from the Annals of Time. Some famous gays:

Leonardo da Vinci (Italian Universal Genius; 1452-1519);
Michelangelo (Italian Sculptor, Painter, Architect; 1475-1564);
Lord Byron (English Poet; 1788-1824);
Walt Whitman (American Poet; 1819-1892);
Peter Tchaikovsky (Russian Composer; 1840-1893);
Willa Cather (American Author; 1873-1947);
Cole Porter (American Composer; 1893-1964);
Lorenz Hart (American Lyricist and Poet; 1895-1943);
Tennessee Williams (American Author; 1914-1983);
James Baldwin (American Author; 1924-1987); and
Mark Bingham (American Hero; United Airlines Flight 93, Sept. 11th).

If you are a Christian who wants nothing to do with homosexuals, then why not be true to yourself and stop "talking the talk," but "walk the walk" by separating yourself from everything associated with homosexuals? To do so, you would have to effectively remove yourself from society, because every aspect of the productive world we live in involves homosexuals. Don't go grocery shopping anymore, because in the "grocery world" there are homosexuals growing, processing, and shipping your food, stocking it on stores' shelves, ringing it up at registers, bagging it, and helping you out to your car. The music you love, the TV shows you watch, the clothes you wear, the cars you drive, the food you eat... *all manner of things involve both heterosexuals and homosexuals.*

■ ■ ◆ ■ ■

The following is excerpted from Rosie O'Donnell's interview with Diane Sawyer on Primetime Live (March 15, 2002).

Diane Sawyer: Do gay parents raise gay children?

Rosie O'Donnell: I had heterosexual parents. Every gay person I know had heterosexual parents. It was modeled in my house. I don't think you choose it. This is what I believe. Who would choose it? It's a very difficult life. You get socially ostracized. You worry all the time whether or not you're in physical danger if you show affection to your partner. You worry that you're an outcast with your friends and with society in general. It's a very difficult life. I don't think anyone would choose it.

(3 minutes, 28 seconds later)
Diane Sawyer: Is there anything you and Kelly do or do not do in front of them (their 3 adopted children), because you think that you have to introduce them gradually or in a different way, physically, to what it is to be gay?"

Rosie O'Donnell: You know, all they see really is love. I mean, we have a lot of friends who are gay and, men and women, and we have a lot of friends who are not gay, and they know every family is different. They know kids in their class who are raised by a grandmother. They have a very diverse school that they go to here in the city. There are other children with gay parents in their class. So, they know that every family comes in a different size and shape but, you know, as for how we act in front of the children, in the same way that heterosexual people act: You never act sexually in front of your child, ever. "Sexually" is not appropriate for a kid, no matter if you're a homosexual or a heterosexual.

The Good Spirit certainly appears to be on Rosie's mind.

■ ■ ◆ ■ ■

One of the greatest injustices thrust upon children is the "behavioral" brainwashing of boys and girls, that boys are to be strong, fearless, assertive, tough, daring, successful, decisive, aggressive, powerful, and dominant, and girls are to be darling, delicate, emotional, overly-cautious, fearful, and submissive. These behavioral extremes breed predator/prey mentalities, the masculine "predator," the feminine "prey."

On one end of the spectrum are the "bully boys," who are programmed to believe that showing love and tenderness is a sign of weakness (femininity). Is it any wonder that such programmed minds often seek to diminish, blame, harm, *even destroy* that which they perceive to be an affront to their macho mindset? *They live in fear of being feminized.* On the other end of the spectrum are the "girly girls," programmed to be so grossly feminized that whining, crying, and blaming becomes routine when their selfish "needs" are not met.

Both extremes begin early on and, if left undisciplined, blossom in adolescence. Between the ultra-masculine and ultra-feminine affectations and behaviors taught by society is a range of *"reasonable normalcy,"* where society's many, various "set" behavioral roles of masculinity and femininity are not so idolatrously worshiped. Still, *no matter your masculinity or femininity,* all that ultimately matters is your Good Spirit.

■ ■ ◆ ■ ■

God made us in His "image," and His Image, His Spirit, is both Male and Female (Genesis 1:27). Every cell in every human body is of male and female components, *naturally,* as we are a genetic mixture of mother and father. Our souls do not have genitals, but do have "maleness" and "femaleness."

Spiritually speaking, the "femaleness" within our souls is Thought, *the Passive-Nature of God's Spirit which builds, considers, and rationalizes our desires*. The "maleness" within our souls is Action, *the Active-Nature of God's Spirit which is that part of us that acts upon our desires*, that gives "life" to our thoughts and desires.

In Genesis, we learn that God, being Creator, ruled over all His Creation. The next in dominance was Adam, the first God-human soul *born of the Creator*. Though Adam's soul dwelt in the physical body of a male, he was a male-female soul until God separated his femaleness from his maleness. Eve, the God-human female soul created of Adam, *born of the created (Adam)*, is the least dominant.

The reason why God is a "He" is because the ruling nature of His Spirit is Active ("maleness"), not Passive ("femaleness"). If Thought ruled over Action, *then thoughts would be more powerful than actions*. But, as it is, actions are more powerful than thoughts/desires. You can have a desire, but if the desire is not put into action, *not manifested in any other way than through thought*, then there is no physical justification that the desire ever existed. So, when the Bible reveals that the "female" is subject to the "male," it is not about women being dominated by men, but about your thoughts and desires ("femaleness") being dominated by your actions ("maleness"). We are instructed to keep the Good Spirit at the forefront of our thoughts and desires (Immaculate Conception), that we only give "life" to God's Savior-Spirit, building His Christ Within.

When we were newly birthed child-minds of God, our "baby" souls were Pure in Action (Active Spirit) and Thought (Passive Spirit), like Adam and Eve. One by one, our minds were innocently, *naturally awakened* to the desire to bring to Life the Knowledge of that which would lead us to know ourselves (the Knowledge of Good and Evil). It is by this cause that we have self-identity, which is individuality apart from our Father-Creator. This is natural for all children of all parents at some point.

Collectively, the souls of humankind are connected with God's Spirit and Mind, which is learning by the warring of the Spirit and the anti-Spirit within our souls, so that He gain the Full Library of the Knowledge of Good and Evil, *further defining Himself*. God's Mind is, *and has always been*, the "Full Library," having Full Knowledge of all that has ever occurred. But His still-expanding Mind and Universe shall have an endpoint. That endpoint shall come 1,000 years after the day of the "fulness of the Gentiles" (the day of the maximum corruption of the unbelievers; the day of the maximum Knowledge of Evil; p. 100). When maximum Evil has been met, so too shall maximum Good be defined, *naturally*. It is upon this moment that the Rapture occurs, followed by the beginning of the hour-long cleansing of "satan's worshipers" (the unregenerately selfish souls of humankind), followed by Christ's Second Coming [the Book of Revelation discloses that the "fulness of the Gentiles" is reached when one-third of the souls of humankind have become unregenerately selfish, or given over completely to the anti-Spirit].

God is the "I AM." We are the only creatures upon Earth who possess the "I AM," or self-identity, being God's Children. We, *unlike the rest of Earth's creatures*, are the "gods" of Earth that thirst for knowledge to understand the "I AM" Within by answering "Who Am I?"

The domination of "male" over "female" is about our struggles with: **1)** our desires ("femaleness") to accept or deny the Spirit; and **2)** our giving "life" to those desires through our actions ("maleness"). The Bible's "male domination over female" is a Message from the Spirit to us that says: *Make your Good Works overrule your selfish desires* ("overcome evil with Good").

■ ■ ◆ ■ ■

One of the big arguments about homosexuality is that it goes against the planet's "natural" order of males always having sexual relations with females. This is disproven in *Biological Exuberance: Animal Homosexuality and Natural Diversity*, an exhaustive study on the matter of same-sex behavior in nature, written by Bruce Bagemihl, Ph.D.

Homosexuality does not go against our natural world, as same-sex behavior occurs in hundreds of species of mammals and birds (squirrels, mice, rats, rabbits, bats, bears, dogs, cats, elephants, monkeys, baboons, apes, sheep, deer, horses, llamas, buffalo, hyenas, koalas, kangaroos, seals, dolphins, whales, ducks, geese, egrets, herons, swans, gulls, sandpipers, bluebirds, sparrows, crows, parrots, and hummingbirds, *to name a few*).

We, *like the animals*, are of flesh and carnal appetites. We, *unlike the animals*, are the free-will souls of God's Children with unmatched intelligence and moral conscience. The Bible reveals that our souls chose to know Good and Evil in order to know and define our individual personhood.

Human sexuality, when consensual, is not the "big issue." As always, the "big issue" is our hearts and motivations. Sex is of the flesh. Souls do not have genitals and, in Heaven, there is no sex (Matthew 22:30), but only Divine Companionship in His Love.

■ ■ ◆ ■ ■

There are homosexuals who object to issues with "straight society" by openly rebelling in Spiritless ways. Regardless of the legally consensual sex that people, *gay or straight*, have in the privacy of their own lives, all of our souls owe their allegiance to God by living in Selfless Goodness *before all else*, in private and in public.

On August 30th, 2002, Bill O'Reilly gave a commentary about homosexuality on his television program, *The O'Reilly Factor*. His commentary was in response to a "kissing protest" by lesbians at a basketball game held by the New York Liberty of Women. Evidently, because there are some lesbian team players, and because some lesbians attend basketball games, and because some lesbians feel they are unrecognized by basketball organizations, a group of lesbians in the audience began passionately kissing to protest their "invisibility." This was their bid for recognition.

Why would anyone want to display his/her sexual passions before the general public? *Because of selfishness, plain and simple.* There is a broad spectrum of "consensual" kissing before the general public that is appropriate, but not when it becomes the mutual "cannibalism" of *sucking face.* The highest, most-excellent love is not sexual, but is divine love... *brotherly love.* Their bid for recognition would have been far-more effective if it exemplified the Selfless, Good Spirit. *Find the Spiritful solution.*

Our world is in hyper-drive regarding sex, where just about every manner of product is sexualized to sell to the public. When corporations deny the Spirit to sell their products (and when people deny Spiritual Enlightenment), they will gravitate to humankind's basest stimulation: lust. *That's just the way it is.* The world is spinning towards greater spiritual corruption with every passing moment. Are you going to buy-in to the corruption around you or are you going to side with the Spirit?

Bill O'Reilly: I don't care what you do in private as long as you are not hurting anyone.

Intimate sexual activity before the general public is not consensual (sin upon only your being), but is sin (selfishness) upon others, namely, the general public... *the witnesses.* Do your intimate sexual activity in private. Of course, this will not make sense to the selfish, who look to the Letter of the Law to uphold their "freedoms." The U.S. has found greatness in its Freedoms by the Law, which shall also be its undoing as the Spirit of the Law continues to be crushed by Letter-of-the-Law legalists. The legalists have lawyered the Constitution so much so that blame reigns over personal responsibility. As the Spirit of the Law is overcome by the Letter of the Law, troubles increase, *naturally.*

Bill O'Reilly: If gays think they will gain acceptance by flaunting their sexuality, they're crazy. All that does is make more people dislike them. It is self-destructive, un-classy, and illogical. So what these public sexual displays are really meant to do is offend people that don't like gays [or] that gays don't like, I should say. They are personal attacks on opponents of homosexuality. That's the "no spin" truth of the matter. But what many gays don't realize is that some Americans who "live and let live" are angered, because their children are being exposed to situations far beyond their years, and when gay activists say, "That's tough," that kids should be forced to deal with homosexuality at an early age, then those activists become the oppressors. Those people become just like the homophobes they despise.

Personally, I am not shocked or particularly offended by public displays of intimate sexual activities, but I can certainly understand how families, *the structural backbone of society,* are offended when people do these things in public. Generally, the public is more tolerant of displays of heterosexual sexual activities, *even encouraging it at times,* though such public, heterosexual displays are as much a denial of the Spirit as similar homosexual displays in public.

The Message of the Spirit destroys the victim mentality, upholding personal responsibility. The lesbian "victims" who feel left out have become the victimizers by thrusting their intimate sexual activity upon the general public. In turn, some of the "offended" public played "victim" and generated their own selfishness (hatred, intolerance, vengeance, etc.) towards these lesbians, *making of themselves victimizers!* It is an endless cycle until the selfish "victim mentality" is broken.

The only way to break the victim mentality is to accept personal responsibility for your life at every given moment. When faced with troubles, do not linger on the "victim road" of blame, vengeance, hatred or any other such Spiritlessness for very long, but come quickly to count your blessings and find a Spiritful solution. There is always a Spiritful solution.

Bill O'Reilly: Americans have the right to live their lives without knowing about your sex life, whatever it is. Keep private things private.

We all have our differences, and most of us know what it is like to be hated by someone else for something or other. Everybody suffers. Gays, blacks, whites, straights, young, old, healthy, good-looking... *everybody suffers.* It is your decision alone as to how you will reconcile the suffering you meet. Do you feed your suffering with selfishness or do you overcome it with the Spirit?

Chapter 11

PRIEST PEDOPHILIA

Some possible misconceptions about pedophilia in corporate Christianity: it only happens in America; it is a recent phenomenon; it only happens to boys; it only happens in the Catholic Church.

■ ■ ◆ ■ ■

#24 - McBrien, Richard (on *The O'Reilly Factor* with Bill O'Reilly; April 18, 2002)

Richard McBrien (*Reverend & Professor of Theology at Notre Dame*)*:* My prediction is that the Pope will ask, that's putting it mildly, he will ask the American bishops, through the cardinals and the president and the vice-president of Conference (referring to the U.S. Conference of Catholic Bishops) to finally institute a national policy that all the bishops and all the dioceses in the United States will follow when cases of sexual abuse by priests come up. Of course, it has to be consistent with the laws of the various states but, you know, it's been over fifteen years since the American bishops were urged by people that they themselves appointed to study the matter, urged to institute a national policy, and they just couldn't agree on doing it. Many bishops, you know, they're kings in their own diocese [and] didn't want to see that power.

(46 seconds later)
Bill O'Reilly: Now, what's wrong with the Hierarchy? What is their problem? Is it them against the world? Is that the way they see it? Are they above the law? What is it?

Richard McBrien: Well, I'm going to get a heck of a lot of e-mails now from your viewers, but it goes back to the Pope. And you said it yourself in your column. He (the Pope) appoints a certain type of man to the Hierarchy. They're not bad men. They're men whose prime directive seems to be to protect the reputation and the welfare of the institutional Church before all else. <u>And in some of these cases, these bishops in question, they didn't do it deliberately, they didn't do it out of some sort of evil motive</u>, but they instinctively put the reputation of the institutional Church and the priesthood ahead of the welfare of children and of potential victims, and when they placed one priest from one place to another, knowing he was a predator, knowing he had this problem, they really put the children in the new pastoral situation in harm's way, and this is criminal activity, not just sinful activity.

Bill O'Reilly: Absolutely. But are they looking out for the Church or themselves? See, my theory is that many of these people, and Cardinal Law (of Boston) is one of them, and possibly Cardinal Egan of New York, are so driven by their lust for power that they love the red hat (referring to their Hierarchal status), that they want the ceremonial obsequience that they get, that they put themselves above the children, and above the law, and above their parishoners, because they want the power. Am I wrong?

(6 seconds later)
Richard McBrien: Let me just say that there's a lot of truth in what you say, but they're human beings. Let's face it. There's a careerism. Even Cardinal Rotzinger, who's going to be at this meeting, has criticized the careerism of bishops.

Bill O'Reilly: That's right.

Richard McBrien: It's there. Let's face it. We may say that the Church is the Body of Christ, it's the Temple of the Holy Spirit, it has a divine dimension as well as a human, but it has a human dimension, and people aspire to positions of power and influence. Some of them do like to prance around in all this finery. It's a seductive thing.

Here, we are taught that some bishops, *who put the reputation and welfare of the Church above the welfare of children and potential victims by moving predatory priests to other dioceses,* did these things without deliberate, selfish motives. Later, these misled bishops are judged "criminal" and "sinful," *and rightfully so,* but how can that be if, *as previously told,* they never truly intended evil by their errant decisions? How is it remotely possible that adult males installed into the great Hierarchy of the Catholic Church do not know that pedophilia is an appallingly serious crime?

The "seductive thing" of the Church is its idolatry, from which was birthed its chronic problem with pedophilia, principally enabled through: **1)** idolatrous confession, *which absolves sins via ritual;* **2)** idolatrous Hierarchy, *which protects its self-exalted authority and image through mystery and secrecy;* and **3)** idolatrous celibacy, *which can become a seriously unhealthy repression of one of the most basic and powerful desires of the human animal: SEX* (celibacy is the sacrificing of sexual nature as a path to Holiness, which is self-serving if your Holiness is not justified by living in the Good Spirit).

■ ■ ◆ ■ ■

The following, excerpted from *Dateline Friday* with Stone Phillips, aired April 19, 2002. The guest is Tom Doyle of the Catholic clergy who, in 1985, without the Church's permission, co-authored a 100-page report about priests and pedophilia.

I offer no commentary about the following, other than I am impressed by both *Dateline Friday* and Rev. Doyle's courage and Spirit in openly presenting such fascinating information about the issue of pedophilia in the Catholic Church.

Stone Phillips: So, Cardinal Law (of Boston) recognized there was a problem.

Tom Doyle: That's correct. He did.

Stone Phillips: This is in the mid-80's.

Tom Doyle: These discussions all were going on in 1985, between January and June of 1985.

Stone Phillips (narrative): Among Doyle's recommendations (from his 100-page report): remove the accused priest immediately from duty until an investigation is conducted; report charges of abuse to police; and never assign priests to new parishes until allegations are resolved. The report also warned that the recidivism, or relapse rate, for pedophilia is second only to exhibitionism, and that people who sexually abuse young children have little chance of being cured. And Doyle was clear: The price of confronting this problem was the demolition of a deeply embedded Church tradition.

Tom Doyle: The secrecy was the first thing that, we believe, had to go, that the bishops had to be totally up-front and honest with the faithful, with the public, as to what was going on. And, unfortunately, the secrecy level in the Roman Catholic Church, traditionally, has been almost pathological in nature.

Stone Phillips: When you finished this report and it was ready to go out, what did you think church leaders were going to do with it?

Tom Doyle: At first, I naively thought that they would look at the problem and maybe not use my report, but use some information, somewhere, to do the right thing.

(12 seconds later)
Stone Phillips (narrative): Undeterred, Doyle and his co-authors mailed the report to every bishop in the United States, but still no action was taken. If anything, Doyle says the emphasis on secrecy only intensified, all in the name of protecting the Church's reputation.

Tom Doyle: The institutional Church is preaching a very stringent moral code and, at the same time, while it's holding the faithful up to these very, very high expectations, it's allowing, you know, the basest form of sexual acting-out among its own clergy.

Stone Phillips: If a priest, like Father Geoghan (a convicted pedophile, who was murdered in prison in Sept. 2003), were to be caught embezzling the Church, skimming from the Sunday offerings, what would happen?

Tom Doyle: They would never transfer him from one parish to another for stealing money.

Stone Phillips: Never?

Tom Doyle: Never. He'd be finished.

Stone Phillips: But for molesting a child, then you can go back to work.

Tom Doyle: I can't understand that, nor can anyone else. Here, you have money, is that more important than the life of a child and their families?

■ ■ ◆ ■ ■

#24 - McBrien, Richard (on *The O'Reilly Factor* with Bill O'Reilly; May 20, 2002)

Bill O'Reilly: The Vatican approved an article, as you know, I don't know whether you've read it or not, but basically said to the Catholic bishops before they meet in June (2002), in Texas, that you should not cooperate with law enforcement authorities in the cases of pedophile priests. Your reaction?

(18 seconds later)
Richard McBrien: Someone in the Vatican bureaucracy certainly gave it a "wink and a nod" and said: You can go ahead and publish it (referring to the article instructing bishops not to cooperate with law enforcement authorities), and we'll sort of stand behind it. Listen, I'm not gonna be here tonight to defend the Vatican bureaucracy, I mean, they do have a tin ear on this question, I mean, from the very beginning, Vatican bureaucrats have regarded this as an American problem, and as an American problem with American peculiarities. There's a strong dose of anti-Americanism in the Vatican bureaucracy, and has been there for years. I think this, they're very dismissive. I don't know if you recall one of the press conferences that was held a few weeks ago. One of the high ranking cardinals in the Vatican got very exasperated at one point and he said, "I notice that all the questions are coming from English-speaking reporters," as if this is a problem that is confined to the English-speaking world.

Rev. McBrien is courageous in the Spirit to speak so frankly about Catholicism's hierarchical, bureaucratic system.

The Catholic Hierarchy has always been a secretive, elitist group surrounded in their own self-made, self-exalted "mystery," so as to appear before the masses as beyond the law, *untouchable*. It should come as no surprise that the Vatican has anti-American sentiments, after all, this country is about freedom, and was founded by peoples escaping the horrors and terrorism of oppressive Catholicism in Europe. Freedom is a formidable enemy of corporate structures that thrive upon enslaving souls to their self-serving agendas.

Church Hierarchy does not want to be questioned. It is precisely due to the freedoms in America that their lawlessness has been ferreted-out, and they don't like it. How much pedophilia goes on unchallenged in lesser-free, predominantly-Catholic nations (Philippines, Mexico, Spain)? Would it be incorrect to suggest that the pedophilia problem is far greater in those nations? *I would certainly think so, yet we hear nothing of it.*

■ ■ ◆ ■ ■

#10 - Galante, Joseph (on *The Oprah Winfrey Show* with Oprah Winfrey and guests David Clohessy of SNAP and author Jason Berry ; July 1, 2002)

Oprah Winfrey (narrative): It's been nearly seven months since the massive sex-abuse scandal involving priests in the Catholic Church first made headlines. Since that scandal broke in January (2002), 250 priests, including 3 bishops and an arch-bishop, have resigned or been removed from parishes throughout the U.S. In response to an enormous public outcry, the U.S. Conference of Catholic Bishops met in Dallas last month and voted to adopt a national sex-abuse policy. That new policy requires bishops to report all allegations of sexual abuse to the police. Priests found guilty of abuse are going to be removed from public ministry and banned from performing public mass, wearing a collar, or presenting themselves publicly as priests. The new policy also states each bishop will be accountable to a national monitoring board, which will be headed by Oklahoma's governor, Frank Keating. Despite the hard-line [that] bishops have taken to end the Church molestation crisis, many victims say, "It is just not enough." They say the plan doesn't account for bishops who covered-up for predator priests, and it allows priests who abused children to remain in the priesthood and perform mass in the privacy of their own homes (narrative ends here).

Joining us is Bishop Joseph Galante of Dallas. Bishop Galante helped draft the new policy proposal, and we understand that the new policy does not punish bishops like, for example, Boston's Cardinal Law, who knowingly transferred abusive priests from parish to parish. A recent poll showed that ninety percent of U.S. Roman Catholics believe that bishops should be held accountable for reassigning abusive priests. Bishop

Galante, what do you want to say to the overwhelming majority of Catholics who believe that?

Joseph Galante: First, I would want to say that, why the document didn't say anything about punishing bishops is because we don't have the authority to discipline one another, only the Holy See does. What it has said, and what bishops have said privately to one another, is to express the anger towards bishops who've done this, and who have done it over a period of time. We also have built-in, both with an Office for the Protection of Youth, and then the advisory board that you mentioned earlier with Governor Keating, strict accountability. One of the big changes this charter brings about is that every bishop has to be accountable to, not just to the bishops, but to this Office for the Protection of Youth and to this oversight committee, and I believe that's the beginning of strengthening the possibilities that you were talking about. Any bishop who would continue to move proven offenders around is really not living-up to what we have promised, what we have pledged, what we have stated, and what we've committed ourselves to, and there is no room for that.

Oprah Winfrey: Also joining us is David Clohessy of SNAP, that is, the Survivors Network of those Abused by Priests, and their membership numbers more than 3,500. David spoke at the Bishops Conference in Dallas and says that the new policy is not the zero-tolerance policy the victims had been hoping for. David, good to see you again.

David Clohessy: Thanks Oprah, appreciate it. Yes, we believe the policy simply doesn't go far enough. There's very little in there about prevention. There's virtually nothing about prosecution, and we all know that the safest place for a child molester to be is behind bars and, fundamentally (rousing applause from audience for 8 seconds), and that fundamentally there really is no accountability. There is no mechanism by which a bishop can be disciplined in any way for these crimes. So it's one thing to pledge, it's one thing to promise but, frankly, we in the Survivor's Network were at the table ten years ago when the bishops made similar promises, and unless there's a real enforcement mechanism, unless a bishop can lose his job for doing this, we're back to square-one in some ways.

(1 minute, 55 seconds later)
Oprah Winfrey: Joining us is Jason Berry, a writer and reporter who has covered the Catholic Church for 17 years. Jason is also the writer of *Lead Us Not Into Temptation: Catholic Priests And The Sexual Abuse Of Children.* Jason says he feels the proposed policy is a step in the right direction, but leaves a lot of gray areas. How so Jason?

Jason Berry: Well, the Vatican has to essentially sign-off on the document in its final form, and that is going to be a source of tension, I think, that will unfold. But there's something else, Oprah, that, I think, we all have to bear in mind. There is a case in Rome that was filed in 1998 by eight men who accused the head of the Legion of Christ, a religious order, this is one of the most powerful priests in Rome (referring to the case of Father Marciel Maciel, Chapter 4) . They've accused him of abusing them when they were seminarians. The Vatican has refused to let these men give testimony in the case. I don't see how the Vatican can speak with moral authority on this issue and help the American bishops in devising a program that will really work as long as this case is left unresolved.

The enabler of Catholicism's priest pedophilia is the corporate system of Catholicism. If The Way of the Good Spirit was the cornerstone of the Catholic Church, the slightest hint of pedophilia would be remedied quickly and legally, and accused offenders would be immediately turned over to the state's legal system, not shuffled around the world to afflict more children.

In March, 2004, Newsweek *magazine gave national statistics from the John Jay College of Criminal Justice, reporting that of the 10,667 people who filed sexual abuse complaints against priests, 81 percent were male. As for the accused priests, 2 percent have received prison sentences.*

Chapter 12

RELIGIOUS TERRORISM

Finding the solution to a problem requires defining its truest source. September 11th was religious terrorism born of lies… *lies about God, jihad, and martyrdom.* Muslim false-religionists, like Bin Laden, teach that *jihad* is the "holy war" against those perceived as "enemies." Jihad is, *before all else,* the "holy war" Within oneself, and is about overcoming your selfishness with the Selfless Spirit. The only war that ultimately matters is the holy war between the Spirit and the anti-Spirit Within you. Both Muhammad and Jesus reveal this, but their Divine messages to humankind are diminished, *even nullified* by religious leaders seeking to fulfill their own selfish, separatist agendas.

September 11th was a global upheaval, greater than any one earthquake, because it was senseless, unnecessary, selfish, and man-made. For many, it was also a spiritual upheaval. Common sensibilities desire for justice to be met, *and to build a future where no such awfulness might ever happen again.*

The difference between thinking evil and doing evil is a change of conviction from selfishness (self) to Selfless Good (God). That simple change of conviction is the "New Mind," or "New Perception"… *The Way of the Good Spirit.* If the warring Jews, Muslims, and Christians of the world believed in the Spirit of God with all their hearts, souls, and minds, then Peace would reign among them. Sadly, due to human selfishness, the corporate-Christian "mindset" blames the corporate-Muslim "mindset" for the horrors of September 11th, when both are intimately and immeasurably responsible, both having hated and fought each other for over 1,000 years at the expense of the lives of their "blind," mostly-Good followers.

Spiritually speaking, September 11th happened because of Spiritless religion alive and well in the corporate "mindsets" of Christianity, Islam, and Judaism. They all think they're One with God's Message, but they're all so very, very wrong. Had these three "brother" religions given their allegiance to the Spirit of Selfless Love and Good Works, teaching and requiring the same from their citizens, they would never have thrust so many evils upon humanity, and would never have tempted and enslaved souls to their self-serving, money-and-power-hungry institutions. If they were teachers of the One Spirit, *then they could never be held responsible if one of their followers misused Scriptures to "sanctify" separatism, hatred, and violence.* Instead, all three Abrahamic religions exalt the Letter of the Law over the Spirit of the Law and, as such, act like magnets for zealous extremists who use Scriptures to suit their own selfish agendas, just like their "parent" religions do. *The fruit falls not far from the tree.*

The Abrahamic religions, *on a global level,* still do not teach the transcendent Way of the Spirit over their separatist, self-sanctified "ways" to God. They thrive to capture and enslave individual minds to their holier-than-thou, corporate mindsets. They call themselves religions of "God," yet are soaked in blood and idolatry.

The world is choking on false religionists who live to propagate their idolatry. Their "mindsets" reject the evident Truth that they are perpetuators of global cults that have conquered the world not through Selfless Love, but through religious selfishness. The villainy of September 11th is added to the long list of crimes against humanity due directly to the Spiritlessness of corporate Judaism, Christianity, and Islam.

Since September 11th, famous Christians leaders have come forth to spew fear, lies, intolerance, and hatred towards Muslims, attacking the person of Muhammad, but seeing not that his Message of the Spirit is One with Jesus' Message of the Spirit. Where Islam has its militant zealots, so does Christianity. Just as there are many Muslims who exalt the Letter of the Law over the Spirit of the Law, so do many Christians. Just as you can take verses out of context in the Koran and use them to support selfish agendas, so can you do the same with the Bible.

As long as Judaism, Christianity, and Islam deny that living and growing in the Spirit is the One Way to Salvation, there will never be Peace among them. Though Christians believe Jesus to be the Messiah, *and though Muslims and some Jews believe Him to be a Divine prophet,* their global, corporate religions deny His Message of the Spirit.

The following shows the Oneness of the revelations given by both Jesus and Muhammad.

- Both Jesus and Muhammad instruct us to be true to God's Spirit in times of peace and in times of troubles.
- Both Jesus and Muhammad exalt the Spirit over idolatry, and yet the man-made, corporate structures of Christianity and Islam are lost in idolatrous, false religion, where they worship things (rituals, confessions, hierarchy, etc.) as the "way" to Salvation, denying the Good Spirit Within as The Way.

- Both Jesus and Muhammad teach the Universality of "as you sow, so shall you reap."
- Both Jesus and Muhammad instruct their followers to overcome evil with Good.

In Islam, the highest value of *jihad* is that of overcoming the holy war Within you, effected only by overcoming your evil with Good. The least and lowest value of *jihad* is to war against another person or tribe, an option not acceptable unless in imminent danger of physical attack.

Corporate Christianity justifies its self-exalted, "Holy" status over Islam by citing revelations in the Bible about the "bondwoman" and the "freewoman." In Genesis, Chapter 16, we are told how Sarai [wife of Abram (later called Abraham)] could not conceive, so she urged Abram to produce a child with her maidservant, Hagar the Egyptian, a slave ("bondwoman"). Hagar's child with Abram, *named Ishmael,* became the ancestral branch that produced the religion of Islam. Later, Sarai conceived and gave birth to *Isaac,* the ancestral branch of Promise that would bring forth the Messiah. The Bible reveals that only those born of the "freewoman" shall know Salvation.

When literally interpreted, Christianity says that they, *the Children of Promise* ("freewoman"), are saved, and that the Muslims, *the Children of Enslavement* ("bondwoman"), are damned.

When spiritually interpreted, the "bondwoman" has nothing to do with Muslims and the "freewoman" has nothing to do with Christians. The two categories of souls by God's definition are Jews and Gentiles (page 55). The "bondwoman" symbolizes the Gentiles, *or to those enslaved to selfishness* (idolatry). The "freewoman" symbolizes the Jews, *or those committed to The Way.* Treading The Way of the Selfless Spirit makes us free from enslavement to self, free from the "bondwoman" (selfishness; idolatry; "the truth shall make you free," John 8:31-32).

America's "War on Terror" has been criticized by Christian pacifists who abhor any killing, *justified or not,* citing Jesus' Messages about "peacekeeping." Peacekeeping, like all other issues, is relative to the individual. On one extreme are zealous pacifists, on the other extreme are zealous warriors. If you believe, *by your Good Conscience,* that peacekeeping means that it is a sin to kill for any reason, than be true to your Good Conscience, *your God-Mind and Spirit Within,* and do not kill under any circumstance. If you believe, *by your Good Conscience,* that peacekeeping means taking up arms to fight, even kill your attacker(s) so as to protect the lives of family, countrymen, or others from attack... *so be it...* this is also peacekeeping. God knows our hearts and motivations, and all things shall be forgiven those who do not deny their Good Conscience (Matthew 12:31-33).

Since September 11th, many have asked: *Why did God allow this to happen?* God "allowed" it to happen because He allows our souls to have free will. It is human selfishness that gives "life" to dis-ease, destruction, and death. Our bodies suffer and die because of the selfishness (anti-Spirit; death) alive in our souls.

We often hear the word "innocent" used when referring to those killed via destructive events. In the case of September 11th, we repeatedly heard how thousands of "innocent" people died on that day. This is true in the sense that none of those people had done anything to be so unjustifiably killed. Legally, they were innocent indeed. But, *spiritually*, none of our souls, not even those within infants, are innocent, and shall reap of sins, sufferings and death. That is the Letter of the Law. But by God's Mercy, we have the Spirit of the Law that always, in the end, overrules the Letter of the Law for those who grow in the Spirit. The troubles and evils we experience and witness are not causeless, but happen for the Glory of the Spirit, so that our souls, *even those who died in the great tragedy*, might draw nearer the Spirit and come to Salvation.

It is commendable to grieve for the loss of others, but the grieving process must not grow overwhelming, where hopelessness and despair take root. Be comforted in the Spirit (the Spirit is the Comforter). In your grieving, seek the blessing in the curse, and Enlightenment will spark. God sees and knows your sorrows and troubles, and instructs you to be courageous, not losing hope, but finding forgiveness and restoring yourself to Inner Peace through His Comforter. All that is of the flesh will pass away, but the Spirit shall live forever Within souls that live in the Spirit (the Mind and Spirit Within the flesh, *and Within your flesh,* is the "man Christ Jesus," the One Intermediary between your soul and God; John 14:16-17, 26). Be comforted in the wisdom that, regardless of human justice, God's Righteous Justice will be met, and all will reap what they sow.

Bin Laden's lust for destruction and murder is just more human selfishness. *Human selfishness* ... the source of all of the sufferings that humankind heaps upon itself. Countries, religions, races, and cultures the world over are guilty of brutality and murder upon others deemed "unclean" or "heretical." History has witnessed Japanese against non-Japanese, Chinese against non-Chinese, Americans against American Indians, Christians against non-Christians, Catholic-Irish against Protestant-Irish, Nazis against Jews, Jews against non-Jews, Muslims against non-Muslims... *the list is seemingly endless.*

Your soul is instructed to lift its Spirit Within above any and all selfish, groupist mentalities that propagate and nurture separatism and blaming. Such mentalities breed destructive, *even deadly* results. Just how many have been shunned, persecuted, tortured, and murdered by separatist religionists "in the name of God?"

Lastly, Muslim extremists define America as the "great satan." Incorrect. The power of "satan" grows Within all who deny the Spirit. It is magnified when groups of people come together to enforce their selfish agendas. The "great satan" grows greatest in groupist or "corporate" mentalities that put their selfishness over God's Selfless, Good Spirit. Collectively, the "great satan" represents the world's Spiritless souls ("Gentiles"), the perpetuators of human selfishness. Conversely, the "Church of Christ" represents the world's Spiritful souls ("Jews"), the builders of The Enlightened Way, so that others might see and follow.

■ ■ ◆ ■ ■

#8 - Falwell, Jerry (on *Saturday Edition* with Andrea Koppel; April 30, 2002)

Andrea Koppel: Reverend Falwell, I'd like to ask you, sir, about some comments that you made in the wake of September 11th, this was during a 700 Club broadcast. And you said, you said you were quoted out of context, so please help me here. You said, "I really believe that the Pagans, and the abortionists, and the feminists, and the gays, and the lesbians who are actively trying to make that an alternative lifestyle, the ACLU, People for the American Way, all of them who have tried to secularize America, I point the finger in their face and say, 'You helped this happen.'"

Jerry Falwell: I didn't say that, that was taken out of context. I said that I misspoke, and I apologized for it. I meant to add, as well, "a sleeping Church," because judgment must always begin at the House of God. And if we, as the believing Church in America, had been claiming Second Chronicles 7:14, praying, walking with God, spiritually alert, I believe that we could have expected God to build a hedge of protection around us. So, I did not finish my statement in that one interview, and I acknowledged it, and said so, and said I was sorry. I believe that Second Chronicles 7:14 is the only hope for our nation and for the world for that matter, which says, "If my people who are called by my name shall humble themselves, and pray, and seek my face, and turn from their wicked ways, then will I hear from Heaven, and forgive their sin, and heal their land." Tomorrow, here in Lynchburg, Virginia, like in thousands of other locations, we'll have our Easter Sunrise service, and thousands will attend here on the campus of Liberty University, and we'll talk not about the terrible things that are happening in the world, but we'll make reference to them, but that we have the message, the message of the death, burial, resurrection of Christ, namely the Gospel, by which men may have their hearts changed. They can be born again, become believers and followers of Christ and, really, the only hope, and I suspect all the gentlemen here will agree with this (referring to the other two preachers on the panel), the only hope for the world is a spiritual awakening centered around the Lord Jesus Christ that changes the hearts of people.

This Protestant "mindset" blames secularists, pagans, feminists, gays, abortionists, and the ACLU for helping to bring about the destructions of September 11th. In his defense, he reveals that his statement was unfinished (he had meant to add "a sleeping Church" to the list). In addition, he faulted others, who took his remark "out of context." *Fine.* But prove it.

The only scriptural "proof" he offers to support his finger-pointing is Second Chronicles 7:14, examined as follows.

Second Chronicles 7:14 (spoken by God; authorship unknown)

14. If my people, which are called by my name, shall humble themselves, and pray, and seek my face, and turn from their wicked ways; then will I hear from heaven, and will forgive their sin, and will heal their land.

Spiritually interpreted, Second Chronicles 7:14 reveals that:

- Those which the Spirit seeks ("which are called by my name") are those which seek the Spirit (Matthew 22:14, page 116)
- If you shall continue overcoming your selfishness by living and growing in the Spirit, ["shall humble themselves, and pray, and seek my face, and turn from their wicked ways"]
- then God shall know your strengthened Spirit, [then God "will hear from heaven," meaning that He shall know ('hear') your strengthened Spirit (the Spirit Within is the Heaven Within; Luke 17:21)]
- and will cleanse your soul, [and will forgive your sins (which happens by way of His Righteous Justice, for as you sow to the Light, so shall you strengthen your Light Within, naturally diminishing your soul's darkness)]
- and will heal your body. [and will "heal their land," referring to the human body. Our bodies are the "land," the "dust of the ground" (Genesis 2:7), the vessels of "clay" created by God, who is the Potter (Isaiah 64:8)]

When literally interpreted, Second Chronicles 7:14 refers specifically to the stiff-necked Israelites who, after entering the Promised Land, grew idolatrous. They denied the Spirit and, in so doing, defiled their Promised Land, which consequently grew barren. By sowing the unfruitful anti-Spirit, their land grew unfruitful.

Since the "fall" of the Israelites after their entrance into the Promised Land (an event that mirrors the "fall" of Adam and Eve from the Garden of Eden), no other nation has had Spiritual Oneness in God (evident by the corruption within every nation). Therefore, Second Chronicles 7:14 is not just towards corrupt nations or groups but, more importantly, towards each of us, individually, revealing that we are ultimately responsible for leading our souls to Salvation or damnation.

This preacher accuses Pagans, abortionists, feminists, gays, and lesbians for so corrupting America that they helped to bring about the destructions of September 11th. He blames, blames, blames (like a typical "Laodicean"; Chapter 5), but does not "see" how separatist, fearful, superstitious, global, corporate Christianity holds far greater responsibility in these matters with Islam and its religious zealots.

Ultimately, the greatest truth of the matter is that the destructions of September 11th were born of selfishness alive in the minds and souls of idolatrous, separatist, corporate religionists, namely, Bin Laden and his "blind" followers, who misused the Koran to "sanctify" their violence against those outside their group "in the name of Allah." This, *of course,* mirrors corporate Christianity's misuse of the Bible to "sanctify" their bloody rise to power "in the name of God."

■ ■ ◆ ■ ■

#8 - Falwell, Jerry (September 23, 2001)

The images replayed on our TV sets of the September 11th terrorist attacks on America will never be erased. The news footage of the World Trade Center buildings and the Pentagon reminded us of an apocalyptic scene lifted right out of the Book of the Revelation. Many in our country are asking, "Why did these terrorists attack America? Why do they hate America so much? The reason is very simple: Genesis 12: We have blessed Abraham. We are the friend of Israel, and because they hate Israel, they hate America.

Hateful Muslims hate because their idolatrous mindsets are blind to the Spirit in the Koran and the Bible (Muslims accept the Bible as the "word of God," but do not accept Jesus as the Messiah). Similarly, many Jews and Christians "hate," as they too are blind to God's Spirit in the Bible. If this were not true, Peace would reign among them.

Those who truly have "Blessed Abraham" are, *by God's definition,* "Jews" (Chapter 4). There are "Jews" and "Gentiles" of every manner, defined as such by their devotion to the Spirit, regardless of their ancestry or religiosity.

■ ■ ◆ ■ ■

#37 - Schuller, Robert (September 30, 2001; on #5's television show)

Referring to September 11th, Mr. Schuller was asked, "Why did God allow this to happen?"

And I said, "Paul (Paul Crouch, #5), the world is made up of good and evil. Take a letter 'o' out of 'good' and you've got 'God.' Put a letter 'd' in front of 'evil' and you've got 'devil.'" There's a God and there's a devil. God didn't do it, the devil did. I don't preach about the devil, because a lot of people use that as an excuse for not being the persons they want to be. I, once, as a young boy, said, "Maybe the devil made me do it," and the preacher said, "I don't think so, you're not that important." I'll tell you one thing, I think intelligent, horrifically intelligent evil was behind what happened in New York, and don't blame God for it. And, for God's sake, don't say that God did it to punish us because of our sins. You want to see God against the devil. The devil destroyed, killed, burned. God came with firemen and policemen and doctors and nurses. Never before have I seen such a dramatic illustration of the Presence of God, a God of love and caring and mercy. Never before have I heard a president (President Bush) put it so bluntly, "This is a war between freedom and fear." That means it's a war between faith and fear. That means that in my 75 years in the Church, I have never, ever before seen the Church so divinely called into service today. We are called to arms. We will be at the front line of this war. How long will it last? Years, probably. The Church is the front line of defense.

(11 minutes, 27 seconds later)

I've been into churches in the United States of America that are closed. In the past 30 years, with all of our peace, with all of our prosperity, and with all of the pleasure devices sold to us, churches are losing. I'm not going to accept that, and you will not accept it. The first week after the towers collapsed, our mail dropped over fifty percent, and the income is down fifty percent. That's gotta be changed drastically. Can't survive that kind of a hit. The terrorists are after hitting the power of America, and the power of America has been something bigger than what you found in the Twin Towers. It's what you found in the synagogues. If you're listening and you're Jewish, get back to the synagogue. If you're a Catholic, get back to your church. If you're a Christian, get back to your church. Your call to arms can call you to war. I'm calling every one of you to war. Every one of you. Not a single one can get an excuse. Build a church. Build and strengthen the one and only institution on planet Earth that is committed to giving people faith in God (rousing audience applause). Then stand up, stand up now to receive my closing prayer. And I look at you standing, and I'm expecting that you will be somebody powerful in the hand of God. Oh God, look at these people, and look at them standing, in their heart and in their head, around the world. The Church needs to be re-strengthened, revived. I pray that you will create a revival in the Church, that every church will go back to the book, back to Jesus Christ, back to the cross, back to Easter's resurrection and build faith. Amen.

America's corporate Christianity is labeled the "front line of defense." The tragedy of September 11th is used as a "call to the masses" to fortify corporate religion in this war between "faith and fear." Why? To "heal" the biggest fear of corporate Christianity... loss of revenue ("...the income is down fifty percent... Can't survive that kind of a hit"). Where is the faith in all this fear? *Faith knows no fear.*

Here, we hear the plea for the Jews to go back to their synagogues, followed by a prayer for every church to go "back to Jesus Christ." Why even say this when Jews don't believe in Christ as the Messiah? *Just more separatism.*

■ ■ ◆ ■ ■

#13 - Graham Lotz, Anne (on *Hannity & Colmes* with Sean Hannity and Alan Colmes; December 11, 2001)

Alan Colmes: You know, I get e-mail all the time from our viewers, and we love getting our e-mail, and a few times a day I get this quote, which I'm sure you've seen. Its all over the Internet, so let's get your response to how its been portrayed. And here's what it said, something you said on the CBS Early Show (aired September 13, 2001): "For several years now, Americans, in a sense, have shaken their fists at God and said, 'God, we want you out of your schools, we want you out of our government, we want you out of our business, we want you out of our marketplace.' And God, who is a gentleman, has just quietly, I believe, backed out of our national and political life, our public life, and removing his hand of blessing and protection." Is that [what] happen[ed] on September 11th? Was this a punishment from God, because of the way He's been treated in the public sector?

Anne Graham Lotz: It's not a punishment. I think it's a consequence of asking God to get out. Romans, Chapter One, in the Bible, says that when we don't repent of our sins and turn to God, He backs away from us, and so I believe He's backing away from us, or He has, and He's lifted His hand of protection all these years. Why is this the first time we've been attacked like this? There's been an invisible wall of protection, I believe, around our country, and I think we just need to invite God back in.

Alan Colmes: Are you suggesting, for example, if we didn't have a separation of Church and State that this might not have happened?

Anne Graham Lotz: I'm not so concerned about separation of Church and State. I'm concerned with separation of State and God, and I think we've taken that to the extreme, so we've actually removed God from our society. That has nothing to do with, or I shouldn't say has nothing to do with, the Church, but that's not the Church.

We are told, "I'm not so concerned about separation of Church and State," but "separation of State and God." Well, in the corporate mindset of Christianity, what's the difference? After all, corporate Christianity sees itself as Earth's "House of God" and "Kingdom of God." It certainly is about Church and State, because the Christian Church holds itself up as God's Elect, *His personal "representative" on Earth.* It is growing as a political force that blames others for *its* problems, though there is none more responsible than *itself,* ultimately, through its teachings of idolatrous religion (separatism, fear, superstition) over The Way of the Spirit.

God's "hand of protection" was last upon the Nation of Israel who, *after having been spiritually purified through their forty years of wandering in the wilderness with Moses*, entered the Promised Land. But because they soon denied His Way, they reaped of the corruption they sowed and, consequently, God's "hand of protection" was lifted from their nation.

Since then, God's "hand of protection" has not been upon any one nation, as all are corrupt in some measure, even America. Had God's "hand of protection" been upon America before September 11th, then why the mass killings of the Civil War? Why the slavery? Why the Ku Klux Klan? *Why is the world filled with Christian religionists who blame, blame, blame when corporate Christianity is directly responsible for leading peoples and nations into selfish, separatist religion? Why, through all these centuries of corporate Christianity, are the blind still leading the blind?*

"And if the blind lead the blind, both shall fall into the ditch," or "bottomless pit" (hell; Matthew 15:14; Revelation 20:3).

■ ■ ◆ ■ ■

#14 - Hagee, John (January 19, 2002)

On September the 11th, when the Islamic terrorists flew their hijacked airliners into the Twin Towers and into the Pentagon in Washington DC, Americans discovered that they were at war, and it is a World War, and it is a war against fanatical Islamic terrorists who believe that killing Americans and killing Jews is according to the prophet Muhammad and according to the will of God, the God being Allah. Question: In war, when one side understands it is at war, as the Islamic extremists, and the other side think that they are apostles of peace, which side has the advantage? Listen to me, this new war America is fighting is a war for the spiritual survival of this nation and the survival of the Western World. It is an attack against our religious freedom. It is an attack against religious speech, freedom of speech. It is an attack against every freedom that you cherish. We are at war with a religious dictatorship for the survival of the Western World, nothing less than that. The attack of 9/11 proved that the Islamic terrorists are willing to use weapons of mass destruction to kill as many Americans as possible, because we are considered infidels.

The anti-Spirit alive in corporate Islam is alive and well in corporate Christianity too. Muslim leaders with selfish agendas can pull anything from the Koran to justify their separatism, intolerance, fears, and judgments towards others, just as Christian leaders can do with the Bible. Both are "blind" to the Spirit alive within their Scriptures. Just as some corporate-Christian "mindsets" in America believe and teach that all homosexuals, abortionists, and non-Christians are hellbound "heretics," so too are there corporate-Muslim "mindsets" who believe, teach, and judge similarly. *Bin Laden's group would never have found support, taken root, and come to such power had corporate Islam taught the Message of the Spirit, as delivered by both Muhammad and Jesus.*

Corporate Christianity is the world's most enduring "World Imperialism," the great Hierarchical Mustard Tree that holds itself as the "way" to Salvation, though Jesus reveals that The Way is the Spirit. The great Church System will not teach the Message of the Spirit, as this would compromise its big-business "way" to Salvation, effectively destroying its idolatrous nature. It most certainly does not want to give up its high-holy rituals and holidays or its beloved fears and superstitions. It surely doesn't want its enslaved masses to learn that The Way to Salvation is ultimately their personal responsibility through, *simply*, devotion to the Good Spirit. This Truth might cause many to flee their corporate "covering," which would mean... *you know*... emptier coffers! Their great fear! With loss of revenue comes loss of power and control.

Why do you think the Temple priests and scholars of Israel wanted Jesus captured? Because the people were abandoning the Temple to follow Jesus, which meant... *you know*... emptier coffers! They were losing power and control over the masses, and because they could not successfully nullify His Good Message, they went after the Messenger. *Yep, the machinery of corporate religion 2,000 years later is still not "built" to exalt The Way of the Good Spirit.*

Among corporate Christianity's services, it also acts to broker the charity of its members. It might be wise to be discerningly judgmental about corporate Christianity's advertised "charity," as it may be quite self-serving. What better way to bolster a "Holy and Righteous" image than by shouting about your wonderful charities to anyone who will listen? How is it that God's definition of charity is so ignored? He tells us that charity for worldly rewards or publicity shall have no reward in Heaven. Why let others, *like churches*, broker your charity? Why not give your charity firsthand, in secret, to whomever you desire, *when the Spirit moves you*. How much of your brokered charity gets to those who need it?

Matthew 6:1-15 (spoken by Jesus; authored by Apostle Matthew)

1. **Take heed that ye do not your alms [Charity] before men, to be seen of them: otherwise ye have no reward of your Father which is in heaven.**
2. **Therefore when thou doest thine alms, do not sound a trumpet before thee, as the hypocrites do in the synagogues and in the streets, that they may have glory of men. Verily I say unto you, They have their reward.**
3. **But when thou doest alms, let not thy left hand know what thy right hand doeth:**
4. **That thine alms may be in secret: and thy Father which seeth in secret himself shall reward thee openly.**
5. **And when thou prayest, thou shalt not be as the hypocrites are: for they love to pray standing in the synagogues and in the corners of the streets, that they may be seen of men. Verily I say unto you, They have their reward.**

6. **But thou, when thou prayest, enter into thy closet, and when thou hast shut thy door, pray to thy Father which is in secret; and thy Father which seeth in secret shall reward thee openly.**
7. **But when ye pray, use not vain repetitions** [like incessant, ritualistic "Hail Marys"], **as the heathen do: for they think that they shall be heard for their much speaking.**
8. **Be not ye therefore like unto them: for your Father knoweth what things ye have need of, before ye ask him.**
9. **After this manner therefore pray ye: Our Father which art in heaven, Hallowed be thy name.** [Pray in this manner: Our Father-Spirit, which lives Within (the Heaven Within), Holy is Thy Presence.]
10. **Thy kingdom come. Thy will be done in earth, as it is in heaven.** [Thy Eternal Companionship come. Thy Way be done outwardly (in the flesh; 'earth'), as it is inwardly (in the Spirit, the Heaven Within; the Kingdom is Within you).]
11. **Give us this day our daily bread.** [Give us this day our daily Sustenance (Life; Spirit; 'manna'; the 'bread of life').]
12. **And forgive us our debts, as we forgive our debtors.** [And forgive us our sins, as we forgive those who have sinned against us (as you sow forgiveness by your Spirit, so shall you reap forgiveness by the Spirit).]
13. **And lead us not into temptation, but deliver us from evil: For thine is the kingdom, and the power, and the glory, for ever. Amen.** ["And lead us not into temptation" is a prayer for our devotion to the Spirit, that we not seek idolatrous temptations (those who seek temptation will naturally be led into temptation, per God's Righteous Justice).]
14. **For if ye forgive men their trespasses, your heavenly Father will also forgive you:** [And if you forgive others their sins, so shall you be forgiven yours.]
15. **But if ye forgive not men their trespasses, neither will your Father forgive your trespasses.** [But if you do not forgive others their sins, neither will yours be forgiven.]

I believe that had I been programmed in any of the exclusive, idolatrous "mindsets" of corporate Christianity, this book would not exist.

My lifelong passion for God, begun in early childhood, was never rejected or hated by my non-religious parents (though our family had its problems, naturally, as all families do to some degree, we were taught to be kind, respectful, hard-working, responsible, loving, helpful children).

I have, many times, suffered afflictions by Christians simply because I was not in their "group." Of course, I know many Christians (Protestant, Catholic, and otherwise) who embrace God's Good Spirit. I have come to understand the all-importance of companionship with such Spiritful souls.

For the sake of those who have been unwittingly deceived by any corporate religion, I sincerely hope that their religious mis-leaders will come to embrace The Way of the Spirit and stop teaching separatism and idolatry as "The Way."

(5 minutes, 44 seconds later)

Historian Paul Johnson writes in the October 15th National Review: "The word Islam does not mean 'peace,' but 'submission.'" And then, Johnson said, "Islam is an Imperialist religion."

So what? So is Christianity. The big-business of Christianity was started and nurtured by the Imperialistic Roman Empire. The structure of Christianity is built upon Imperialism, with its self-serving, idolatrous hierarchy having elitist power and influence over their followers' money, votes, minds, souls, and Good Spirit.

(continued)

In the Koran, those who do not submit to Islam should be killed. That means death to Christian and death to Jew. Now, I ask you: Is that tolerant?; Is that peaceful?; Is that a "sister faith" to Christianity? Let's read some selected verses from the Koran, which is the Islamic Bible, in the aftermath of the 9/11 attacks to increase our understanding of the basis of their faith. Sura 5, Verse 85, "Sura" is a chapter, Sura 5, Verse 85 prophesies an inevitable conflict between Muslims and non-Muslims: "Strongest among men in enmity to the believers," the believers being the Islamics, "will you find the Jews and the Pagans." You (pointing to the audience) are the Pagan in their view. Sura 9, Verse 5 states, "Then fight and slave the Pagans where you find them, and seize them, beleaguer them, and lie in wait for them in every strategy of war." That's in their Bible. The Koran insists that no matter how mighty a nation is, it must be fought until it embraces Islam.

Here, we see how Christianity accuses Islam of that which Christianity is likewise guilty. Muslims who pluck quotes from the Koran to support their selfish agendas are no different than Christians who use selected Bible verses to do the same. And all the while they ignore God's One Message.

In the Koran, its reference to "believers" represent the Spiritful, and the "Jews and the Pagans" represent the Spiritless (naturally, they view Jews as "unholy" as, historically and currently, they have lived to oppose each other). Nevertheless, the Koran, like the Bible, provides the superseding Message of the Good Spirit that transcends all "groupist," worldly labels ("Muslim" and "Jew").

Christians who spew erroneous, ignorant, hate-stirring propaganda about Islam are no better than Muslims who do the same about Christianity. They breed separation from the Spirit, separating their own souls from God even more.

■ ■ ◆ ■ ■

#6 - Davis, Maury (on *Hannity & Colmes* with Sean Hannity, Alan Colmes, and guest Asma Hasan, author of *American Muslims;* February 7, 2002)

Sean Hannity: Do you believe Islam is evil?

Maury Davis: Yes. And I want to be able to make some qualifying statements. I've heard some things said about some of the sermons I've preached. I don't believe that Muslims are evil. I believe that the religion of Islam has the ability to produce a rage in people that many of us don't understand in America. And I've read the lady's book, or parts of it today that are on the program tonight (referring to Asma Hasan's book, "American Muslims"). And I'm dealing with mostly third-world countries. I have a lot of ministry in Northern Africa, where we work with a lot of Muslim people. And when you're dealing with the fundamental element of the Muslim faith, I believe it is a threat to the United States of America.

Sean Hannity: Is Islam evil in its religion? Would you say that yourself?

Maury Davis: Well, I think Islam is a threat to the Constitution of the United States of America and to our way of life for a number of reasons. I have not spent a lot of time studying Islam until September 11th, and I began to hear a lot of talk about "What is Islam?" and "What is a Muslim?" and I wanted to study it, and I discovered there were different kinds of Muslims as there are different kinds of Christians.

Sean Hannity: But, but, wait a minute, if you think, by definition, Islam is an evil religion, as you're saying, that's what you believe, we have freedom of religion in this country, should people be free to practice that religion?

Maury Davis: Absolutely. I believe in the freedom of speech, in the freedom of religion for every person that is a part of the United States vision and this great country we call America, but I believe that tolerance has been pushed beyond intellectual abilities.

Sean Hannity: All right. Asma, let me go to you. You and I have discussed this on the program before. I don't like to go after peoples' deeply held religious views or their faith, because that's so deeply personal. My only criticism has been the fanatical, extremist interpretation of a religion, and it comes from all faiths, it's not just one, and that's what we get to here. How do you juxtapose that with what the pastor is saying here?

Asma Hasan: Well, I think what the pastor is talking about is a reality for sure, it exists, and the stereotypes exist for a reason. However, he's being selective about the sources that he looks at. If you were to read Karen Armstrong, for instance, or my book, you would find out that Muhammad founded one of the world's first democracies. He wrote a Constitution in Medina recognizing the rights of religious minorities and, you know, Pastor Davis is acting as though he isn't calling me evil or other Muslims evil, but when you call Islam evil, I think you're calling the people who follow it evil as well. And it's very clear for anyone who reads the Koran, a good translation, that evil is something that's condemned. It says many times in the Koran, "Forbid the evil, enjoin the good," and that's what Islam is about. And we accept Jesus as well.

Alan Colmes: Let me put up some of the parts of the Koran, which I spent some time reading today, you'll be happy to know. Pastor, let me show you the part where it says, for example, "Thus, if they let you be, and do not make war on you, and offer you peace, God does not allow you to harm them" (Koran, 4:90). Or let me show you the part that says, "whoever took a life, unless it be for murder or for spreading disorder on earth, it would be as if he killed all mankind; and whoever saved a life, it would be as if he saved all mankind" (Koran 5:32). Does that sound warlike and vicious to you?

Maury Davis: No sir, and if you read the entire Koran, you'll discover that the Koran is almost a flip of the Bible. The Bible starts out with law and moves to grace. Mohammed started out as a very peaceful man and ended up a conqueror who was involved in 65 wars. And when you look at the Koran, there are many verses in there that, if you don't put the whole picture together, would not come out. The young lady (referring to Asma Hasan) misunderstood something I said earlier and, in her book, she writes that her stance would not be acceptable in most mosques in the United States of America. I believe that there are Muslim people that are as peace-loving and as kind and as wonderful in this country as there are Christians, but the Islamic faith, as finished by the prophet Muhammad, is a different faith than we've been raised with in the United States of America. Let me give you some Scriptures. The Scripture says in Sura 2:2:28 that men are superior to women. It says women have half the rights of men in the Sura 2:28:2. It says that the man may punish the wife by beating her, Sura 4:30:4. And the point is, I met with Iman Abdullah here in Nashville yesterday, and I went over these Scriptures with him and talked to him about the multiple marriage...

Alan Colmes: Pastor, we only have moment left. I don't mean to interrupt. I'm very sorry, but we just have to move the show along, we only have time for one more question. Is Osama Bin Laden any more representative of Islam than Paul Hill, for example, who committed a murder in an abortion clinic, is of Christianity?

Maury Davis: I don't believe that a man who would commit a murder has known the Lord or been born again, and I can't speak for Osama Bin Laden as a Muslim [could].

Alan Colmes: Asma, do you think the Bible, the Christian Bible or the Old Testament, which the Jews and the Christians both read, is that violent?

Asma Hasan: Well, obviously there are passages in there that are violent, and when you take them out of context, like the pastor is doing with the Koran, and when you rely on mistranslations, specifically like the one's he just talked about with women, if he'd actually read my book, he would know that those are mistranslations, the specific ones that he's talking about, saying that women are inferior. Any religious faith, any belief system taken out of context, manipulated for people who want to become famous and sensationalized, that's going to happen.

Ecclesiastes 7:25-26 (likely authored by King Solomon)

25. I applied mine heart to know, and to search, and to seek out wisdom, and the reason of things, and to know the wickedness of folly, even of foolishness and madness:

26. And I find more bitter than death the woman, whose heart is snares and nets, and her hands as bands: whoso pleaseth God shall escape from her; but the sinner shall be taken by her.

Corporate Christianity has, for the better part of its existence, denied women the same rights as men, teaching that the male is superior to the female, not understanding that God's Spiritual Message is talking about the "maleness" and "femaleness" within every living human soul (Chapter 10).

Ms. Hasan is correct. Both the Koran and the Bible can be taken out of context to support selfish agendas (Ecclesiastes 7:26, above, could certainly be used against women).

■ ■ ◆ ■ ■

#11 - Graham, Billy (aired December 8, 2001, live from Fresno, CA)

Now, tonight, our world has been turned upside down. <u>You will not be able to live the life that your parents had hoped you would live or you thought you would live</u>. It's a different world. It's gonna be felt in every part of our society for years to come. We're in a situation in Afghanistan that is extremely serious. I remember when the British were trying to take Afghanistan and they went through the Khyber Pass, and at one point in the Khyber Pass it's only about sixty feet wide, and the British were slaughtered. They had to give up. Then the Russians came. They wanted to make Afghanistan a part of their Empire. They too had to leave. No one has ever really conquered Afghanistan. And what we're seeing now, as the president (President Bush) said, is a strange new war. And we're in for troubled times, and difficult times, and we're going to have to rethink our lives. <u>But in the midst of all of that, there's one hope, and that is the hope that Jesus Christ said that He's coming back again</u>. He said, "If I go and prepare a place for you, I'll come again."

Is it not *utterly hopeless* to teach "You will not be able to live the life that your parents had hoped you would live or you thought you would live?" This is no Good blessing upon an audience, but an ill "blessing" of hopelessness. But why? To then teach that the "one hope" is Christ's Second Coming. *What does the hope of His Second Coming have to do with teaching His Message of the Spirit?* His eventual Second Coming may be the "one hope" to this preacher, but the Bible reveals that our One Hope is our devotion to His Good Spirit.

(continuing)

Without hope, our nation could not go on. Since September the 11th, we've begun singing again a hymn we used to sing often. In fact, it was sort of the theme of our crusades for some years: "Mine Eyes Have Seen the Glory of the Coming of the Lord."

Now, the coming of Christ is taught in all the great creeds of the Church. The Nicene Creed says, "He shall come again with glory to judge both the quick and the dead." Charles Wesley, the great Methodist, one of the founders of the Methodist Church, wrote seven thousand hymns, and in five thousand of them he wrote of the coming of Jesus Christ. When Queen Elizabeth the Second was crowned, the Archbishop of Canterbury laid the crown upon her head with this statement, "I give thee, O Sovereign Lady, this crown to wear until he who reserves the right to wear it shall come."

After delivering a message of such hopelessness, we are then taught that "Without hope, our nation could not go on," meaning that without Christ's inevitable Second Coming, America could not go on. *Does any of this make sense?*

It is true that both Nicene Creeds (the Nicene Creed of the Nicaean Council in 325 and the Nicene Creed of Constantinople in 381) declare Jesus as judging "the quick and the dead" ["the quick," referring to those quickened unto Salvation via the Spirit Within (Romans 8:11), and "the dead," referring to the unregenerately selfish, or those "dead to the Spirit"].

Who cares what the Nicene Creeds say? *Corporate Christianity cares, very much, because the Nicene Creeds are highly-summarized, Letter-of-the-Law interpretations of Jesus' Gospel created to serve the big-business of corporate religion.* Both Nicene Creeds are springboards for idolatrous worship. Both were written at a time when the laity was not allowed to possess or read the Scriptures. The newly-birthed Roman Church had wrested absolute control over the Scriptures, *interpreting them to their will,* and have been feeding the masses their exclusive "way" to Salvation ever since.

One of the first major incidents of the Inquisition happened in 1229 when Pope Gregory IX learned that lay people had gotten hold of the

Vulgate (the Bible written in Latin), a situation that was immediately arrested. Knowledge is power, and the Roman Church was not going to compromise their power and control over the masses by allowing them access to the Bible. *God forbid they should read the Bible and possibly come to learn Jesus' Message of the Spirit for themselves.* After all, the Bible reveals: **1)** that no corporate church or any man-made thing is Mediator between a soul and God; **2)** that Jesus does not care if you believe in Him or not, but that you do not deny your Good Spirit and Conscience; and **3)** that ritual baptism is worthless without the *Baptism Within*, which is justified only through devotion to Selfless, Good Works.

A Methodist composer is praised for writing about Christ's Second Coming 5,000 times in 7,000 hymns. Are we to believe that this is some sort of proof that His Second Coming is our "one hope?" And what about what the Archbishop of Canterbury said when crowning Queen Elizabeth II? Are we to believe that her crown is Jesus' Crown when He comes back? Doesn't this belief lift Queen Elizabeth to "High Priest" status, making her our living, personal representative of Christ on Earth? When Jesus returns, will He first stop at Buckingham Palace for His man-made adornment? What does He need with corrupt, worldly treasures?

(continuing)

I think of it, you know, when I watch the news, and listen to the news, and read the news. Who could restore order to the world? What one man, what one ideology can govern the world? And we don't have many answers to that unless we mention what Jesus said, "Behold, I show you a mystery. We shall not all sleep, but we shall all be changed in a moment, in the twinkling of an eye at the last trumpet, for the dead shall be raised." Christ's coming again is mentioned in the New Testament you know how many times? Over three hundred times.

Incorrect. Jesus did not make that statement ("Behold, I show you a mystery..."). Apostle Paul did, in First Corinthians 15:51-52. It refers to the Rapture, when the true and faithful to The Way, *Christian or not*, shall be translated, *body and soul*, from Earth to Heaven one-hour before Christ's Second Coming on the last day of the seven-year Tribulation Period (Chapter 6). Let us not forget that there will be Christians who, because of their selfishness (idolatry), shall not be raptured. This does not necessarily mean that they shall not come to Salvation, as the Millennial Kingdom serves as the final period for the Redemption of the unsaved, during which the "sheep" (the unsaved believers) shall be further separated from the "goats" (the unsaved unbelievers).

■ ■ ◆ ■ ■

#12 - Graham, Franklin (on *Hannity & Colmes* with Sean Hannity and Alan Colmes; February 22, 2002)

Franklin Graham: I certainly love Muslim people, and want to reach out to them. I do have some problems with the teaching of Islam as it relates to their treatment of women and to their treatment of non-Muslims, especially Christians and Jews, and I find some of this teaching very disturbing, and it really bothers me, but I want to reach out to Muslim people and love them, and help them, and that's why we are in Afghanistan right now, working in that country with medicine, and we work in a number of Muslim countries around the world, and we've been doing that for over twenty-five years (referring to his Charitable Organization, *Samaritan's Purse*).

Alan Colmes: When you called Islam, the phrase you used was "an evil and wicked religion," do you want to rephrase that? Was that taken out of context, or would you like to put that in a frame that might be more understandable or palatable for those that might be of the Islamic faith?

Franklin Graham: Well, Alan, again, I have some real problems with these teachings. I have a hospital in the Sudan, and our hospital, a year before last, was bombed on seven occasions. We've had people killed in our hospitals. There are churches that have been burned. Christians, over two million Christians have been killed in the Southern Sudan in the name of Islam, and this is a real concern to me, and here's a country, an Islamic country, that still practices slavery. Here we are in the new millennium, and black Africans are still bought, sold, and traded in slavery in the Sudan, and I have some problems.

Alan Colmes: Do you believe that Islam is an evil religion, do they, that's what you're saying, do they worship the same God as the Judeo-Christian God? Is it a different God?

Franklin Graham: No, it's a different God. The God that we worship that has, that's a Father, and He has a Son, and His name is Jesus Christ, who came to this Earth to die for the sins of mankind. And, of course, in Islam, their God is not a Father. He does not have a Son and, of course, if you said that He has a Son, that's blasphemous to a Muslim. And, of course, their picture of Heaven is completely different of the Heaven that we look forward to being [in] someday. It's a completely different view. And so, yes, it is a different God, but, listen, we love Muslim people, and I would reach out to them everyday in love. And we don't have a problem with Muslim people, but the religion I find some problems.

Mr. Colmes' pointed question is never directly answered when he asks this preacher about having judged Islam as "an evil and wicked religion." Instead, a passive answer is given, describing Islam as having "some problems." *Didn't we see this "relative" dancing-around-the-question earlier, in Chapter 1, with his corporate-minded sister, Anne Graham Lotz?*

The Muslim "Allah" is the God of the Bible. Though Muslims accept Jesus as a Divine prophet, they do not accept Him as the Messiah, which is of no consequence to Jesus, as He cares not if we speak against Him, but that we do not deny the Spirit (Matthew 12:31-33). Additionally, Muslims do not accept that God is Three-in-One, *the Three Persons of the Father, the Son, and the Holy Spirit.* Instead, they believe that God is One. The Muslims worship the One God and call Him "Allah." Allah is the God of the Bible, but just not recognized as being divided into Three Persons.

America gives billions of $$$ in aid to the world's poor countries, but some of these countries, *run by corrupted government officials,* do not funnel those $$$ down to the suffering populations. If they did, there would be no need for sympathetic outside forces to set up "camp" in these countries, to dole out food, medicine, schooling, and $$$. Christians have poured millions into setting-up such camps. Helping the poor, *which are Good Works,* can be born of Selfless and/or selfish motivations. *Is it not possible that this charity also has self-serving motivations, namely, intent to convert downtrodden, suffering Muslims into Christians, to "save" them in the name of corporate Christianity's idolatrous vision of Jesus?*

You've got poor, uneducated, miserable souls suffering with constant hunger and dis-ease, all taught to be Muslims, but getting no aid from anyone, and along come corporate-Christian "mindsets" who build buildings and administer aid, food, education, and their "God." *Is it too difficult to understand that millions of these impoverished, starving people converted to Christianity because the aid, comfort, food, and schooling brought by Christians revolved around "saving" their "heretic," Muslim souls?* And wouldn't the conversion of millions of desperate Muslims into Christians be seen as an affront to the corporate Islamic structure that has ruled that region for centuries? Could this be why Islamists, *according to Graham,* have killed over two million Christians? If so, then it is reasonable to conclude that these Muslims-turned-Christians would not have been killed except for Christianity's well-intentioned, but self-serving charity.

The "over-two-million Christians" killed had to have been mostly impoverished Muslims-turned-Christians. Had 2,000,000 American Christians, or even 1,000 been killed in Africa, America would be outraged. Evidently, the Muslims are ticked-off that Christians have barged in with a smile and a helping hand, *not to genuinely help for want of nothing in return,* but helping so that they can increase the world's number of "saved Christians." The bonus for these charitable Christians is that they receive such adulation for their "Holy" work, though their charity is stained with selfish motivations.

But for corporate Christianity's selfish charity, *motivated to convert Muslims instead of giving aid selflessly, wanting nothing in return,* these converts might not have been slaughtered by the millions. Selfless Charity does not exalt religious conversion, but exalts only the Good Spirit that feeds and breeds the Good Spirit.

I thought you might find the following interesting, as it mentions Mr. Graham's charitable organization, *Samaritan's Purse*. It is an excerpt from *Politically Incorrect*, aired May 11, 2002. Joining host Bill Maher are supermodel Molly Sims, host of MTV's *House of Style*, and Frank Turek, a Christian motivational speaker and the author of *Legislating Morality*.

Bill Maher: Have you heard about this thing. It is related to the moral depravity of our times, but I saw it, it was all over CNN today. Some camera guy, some moral reprobate is hiring bums, giving them money to fight each other, and then he films it, and the videos are, of course, "flying off the shelf," because this is America. They are paying bums to fight.

(1 minute, 19 seconds later)
Molly Sims: It's exploitation. It's gross.

Bill Maher: It's so gross, but people buy it. And I love the way these guys (referring to the producers of the 'bum' fights) say, "Well, we're not forcing anybody to do it."

Molly Sims: But if your homeless, if they're going to give you money, you're gonna to do it.

Bill Maher: Right. And I thought I wasn't going to relate this to religion, but I guess I am, because, you know what, that's the same thing that missionaries do. They go to a place that's devastated by an earthquake where the people are poor, and they say, "You don't have to believe in Jesus Christ, but this sandwich... (Mr. Maher pauses, the audience applauds)... pretty much comes with accepting Jesus Christ."

Frank Turek: Bill, they do it the other way, Bill.

Bill Maher: Oh, no they don't.

Frank Turek: They give them the sandwich, and then they speak to 'em about the Lord.

Bill Maher: Yeah, but I tell you, the Lord goes down much better on a full stomach.

Frank Turek: He does. He does. You're absolutely right. You're absolutely right. There's no questions about it. So, what's wrong with that?

Bill Maher: Okay, well, I mean, but when missionaries show up where there's been an earthquake and they go, "Boy, look at this place, your God really sucks, I tell ya'. I don't know what kind of God allows this destruction to happen, but have you seen our brochure? Don't believe that stuff you hear about the kids (referring to crimes of pedophilia by Catholic priests, kept secret and perpetuated by Church Hierarchy)."

Frank Turek: Nah, come on. Franklin Graham's Samaritan's Purse, they do great work. Don't lump 'em with all the (sentence ends).

Franklin Graham's *Samaritan's Purse* is a charitable Christian Missionary organization. I would certainly think that this organization is not forcing impoverished, diseased Muslims to become Christians by withholding food and medicine. These Christian missionaries are like "saviors" to some Muslims, whose own churches and countries provide them little to no aid. Along come Christians with food, clothing, medicine, books, and schooling. They show much love and care, looking to indoctrinate them, so that they might change their religion from Islam to Christianity. *I would convert too if in the same desperate situation. Absolutely.* But, evidently, this has enraged fundamentalist Muslims so much so that they are annihilating these Muslims-turned-Christians "in the name of Islam." These massacres must be, in part, due to corporate Christianity's selfish desire to convert grievously impoverished Muslims, *not giving of their charity Selflessly, for want of nothing in return,* but selfishly, to gain converts.

That so many have be murdered and the "mission" continues on "as is" should be criminal and should be forced to stop. *Stop it*, or give your charity without pushing idolatrous, corporate Christianity upon these suffering souls. Do not put their lives in danger by converting them. Respect their religion, for the Spirit cares not about one's religious membership (or lack of). Show them your Selfless Goodness, compromising not their religion and their lives, asking for nothing in return. *Of course, this will probably not happen.* Idolatrous Christianity doesn't care that millions are being murdered for having converted, because as far as it's concerned, at least they were "saved," otherwise they would have gone to hell. *When will this insanity stop?*

Chapter 13

MISCELLANEA

#14 - Hagee, John (January 9, 2000)

People are going around on national-television talk shows, expounding their concept on whether the Bible is right or not, and there are many ways to God. I saw a lady the other day on The Jerry Springer Show, she looked like, conservatively, she must have weighed four-hundred pounds, and had the IQ of twelve, expounding about whether or not the word of God was relevant or whether there were many ways to God or not. Let me tell you something: You don't have a vote. The Bible says, Jesus speaking, "I am the way, and no one cometh unto the Father but by me." He is the Creator, we are the created. He is the Shepherd, we are the sheep. He is the Potter, we are the clay. We don't tell Him, He tells us, and then we do it.

Is it not Christless and mean-spirited to judge this woman's spiritual seeking by way of her fatness and supposed low intelligence? *At least she is seeking.* God promises that those who seek shall find.

■ ■ ◆ ■ ■

#14 - Hagee, John (December 26, 1999)

America's full of macho wife-abusers who slap their wife around like a beach ball. I pray that next time you swat your wife, God withers your arm at the elbow. If that doesn't happen, I hope she plants an iron skillet right between your eyes, in love, of course.

Why pray for the husband's arm to wither? And what happens if God doesn't wither his arm? *The wife is called to vengeful violence* ("vengeance is mine, sayeth the Lord"). We are not to exact vengeance, but overcome evil with Good, continuing upon The Way as best we know.

Why not instruct the wife to separate from such inhumanity as soon as possible? Instead, she is to take vengeance in the name of "love" that could kill her husband. With such Spiritless teachings from the pulpits, is it any wonder why so many Christians fill America's prisons?

(3 minutes, 36 seconds later)

Who controls your mind, the Holy Spirit or Hollywood? Your mind is like a computer: "trash in, trash out." When you watch forty hours of American television full of sex and violence, it's "trash in." All that can come out of you is "trash." The Holy Spirit cannot live in a "trash dump."

Let's see if I've got this right: *The Spirit can live on Earth, our planetary home upon which evil thrives, but cannot live in a mind that has viewed sex and violence?* If the Spirit cannot live in a mind that has viewed sex and violence on television, then how can it live in a mind that teaches false religion?

Knowledge is Power. We are instructed to be wily as a fox, but gentle as a lamb in this world, which means that we are to be educated about worldliness, that we might not fall prey to it, deceived away from the Spirit. Films, *even films depicting the nature of such things as sexual lust, murder, and violence*, can be valuable sources of learning. The Spirit knows no fear.

This book was not a "trash in" experience, although I subjected myself to over 700 hours of religious "trash" to get it written. *Good things can come out of trash.*

■ ■ ◆ ■ ■

#35 - Rogers, Adrian (May 11, 2003)

Friend, what is the greatest power known to man? Is it the devastating power of a hurricane? Is it atomic power? Monetary power? Military power? Listen to me, beyond the shadow of any doubt, the greatest power known to man is prayer, because prayer engages Almighty God in our lives.

Once again, denial of the Spirit. It is not prayer that is the "greatest power" and that "engages Almighty God" in your life, but the Spirit Within you. When will preachers exalt the Spirit over idolatrous rituals? Your ritualistic prayer is only as powerful as your soul's devotion to the Spirit. Get off your knees and go out and let your Good Spirit Within shine upon the world, for that is Truest Prayer.

Jesus gives us only One Prayer to pray (The Lord's Prayer), and yet corporate Christianity has formulated all sorts of idolatrous, ritualistic prayers for every occasion. No matter all your religiosity and prayers, God will never be "engaged" in your life if you do not engage your life in His Spirit. Those who keep their Good Spirit to themselves shall lose it, and be damned (per Jesus' Parable of the Talents, Chapter 3).

■ ■ ◆ ■ ■

#9 - Finley, Mark (May 11, 2003)

We've already seen that God is Love, and whatever that means, it at least means that love is an overriding characteristic of God, but notice that not only does God love, but He is commanding that we love as well. And here's the amazing thing: The first and greatest commandment is the one commandment that God cannot force us to obey. I'd like you to think carefully about this with me. God could force you not to commit adultery, if He chose. God could force you not to steal, if He chose. God could force you not to lie. See, He could program our brains so we didn't do any of those things, but He could not force us to love Him, because love, to be love, must be free.

Here is tortured logic that does not accept the Truth that God is Love, but questions it ("whatever that means"). To say that Love is an "overriding characteristic" of God lessens the rock-solid Truth that God *is* Love.

We are taught that God, if He wanted, could force you not to commit adultery. No, no, no. *Never.* When the Bible says, "With God, all things are possible," it means that all things are possible *by the Good Spirit.* But it doesn't mean that the Good Spirit can change its very nature. It would be against God's Spirit to force you to do nothing/anything. God does not "program" us in any way, as that would make Him a manipulative slave-master, not only denying His Righteous Justice ("as you sow, so shall you reap"), but denying the very nature of His Selfless Spirit.

■ ■ ◆ ■ ■

#29 - Patterson, Gilbert E. (May 26, 2003)

There is nothin' broken in your life that God cannot fix. Yeah, you talkin' about Mr. Fix-it. One of the automobile manufacturer's talk about Mr. Goodwrench, can fix anything that happens to your car. I want you to know, God's got a way of fixin' anything that can happen in your life. He is the original Mr. Fix-it, and if you let Him... (sentence ends). You see, the thing about it, you don't let Him. We have a tendency of tryin' to tell Him how to do stuff, but He's got His own way of doin' what needs to be done. Yet some of you all have even prayed for God to save a particular family member and, the next thing you know, that family member suddenly gets sick or gets hurt in an automobile accident and has to lie up in the hospital for six months. And you talkin' [to the] Lord, "I want you to save him, I didn't tell you to kill him." But God said, "I got to stop him so I can talk to him." Yeah, you see, a lot of time God is workin' on your case, and you don't understand what He is doin'. But when you turn it over to Him, you got to let Him do it His own way. He's not gonna do it your way. He's got a way where He can do everything that needs to be done. But the end result is, when He gets through workin', that thing is gonna be fixed, and it's gonna be fixed forever. Glory to God.

Here, God is envisioned as a manipulative God who personally holds your life and death in His hands, and is going to do things His way regardless of your will and prayers. Incorrect. Your life and death is always, ultimately your responsibility. God does not bring you dis-ease or death. You do, through your soul's unreconciled darkness.

God is the Good Spirit Within that only you have the power to Glorify or crucify. Truest Prayer comes by conducting the Good Spirit. So too does Truest Healing. Those who need healing can only, ultimately, effect the healing process within themselves by sowing to the Spirit.

We are not to fear dis-ease and death of the body, but of the soul, because the flesh is temporary and the soul eternal. So, amidst life's sufferings, we are to keep our eyes on the Prize by taking care of our wellness and staying true to the Spirit.

■ ■ ◆ ■ ■

#28 - Parsley, Rod (May 16, 1999)

A Holy Ghost invasion is taking place. Man your battle-stations. Ready your weapons. Lock and load. The revolution has begun. Let it begin with a shout unto Him who has not only called us to war, but has called us to win. Touch somebody and tell 'em, "I'm gonna be a part of a revolution. I don't have to be right. I don't have to be regarded. I don't have to be rewarded."

Where is the Spirit in all this? Here is a call to arms, to "lock and load" your weapons in a war that does not have to be "right." How many misled zealots have heard this type of preaching, influencing them to violence?

(3 minutes, 21 seconds later)

I'm trying to find me somebody that won't take it any more. You're just not gonna put up with it any more. You're tired of the devil running through your family. You're tired of ancestral curses. You're tired of drug lords runnin' your neighborhood. You're tired of abortion doctors lining their pockets with millions.

Jesus' Gospel is not about being "tired of the devil" that pollutes the world, but is about cleansing your "world" by overcoming your selfishness with the Selfless Spirit.

Romans 12:21 (authored by Apostle Paul)

21. Be not overcome of evil, but overcome evil with good.

(11 minutes, 40 seconds later)

He's (God) waiting on you to become a member of a revolutionary army that's not just about ready to let the world go to hell.

Here is a call to a Christian "holy war" that paints a picture of strategy, weaponry, and motive, a war that seeks no reward and *does not have to be right*. The "war" theme from this ministry continues, as follows.

■ ■ ◆ ■ ■

#28 - Parsley, Rod (July 24, 1999)

Time is running out. Our world is plummeting madly into midnight, unaware that a Holy God is coming to judge mankind. God is stirring the hearts of his remnant Church to reap this millennium's "final harvest" of souls. God has always had a remnant of people set apart and ready to go to war, a group of revolutionary, remnant warriors ready to step out of the comfort zone and into the combat zone for Jesus Christ. I'm asking you to heed this call to action. It's time to take up your arms and invade the smoke-filled corridors of the doomed and the damned and set this lost and dying generation free. Time is running out. This is our last charge in this final year in this millennium. As part of this battle, I must have your financial support to continue this soul-winning outreach.

More fear-mongering, followed by a cry for money to support a "soul-winning outreach." And for what? *To step into the "combat zone for Jesus Christ" by taking up "arms" and invading the "doomed and the damned."* Could this not be construed as a call to militant, violent action against non-Christians and others labeled "hellbound?"

(10 seconds later)

If you can help with a gift of $100 or more, I want to place in your hands this beautiful medal of honor, a special keepsake to mark your cherished dedication to the cause of Christ. As you place it on your desk or bookshelf, I believe it will serve as a cherished reminder of your dedication to winning souls.

Luring listeners to give at least $100 to receive some insignificant, man-made "medal" is nothing more than selling idolatry. No surprise, as this is the *modus operandi* of corporate religion, which peddles idolatry to enrich itself.

■ ■ ◆ ■ ■

#28 - Parsley, Rod (October 3, 1999)

You need to get mad. You need to get tired of your family members being on crack. You need to get tired of pornographers in this city driving Mercedes-Benz's and you driving something held together with Christian bumper stickers. You need to get violent.

■ ■ ◆ ■ ■

#19 - Jones III, Bob (on *Larry King Live* with Larry King; March, 2000)

Larry King: But if you call the Pope the anti-Christ, you will offend Catholics, I mean, that's logical to think that, right? Just as if I said something derogatory about Jesus Christ, I would offend you?

Bob Jones III: Yes, but, you know, the Westminster Confession of Faith, which is supposed to be believed by all Presbyterians that have embraced the Westminster Confession, is their doctrinal basis. Article 6 of the Westminster Confession calls the Pope an anti-Christ. There's a long tradition for this. In fact, Wycliffe, that I talked about a while ago, in the 14th century, he called the Pope an anti-Christ. So, Protestants do not, you know, the Pope doesn't go down well with Protestants, okay?

That the Catholic Pope doesn't "go down well with Protestants" is no surprise, as both groups have hated, fought, and killed each other for nearly six centuries. It lives on today. *Look at Northern Ireland.* It's the same ol' story where you've got "Good Catholics" and "Good Protestants" using the Bible to "sanctify" their ill-will and violence "in the name of God," blind to the Truth that God "hates" (rejects) their selfishness.

Christianity and its many sects love their separatism. Separatism rejects Oneness, and dangerously tempts hate, self-exaltation, intolerance, persecution, vengeance, etc. Be not deceived by separatist groups that call themselves "peaceful," as their "peace" is always temporary, *lasting only as long as things go their narrow-minded way.* Separatists fester in self-righteousness, and live to impose *their way of life* as The Way of Life.

■ ■ ◆ ■ ■

#23 - Mann, Gerald (June 6, 1999)

And the only cure for addiction is what the people in AA call the "higher power." The twelve steps of Alcoholics Anonymous is the greatest spiritual movement in this century, and it's because it deals with the problem. How do you deal with addictions? How do you deal with your sins and your proclivities to do wrong? There are three steps which I've reduced to my own language: I can't, I cannot; He can, "higher power"; and the third step is "I'll let Him."

Evidently, the only cure for any kind of addiction is:

1) I tell myself that I <u>can't</u> stop my addiction;
2) I then tell myself that God <u>can</u> stop my addiction;
3) I will <u>let</u> God cure me of my addiction.

The first step must be "I can," not "I can't" because, *after all*, God has given us the free-will power to make changes to our own lives. Only we can ultimately change our minds and souls. Without this most-fundamental realization, no change will occur. Overcoming destructive, selfish behavior requires that the destructive behavior not be given "life" anymore. Though there are several avenues that help to lead alcoholics to wellness (Alcoholic's Anonymous, abstinence, recovery clinics, etc.), it is always ultimately up to the individual to conquer his/her affliction.

The second step must be, "God will" bring healing, not "God can" bring healing. If you repent of your selfishness, *the healing Spirit will grow Within, naturally*. God's Promise is that those who sow to the Spirit shall build the Spirit Within. His regenerative Spirit is available to every living sinner at all times, for God "sendeth rain on the just and on the unjust" (God's Spirit is there for us for the taking; Matthew 5:46).

The third step cannot be "I'll let Him" cure me, as the healing process is already underway via the second step. The third step should be, *naturally*, thanksgiving. Rejoice, and be humbly thankful for His regenerative Spirit. And don't look back (continue forward in the Spirit, not falling back into your selfishness).

Do you know what can happen when you look back upon the "hell" you left behind? When Lot's wife looked back upon the hellish destruction of Sodom, she turned into a "pillar of salt." Her "salt of the earth" was not a pillar of His Spirit of Life, *which had just saved her life*, but a pillar of selfishness. Those who have been led away from destruction (selfishness) may return to destruction if they look back. When walking The Way to the Light, the shadow is cast behind you. Do not look back onto the shadow, as it may tempt you to covet the shadow and lead you to stumble upon The Way.

■ ■ ◆ ■ ■

#39 - Swaggart, Jimmy (June 6, 1999)

It took God far greater power to redeem man than it did to create the worlds. God, according to the writer of Hebrews, was able to create the world, the Universe, the some trillions of trillions of stars in outer space, and I'm not exaggerating. And the Psalmist said He (God) even names them all. He was able to do that merely by His word. He literally spoke them into existence, and that's the power beyond our comprehension, beyond the minds of man, or of men,

I should say. But when it came to redemption, the Lord could not speak redemption into existence. He had to come effect a work, if you will, a work, as Paul said, which was not done in a corner, which incorporated literally thousands of years, some four-thousand years to be exact and, in the Mind of God, it was even done in Eternity past, before the world was ever formed or the foundations ever laid.

We are taught that it took God greater power to redeem man than to create the Physical Universe, and that God could not speak Redemption into existence. *God never redeemed "man,"* but offers Redemption through His Way of the Spirit. *God never spoke Redemption into existence*, but His Plan for the Redemption of sinful souls was *naturally predetermined* before any of our souls ever sinned (Chapter 7).

(2 minutes, 44 seconds later)

That He had to destroy the world by water, saving only Noah and his family, or the whole of humanity would be eternally lost, because of its corruption that threatens to destroy itself.

All life on land was not destroyed and re-inhabited by Noah and his passengers. The "earth" that was deluged in Genesis 7:24 was the "land" upon which Noah lived, in an area of the Eastern Mediterranean [the Hebrew translation of "earth" is "land," or "country" (Genesis 6:17 and 7:24)].

Is it possible that Noah's Flood was a regional flood that covered a massive area of the land upon which he lived? *You bet*. Genesis 6:4 tells of mighty men of renown ("giants") inhabiting the world before the flood came, who still existed after the flood [the "giants" ('sons of Anak'; 'children of Anak') were present upon Earth after the flood (Numbers 13:33; Deuteronomy 9:1-2), along with their city (Hebron, the city of Arba, the father of Anak; Genesis 13:18, 23:2; Joshua 15:13, 21:11)].

If the giants had been killed by the flood, how is it that the Bible reveals their existence after the flood? Do we assume that the new race of humanity, born of Noah's children, spawned more giants? We are not given that knowledge, but are told that this race of giants was alive and well before and after the flood.

Furthermore, if "every living substance was destroyed which was upon the face of the ground" by Noah's Flood (Genesis 7:23), then how is it that an olive tree survived? Wouldn't all trees, plants, and seeds have perished, all being of living biological substance? And yet a dove returned to Noah's Ark with an "olive leaf pluckt off" (Genesis 8:11).

Through intensive studies of Earth's geological record, geologists and scientists have determined that no flood has ever inundated all the continents simultaneously, ever.

■ ■ ◆ ■ ■

#2 - Breese, Dave (September 19, 1999)

Israel, looking at what Jesus said to them about the Kingdom of Heaven, they said, "We will not have this man to reign over us." Instead of saying, "yes," they said "no" to the offer of the Kingdom. And the consequence of that hideous decision exists down to this very day. The consequences have been of greater impact upon the world than any other rejection or any other legal thing that has happened in all of history. Israel was offered, "Say 'yes' or 'no' to the Kingdom of God." Israel, after thinking for just a moment, they said, "no," and the result has had its result in your life and in mine, and especially upon the Nation of Israel. We are able to look back at the consequences of that rejection, and you and I can see that the result was terrible beyond description. The result would leave people speechless when they think about what might have happened and what did happen. One of the things that happened was that Israel had God turn His back upon them. Israel rejected Jesus Christ as its Messiah, the world's most foolish decision.

Incorrect. Israel's rejection of Jesus was inevitable, given the historically rebellious, idolatrous nature of the Israelites towards God's Invisible Spirit. Because of their rejection, the Message of God's Spirit and Grace was blessed upon the non-Israelites. The following Biblical excerpts confirm that Israel's rejection of Christ became the greatest of blessings upon the non-Israelites, and will, *in the end*, reap the greatest of blessings for the Israelites.

Romans 11:11 (authored by Apostle Paul)

11. **I say then, Have they stumbled that they should fall? God forbid: but rather through their fall salvation is come unto the Gentiles, for to provoke them to jealousy.** [Have the Israelites rejected Jesus' Spirit that they should never come to know Salvation? God forbid, but rather by their rejection, The Way of Jesus became embraced by non-Israelites to provoke the Israelites to jealousy.]

Romans 11:30-32 (authored by Apostle Paul)

30. **For as ye in times past have not believed God, yet have now obtained mercy through their unbelief:** [For as they (non-Israelites) have not believed in God in the past, they have now obtained His Grace (His Spirit of the Law) through the Israelites' rejection of it.]
31. **Even so have these also now not believed, that through your mercy they also may obtain mercy.** [Even now, the Israelites do not believe in The Way of the Spirit, that through the non-Israelites' belief they shall believe (the merciful, non-Israelite nations of Britain, France, and America were among the first to grant Jews religious freedom and, in 1948, were vital to the birth of the State of Israel).]
32. **For God hath concluded them all in unbelief, that he might have mercy upon all.** [God saw they all denied His Way (thus causing themselves sufferings, that they might learn Mercy unto all), that He might have Mercy on them all.]

■ ■ ◆ ■ ■

#4 - Clark, Eugene (September 26, 1999)

You know, it's one of the great myths of the crazy times in which we have lived, which feminism has said [that] women were kept down forever, through the Middle Ages, you know, women were oppressed right up to our own time and, in 1960, women were finally liberated. Just utter rubbish. Rubbish. If there was any restriction on women, and there were, like with credit, for instance, and with how married women could assign certain monies, that was quite restricted. You know where it came from? The Code Napoleon. It had nothing to do with Christianity or the Middle Ages.

Isn't it a historical fact that Christian women in predominantly Christian nations have suffered oppression of all sorts? And the oppression still continues, even in America. [Some reports say that America's women and men, overall, receive equal pay and benefits. Other reports say that American women are often paid less than their male co-workers for doing the same job. Personally, I have witnessed the latter many times.]

Letter-of-the-law interpretations about male domination and female submission "sanctified," to many, oppression of women. It's not just women who have suffered from false teachings, but also children, blacks (slavery), Jews, homosexuals, abortionists, etc. Corporate Christianity's greatest oppression is its *oppression of the Spirit* through its mass-enslavement of human minds and souls to its idolatrous religion.

■ ■ ◆ ■ ■

#22 - Long, Eddie L. (March, 2000)

Eddie L. Long: The Lord's Prayer actually is a warfare prayer for barefoot folk. First, talks about the kingdom: "Our Father who art in heaven, hallowed be thy name. Thy kingdom come, thy will be done on earth as it is in heaven." Next thing it says is: "Give us this day" what? "Our daily" what?

Audience: Bread.

Eddie L. Long: Watch this. Watch this. Watch this. Watch this. That ain't just giving you a plate of food. Your "bread" is whatever's in front of you that's keeping you from your destiny.

The Lord's Prayer (page 188), given by Jesus Himself, is a Divine instruction to us to live in Peace, not warfare.

Our "daily bread" has nothing to do with things that hinder us from Heaven. "Give us this day our daily bread" is about the Life-giving sustenance of the Spirit.

In the Old Testament, after the exodus from Egypt, God provided the Israelite multitudes with "bread" that rained down from above, called *manna* (Exodus 16:15).

Spiritually speaking, "bread" is the Spirit that God gives daily to those who choose to "eat" it.

■ ■ ◆ ■ ■

#27 - Murray, Gerald (on *The Factor* with Bill O'Reilly; October 11, 2002)

Bill O'Reilly: In the "Back of the Book" segment tonight, intense controversy surrounding another prince of the Roman Catholic Church, Bishop William Murphy of Long Island, New York. As an assistant to Cardinal Law in Boston, he was up to his neck in the priest pedophilia scandal, and now has caused an uproar all his own. The bishop has spent nearly $1,000,000 renovating a residence where he will live. With us now is Father Gerald Murray, the pastor of St. Vincent De Paul parish in lower Manhattan. Now, your parish is a tough neighborhood, it's a poor neighborhood. When you see a guy, a bishop, who is twenty-five miles away from you, renovating to the tune of $1,000,000, how does that make you feel?

Gerald Murray: I'm not that upset, because he already has a residence that's worth a million dollars or more where he lives, and he's gonna sell that. He's gonna use the proceeds to pay for this.

Bill O'Reilly: Practically, I understand it but, philosophically, I don't.

Gerald Murray: I don't mind that we give our bishops the kind of ample living space where they can have guests, and entertain priests and donors. It doesn't bother me that much.

Bill O'Reilly: A million dollars?

Gerald Murray: Well, he had a problem. His budget was $500,000 and went over by $300,000.

Bill O'Reilly: It went over?

Gerald Murray: Yeah, and that's the problem. I don't know how that happened, and I...

Bill O'Reilly (interrupting): All right. Umm, it's hard to imagine Jesus Christ would want to rehab his residence to the tune of $800,000. I can't. Can you? Can you imagine that?

Gerald Murray: Well, I think if Christ came down to Earth we'd probably invite Him into the Vatican, which is worth a lot more that that.

Bill O'Reilly: I don't think He'd live there.

Gerald Murray: Uh, maybe not, but, you know, as human beings we tend to give what we can to the people that are leaders, and in the Church we honor our bishops by giving them something that's, uh, you know...

Bill O'Reilly (interrupting): So, you don't think that this is out of line, an $800,000 rehab of a residence for Bishop Murphy alone, alone, by himself, to live there. And just so the folks know out there, he spent $120,000 on appliances, including large oriental rugs, a double sub-zero refrigerator, a professional range-top, and a wine cooler. Pipe organ was brought in for the church, this is separate, $1,000,000, originally it ended up costing $1,600,000. Now, father, you do work with the indigent poor. All right? You feed them, they're down in the basement. Again, twenty-five miles away from a guy who wants a chandelier and an oriental rug. C'mon. This is not what Christianity, I believe, is supposed to be. I don't want to say bad things and get you in trouble, but I don't think Jesus would be real happy with this renovation.

Gerald Murray: Well, you know, Jesus Christ set up a Church in the world, and people, traditionally, want their bishops to live in decent and, even circumstances which they would feel comfortable inviting anybody in.

Bill O'Reilly: Lavish circumstances? Do you think that Catholics of the country and the world want their bishops to live in lavish conditions?

Gerald Murray: I don't think lavish is... (sentence ends). "Lavish" is a relative thing.

Bill O'Reilly: This is lavish, father. This is lavish.

Gerald Murray: Uh, lavish, yes, in one sense, because it's a lot of money, but he's got the money to pay for it. Somebody gave the diocese a house that's now worth $1,000,000.

Bill O'Reilly: But he could give you half that money (for the charity works at St. Vincent De Paul), couldn't he?

Gerald Murray: Well, my cardinal is very generous and does give me a lot of money to help me in my parish.

Mr. O'Reilly is correct. The luxury that Catholicism bestows upon its Hierarchy speaks for itself, this story being but the "tip of the iceberg."

Christ did not set up the "Church" of idolatrous, big-business religion in the world. Spiritually-corrupt humans did that. The members of His Church are those, *Christian or not*, devoted to His Good Spirit.

The "worth" of the Vatican is, in dollars, most likely priceless, but is of zero worth to Christ who, if invited in, would not enter. He stands outside the self-serving, political, lukewarm "Laodicean churches" of corporate Christianity (Chapter 5). He will not enter, revealing to us that they are "Christless" churches. Nevertheless, He tells us there are Catholics and Protestants devoted to His Good Spirit though they accept and practice man-made rituals and religiosity. *Jesus' Open Door to Salvation is for all who lift His Selfless, Good Spirit above selfishness.*

■ ■ ◆ ■ ■

#37 - Schuller, Robert (May, 2000)

Now, how do you say "thank you" to people who made such a sacrifice that we might live? The way we say "thank you" to all of those we remember on Memorial Day is to make a difference for good in our country, in our community, in our nation, in our society, to become the best people, the most creative and productive people, to give back to the world a life that is beautiful. How do you say "thank you" when someone has made a great sacrifice for you. I ask that question even now, because many of you are going to make a very significant sacrifice to keep this Hour of Power alive. It will be a summer gift of $150, or $30 a month. You will hear me, and you will know that I am telling the truth when I say that without another 50,000 friends giving an average of $150 for this summer, this program will be dead when September comes around, because the costs remain as high as ever, and the income has dropped, and we need special help. We ask for 50,000 people to keep us through the low summer season with a special income gift, the gift of $150, or $30 a month. And how do I say "thank you" when you make that sacrifice? We have sculptured the three angels: "faith"; "hope"; "love". And we sculptured them in pewter, and we made them small, and attached them to something that you can put in your hand, because we want you to get this message, not just on Sundays, but through the week, and you'll pick up a ballpoint pen, and there is a beautiful, sculptured, pewter angel holding a heart, that's "love." And then you'll pick up a letter opener, and there is the beautiful angel of "faith" holding the cross. And then you, like I, will need a magnifying glass more than you want to admit, and there will be the angel of "hope" holding the anchor. These three sculptured angels, you can't find them, buy them any place. You can only expect to get them one place, from the Hour of Power, Robert Schuller, the touch of faith, hope, love. We're asking for a gift of $150, or $30 a month for May, June, July, August, and September, and I will bill to you these wonderful, precious, pewter-sculptured angels.

We are given a Memorial Day "honor" for the war-dead, followed by *selling* idolatry. The centerpiece of this exceptionally wealthy ministry is its "crystal" church (reportedly costing twenty million dollars), and yet after decades of financial success, its TV program will end without at least $7,500,000 in "gifts" within five months?

Is something a "gift" when there is, *in return*, a receipt of merchandise with monthly billing? This transaction is nothing more than a purchase of graven images, denying God's clear instruction about idolatrous religion (Leviticus 26:1).

"You will hear me, and you will know that I am telling the truth when I say that without another 50,000 friends giving an average of $150 for this summer, this program will be dead." Evidently, the reason these "gift" idols were created is because "we want you to get this message, not just on Sundays, but through the week." *Are we to believe that buying and owning Christian idols serve the Good Spirit?* God's Spirit is not alive in idols and graven images, but Within you, *brightly shining His Light through your devotion to His Goodness.*

(5 minutes, 46 seconds later)

Where did evil come from? Why does God allow suffering? The answer to that question is to understand what (sentence ends). (Name of person deleted) put it this way, he defined evil, he said his 8-year-old son gave him the definition: "evil" is "live" spelled backwards. Very significant. "Evil" is "live" spelled backwards. Okay? You know what evil is? "Evil" is "freedom." That's what it is. Freedom without a Lord. Freedom without a Lord. Now, I've said to several people, "Don't ask me why God allows suffering." That's a shallow question. Ask the deeper question, "Why would God create human beings and not control them at all times?"

(52 seconds later)

He (God) chose to give us free will, and that's the one thing God would not eliminate. The only way God could eradicate, and eliminate, and protect us from suffering, and sin, and evil would be to eliminate the power for any person to make free choices. And that, God cannot do, will not do. Why? Why not? Because of freedom. <u>It's the highest of all human values</u>. <u>Eliminate freedom and you eliminate life</u>.

(2 minutes, 20 seconds later)

Freedom is the bridge between God and man. It's the core, the tap root of our human dignity, or our pride of personhood.

Is it not pandering to the audience to exalt "freedom" as "the highest of all human values" on Memorial Day? Jesus says, *"If ye continue in my word, then are ye my disciples indeed: And ye shall know the truth, and the truth shall make you free"* (John 8:31-32), which is not about the issue of freedom, but about the Spirit. It is the Spirit that frees us from human selfishness (idolatry), the source of sins, sufferings, and death. Without the Light, we would be enslaved to darkness forever.

The Spirit Within is the "highest of all human values." Spirit is the "currency" of God that we, of our own free will, choose to invest or hide (per the Parable of the Talents, Chapter 3).

It is clever enough for an 8-year-old to realize that "evil" spelled backwards is "live," but to lift this obvious realization into something profound makes no sense. Are we to believe that to live is evil? It is by God's Spirit that we live, that our impure souls might be saved. "Evil" spelled backwards is "live"... so what? "God" spelled backwards is "dog." *Arf, arf.*

"Why does God allow suffering?" *"Don't ask me why God allows suffering. That's a shallow question."* What teacher of the Spirit would dismiss this question when it is obviously not "shallow?" When corporate religionists do not have the answer to smart, thoughtful questions about God, they turn to such patent responses as: "Don't ask such questions... just have faith"; or "Don't question the mystery of God"; or, in this case, "That's a shallow question."

The corporate mindsets of Christian leaders, *generally speaking, as seen throughout this book,* deny "as ye sow, so shall ye reap" *unless it serves their selfish wants and needs.* They refuse to acknowledge that Jesus spoke of reincarnation. They do not want to teach the evident Truth that faith is justified by Selfless, Good Works, but rather teach that Salvation comes through idolatrous, man-made rituals. They do not want to tell you that tithing is about giving of your Spirit Within, but rather teach that tithing is about giving $$$ to their churches, threatening you with God's "wrath" if you do not tithe fully. They do not want you to know that you are ultimately responsible for your life's choices and decisions, but are "saved" by making the one decision to follow their "way" to Salvation. They do not want you to know that your soul will be righteously judged of itself by its devotion (or lack of devotion) to its Good Conscience. They do not want you to know that what separates the "sheep" from the "goats" is the Spirit Within, but insist that everyone not part of their separatist, man-made, big-business, corporate system is going to hell.

Instead, when asked a question that puts them on the spot, it's a lot easier to simply say, *"That's a shallow question."*

■ ■ ◆ ■ ■

This intensive, 5-year work that you have almost finished reading has proven, unquestionably, that the Ichi-ban (Number One) feeder of separatism, superstition, and fear in the Christianized "world" is Christianity itself, which *still* exalts idolatrous dogma over the Spirit. Had it built itself upon The One Way of God's Selfless, Good Spirit instead of holier-than-thou separatism and in-the-name-of-God brutality, all the awfulness in Christianity could never have taken root.

Institutionalized Christianity bears responsibility for having led its followers into the idolatrous dogma and corporate selfishness that "sanctified" the Crusades, the Inquisition, and the slavery of peoples. Even both World Wars could not have sparked if Western Civilization's greatest religion, Christianity, had been founded upon exemplifying and teaching The Way of God's Spirit.

There is no hope for corporate Christianity, as a whole, to grow One in the Selfless Spirit, because its primary "business" is business-survival... *money, power and control.* The book of Revelation foresees the "end times" Church as being indifferent to The Way, having wasted so much of its Good Spirit for self-serving "worldly" agendas (politics, separatist dogma, power, control, etc.). And though there is no hope for the whole of corporate Christianity, there is always hope for you, the individual soul, to ascend to Oneness in God by treading The Way of the Spirit, *as He showed to us.*

No man-made Church system is The Way. *The Way is Within you.*

The great, global system of corporate Christianity is like a titanic ship that thinks itself unsinkable upon the River of Life. Be not deceived, the Good River of God's Spirit will suddenly rise and sink it (Matthew 21:42, 44). Fear not the Good River, but rather the idolatrous structures that keep you from swimming in It.

Matthew 22:42, 44 (spoken by Jesus; likely authored by Apostle Matthew)

42. **The stone which the builders rejected, the same is become the head of the corner.** [The "rock" Spirit ('stone') that the builders of Christianity rejected is the cornerstone of Christ's One Church.]

44. **And whosoever shall fall upon this stone shall be broken: but on whomsoever it shall fall, it will grind him to powder.** [Those who submit to the Spirit ('fall upon this stone') shall reap what they sow, and be broken of their worldly ways. Those who reject the Spirit shall reap what they sow, and be rendered powerless forever, "ground into powder."]

REFERENCES

LITERARY REFERENCES

Allen, Oliver E., and Sam Welles, eds. *The World's Great Religions.* New York: Time Inc., 1957.

Bagemihl, Bruce, Ph.D. *Biological Exuberance: Animal Homosexuality and Natural Diversity.* New York: St. Martin's Press, 1999.

Bremness, Lesley. *The Complete Book of Herbs.* London: Viking Penguin Inc., 1988.

Chadwick, Owen. *A History of Christianity.* New York: St. Martin's Press, 1995.

Coogan, Michael D., and Bruce M. Metzger, eds. *The Oxford Companion to the Bible.* New York: Oxford University Press, 1993.

Corcos, Georgette, and Rachel Gilon, eds. *The Glory of the New Testament.* New York: The Jerusalem Publishing House, Ltd., 1984.

Cord, John. *Revelation Earth.* Santa Barbara: EternaLight Publishing, 1999.

Cotterell, Arthur. *A Dictionary of World Mythology.* New York: G.P. Putnam, 1980.

Cowan, Thomas. *Gay Men & Women who Enriched the World.* New Canaan: Mulvey Books, 1988.

Crystal, David, ed. *The Cambridge Factfinder.* New York: Cambridge Press, 1994.

Eliade, Mircea, ed. *The Encyclopedia of Religion.* New York: MacMillan, 1987.

Fraser, Antonia. *King James VI of Scotland, I of England.* New York: Knopf, 1975.

Gardner, Joseph L., and Josephine Reidy, eds. *Who's Who in the Bible.* Pleasantville: The Reader's Digest Association, Inc., 1994.

Greif, Martin. *The Gay Book of Days.* New York: Carol Publishing Group, 1982.

Grun, Bernard. *The Timetables of History.* 1946; rpt New York: Simon/Schuster, 1975.

Hadley, Janet. *Abortion: Between Freedom and Necessity.* Philadelphia: Temple University Press, 1996.

Hendrickson, Robert. *Encyclopedia of Word and Phrase Origins.* New York: Facts on File, Inc., 1997.

Hylton, William H., and Claire Kwalchik, eds. *Rodale's Illustrated Encyclopedia of Herbs.* Emmaus: Rodale Press, 1987

Ironside, H.A. *Revelation.* Neptune: Loizeaux Brothers, 1920.

Kaufmann, K. *The Abortion Resource Handbook.* New York: Simon/ Schuster, 1997.

The KJV Parallel Bible Commentary. Nashville: Thomas Nelson, Inc., 1994.

LaHaye, Tim. *Revelation Illustrated and Made Plain.* Grand Rapids: Zondervan Publishing House, 1973.

MacMullen, Ramsay. *Christianity & Paganism in the Fourth to Eighth Centuries.* 1928; rpt New Haven: Yale University Press, 1997

McGee, J. Vernon. *Revelation.* 3 vols. La Verne: El Camino Press, 1979.

The Oxford Dictionary of the Christian Church. London: Oxford Press, 1958.

Piper, David. *The Kings and Queens of England and Scotland.* London: Faber and Faber, Ltd., 1980.

Prophet, Elizabeth. *Reincarnation: The Missing Link in Christianity.* Corwin Springs: Summit University Press, 1997.

Revelation: A Commentary Based on a Study of Twenty-Four Psychic Discourses by Edgar Cayce. 1945; rpt Virginia Beach: A.R.E. Press, 1993.

Roleff, Tamara L, ed. *Abortion: Opposing Viewpoints.* San Diego: Greenhaven, 1997

Schwarzwaller, Wulf. *Abortion Wars: A Half-Century of Struggle, 1950 - 2000.* Los Angeles: University of California Press, 1998.

Solinger, Rickie, ed. *The Complete Book of Herbs.* London: Viking Penguin, 1988.

The Way to the Kingdom. 1932; rpt Marina del Rey: DeVorss & Co, 1988.

VIDEO REFERENCES

Crime Stories: Crimes in the Name of God. Executive Producer: Steve Rosenbaum. Court TV.

Frontline: Assault on Gay America. Executive Producer: Michael Sullivan. PBS: WGHB Educational Foundation, 2000.

In Search of History: Beyond the Grave: The Afterlife. Executive Producer: Bram Roos. The History Channel, 1995.

INTERNET REFERENCES

http://www.2think.org/abortion.shtml

http://www.2think.org/sagan_abortion.shtml

http://www.adherents.com/rel–USA.html

http://www.jesus-is-lord.com/rumors.htm

http://www.naral.org/actnow/10_facts_ab.html

http://www.pbs.org/now/society/religionstats.html

http://www.prochoice.org/facts/factsheets/fs4.htm

http://www.religioustolerance.org/abo_pba.htm

http://www.roman-emperors.org/conniei.htm

http://www.starvation.net

http://www.truth101.org/vs-ab-abortion.html

INDEX of PREACHERS

#13 - GRAHAM LOTZ, Anne AnGeL Ministries; 5115 Holly Ridge Dr., Raleigh, NC 27612; www.angelministries.org
13-14, 185, 196

#14 - HAGEE, John Pastor, John Hagee Ministries; PO Box 1400, San Antonio, TX 78295; www.jhm.org
iii-iv, 24, 31, 38, 67-68, 80, 93, 98, 102, 110, 132, 145, 160, 186, 199

#15 - HILL, E. V. Dr. & Pastor, Mt. Zion Missionary Baptist Church; 1308 E. 50th St., Los Angeles, CA 90011
89-90

#16 - HUCH, Larry Pastor, Larry Huch Ministries; 7600 NE Glisan, Portland, OR 97213; www.newbeginnings.org
17, 45, 67, 81

#17 - HUCH, Tiz Pastor, Larry Huch Ministries; 7600 NE Glisan, Portland, OR 97213; www.newbeginnings.org
36

#18 - JAKES, T. D. Bishop, The Potter's House; 6777 West Kiest Blvd., Dallas, TX 75236; www.tdjakes.org
24, 41-43, 85, 112, 115

#19 - JONES, Bob III Pres., Bob Jones University; 1700 Wade Hampton Blvd., Greenville, SC 29614; www.bju.edu
55, 105-106, 155, 204

#20 - JONES, Noel Bishop, Noel Jones Ministries; 8401 S. Hoover St., Los Angeles, CA 90044; www.noeljonesministries.org
115

#21 - KENNEDY, D. James Minister, Coral Ridge Ministries; PO Box 40, Ft. Lauderdale, FL 33302; www.coralridge.org
3, 87, 113, 129, 140, 156-157

#22 - LONG, Eddie Bishop, New Birth Ministries; 6400 Woodrow Rd., Lithonia, GA 30038; www.newbirth.org
24, 208

#23 - MANN, Gerald Dr., Gerald Mann Ministries; PO Box 160100, Austin, TX 78716; www.gmm.org
24, 204

#24 - McBRIEN, Richard Reverend & Professor of Theology, University of Notre Dame, Notre Dame, IN 46556; www.nd.edu
170-171, 173

#25 - MEYER, Joyce Life In The Word; PO Box 655, Fenton, MO 63026; www.joycemeyer.org
26

#26 - MOHLER, R. Albert Pres., Southern Baptist Theological Seminary; 2825 Lexington Rd., Louisville, KY 40280; www.sbts.edu
154

#27 - MURRAY, Gerald Priest, St. Vincent De Paul; Archdiocese of NY; 1011 First Ave., New York, NY 10022; www.ny-archdiocese.org
209-210

#28 - PARSLEY, Rod Pastor; Breakthrough Ministries; 4595 Gender Rd., Canal Winchester, OH 43110; www.breakthrough.net
19, 23, 27, 52-53, 81-82, 95, 102-104, 112, 202-204

INDEX of CELEBRITY INTERVIEWERS

INDEX of BIBLICAL VERSES

INDEX by SUBJECT

About the Author

John Cord holds a B.S. degree in Premedicine and is a lifelong, independent scholar of the Bible. His desire to expose the hypocrisy and selfishness of big business, corporate Christianity grew out of his childhood experiences in Japan. The finest English-speaking school in his neighborhood was a Catholic school, open to the public, where he found himself the only non-Catholic in his class during his five years of attendance (1st–5th Grades). One wintry morning, his 4th Grade teacher stopped lecturing, pointed at him and yelled, "You are going to hell because you are not a Catholic." That moment was the "turning point," and he suddenly knew that God didn't care what religion he followed, but that he be a good soul, loving and helping others (God is love; and he that dwelleth in love dwelleth in God, and God in him; First John 4:16).

This "awakening" soon led him to want to read and study the Bible for himself, to see where it taught that only Catholics go to Heaven. The second time he read the Bible through, he summarized every chapter and story in longhand, and it soon became evident that the entirety of the Bible was about The Way of God's Spirit and about His Spirit of the Law over the Letter of the Law.

Cord's work proves the Bible's Message of the Spirit, tearing down Christianity's walls of separatism, fear and superstition.

www.TheChristianRightOrWrong.com

Printed in the United States
33868LVS00004B/67-75

9 781577 331797